COURT-MARTIAL
A Black Man in America

COURT-MARTIAL
A Black Man in America

JOHN F. MARSZALEK, Jr.

Copyright © 1972 John F. Marszalek, Jr.

This book published simultaneously in the
United States of America and in Canada
   Copyright under the Berne Convention

All rights reserved. No part of this book
may be reproduced in any form without the
permission of Charles Scribner's Sons.

A–11.72(V)

Printed in the United States of America
Library of Congress Catalog Card Number 73–38382
SBN 684–12844–6 (cloth)

FOR JEANNE

This is an extraordinary case. It will go down in the books as one of the most remarkable on record.
—Richard T. Greener to Alexander Ramsey, August 14, 1880

I can, I must, I will win a place in life.
—J. C. Whittaker, Buffalo, New York, May 31, 1882

CONTENTS

LIST OF ILLUSTRATIONS

PREFACE

The last two decades have seen upheaval and change in almost every field of human endeavor but nowhere more than among the black people of the United States. Three centuries of resistance to injustice has been intensified, and some victories have been won. Even in the study of American history there has been a fundamental change. Black faces are appearing in history books in other than the slave situation; the factual role of the Afro-American in the life of the United States is finally receiving attention.

This book is an attempt to add to this study. It is the story of one man's battle against discrimination and injustice. While it concentrates on one element—life at West Point, the mysterious nighttime incident, and the subsequent trials and political machinations—it gives insight into much more.

Johnson Chesnut Whittaker, born a slave in 1858, lived through the Civil War, Reconstruction, the period of the development and establishment of Jim Crow segregation, World War I, and the black migration from the South. He experienced the attempts to integrate one of the national schools, the United States Military Academy, and was a pioneer in the establishment of black education. In his hitherto unstudied life can be seen the struggle of black people to emerge from slavery into a full share of the American dream. His life provides an unusual opportunity to study a black man in depth and learn more about black people and even more about American democracy.

The court of inquiry and court-martial alone are significant expositions of American attitudes and beliefs. They are as dramatic and important as any court-martial or trial in American history. They are to post-Civil War America what the Scopes trial was to the 1920's, the Scottsboro trial to the 1930's, or the Calley trial to the 1970's. The Whittaker trials not only tell the story of famous individuals; they also reveal the innermost soul of an age and a people.

This work is based on documents and personal interviews. Finding the appropriate material and people was a historical adventure in itself, consisting of discovering pertinent information in mounds of official documents and personal correspondence in the usual depositories but also in small South Carolina courthouses, dusty attics, and the memories of surviving witnesses. Without the active cooperation of scores of persons, much of the story that follows could not be told. The individuals who knew the subject of this book or are the caretakers of pertinent documents went out of their way to be of help. Their unselfish interest and aid made the writing of this book possible.

J. C. Whittaker's family was most gracious in providing information and photographs. Granddaughter Cecil Whittaker McFadden and daughter-in-law Marian Horton, the remarried widow of John Whittaker, both of Detroit, Michigan, received the author and his wife graciously and were generous with their time and information. In South

Carolina, Whittaker's home state, whites and blacks were equally kind. They are listed below: Mrs. Charliese P. Sheffield, Registrar T. J. Crawford, Professor and Mrs. Reginald Thomasson, Head Librarian Barbara Williams and the entire staff of the library named after Whittaker's son, the Miller F. Whittaker Library, all of South Carolina State College, Orangeburg, South Carolina; in Camden: Mrs. W. A. Boykin of the Camden District Heritage Foundation and distant relative Dr. Theodore Whitaker; in Sumter: Attorney George D. Shore, Jr.; County Superintendent of Education Buford Mabry; E. C. Jones, D.D.S.; William F. Bultman, Sr.; distant relative Anna Louise McDonald; and Dr. Hugh Stoddard, Superintendent of Sumter School District #2.

A host of libraries and librarians provided aid: Rita A. Nies, Grace Davies, and Bernard Schroeck of the Gannon College Library; the staff of the Manuscript Division of the Library of Congress; Elmer O. Parker, Joseph B. Ross, and a host of others at the National Archives; Sara Fuller of the Ohio Historical Society; Watt P. Marchman and Ruth Ballenger of the Rutherford B. Hayes Library; Stanley P. Tozeski of the United States Military Academy Archives and Marie Capps of Special Collections; Kimball C. Elkins of the Harvard University Archives; R. Nicholas Olsberg, T. M. Bolivar, and others of the South Carolina Department of Archives and History; Mrs. Granville T. Prior, South Carolina Historical Society; E. L. Inabinett, Clara Mae Jacobs, and Juliana B. Dinney of the South Caroliana Library, University of South Carolina; Patricia McClure and Dorothy B. Porter of the Howard University Library; Ruby J. Shields of the Minnesota Historical Society; Sharon E. Knapp, William R. Perkins Library, Duke University; Carolyn A. Wallace, Southern History Collection, University of North Carolina; the staffs of the Erie (Pa.) Public Library and the Buffalo and Erie County Public Library. Countless other librarians and archivists too numerous to mention searched their collections for Whittaker material.

Thanks are also due to clerks and probate-court personnel of South Carolina counties, particularly Kershaw, Orangeburg, and Sumter; Bill Eaton of the Buffalo *Evening News;* D. A. Wisener of Oklahoma City, Oklahoma; Cecil J. Williams of Orangeburg; Frances H. Smith, Clerk, South Carolina Supreme Court; Mr. and Mrs. Douglas Dedman and Miss Anna Mae Marszalek of Batavia, New York; Mr. and Mrs. Stanley Marszalek of Albany, New York; Mr. and Mrs. John Marszalek, Sr., and Sister Rosalie Marie G.N.S.H. of Buffalo; Barbara Melton of Killeen, Texas; Mr. and Mrs. John Kozmer of Niles, Michigan; Mrs. Ralph Dowden, John Cunningham, and James X. Kroll, all of Erie; Major W. Scott Dillard of the United States Military Academy; Captain William R. Robie of the Judge Advocate General School, U.S. Army; Elinor Wilson of California; Norman Kotker and Linda Spencer of Charles Scribner's Sons; and registrars and officials of colleges and universities too numerous to mention. All were in various ways instrumental in the completion of the book.

Special thanks are in order to student assistants Edward Grode, Paul Kovacs, David Lastowski, Margaret Orler and Patrick Casey, for their loyalty and hard work and the Gannon College Faculty Service department, Kay Medairy, Rosemary Stewart and Lenore Mulcahy, for their typing skills and their never-flagging enthusiasm. James F. Sefcik of the Gannon History Department read the entire manuscript and offered encouragement, criticism, and both intellectual and personal camaraderie. Gannon College provided two faculty research grants, and a summer grant was awarded by the National Endowment for the Humanities.

used in various sections of the book with permission of the magazine.

Most of all, this book is the result of the patience and the loving understanding and inspiration of my wife, Jeanne Kozmer Marszalek. She helped in more ways than even she knows.

Any merit this book may have is the result of the generosity of these kind people. The fault for any deficiencies lies only with the author.

J. F. M., JR.

Chapter 1

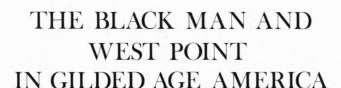

THE BLACK MAN AND
WEST POINT
IN GILDED AGE AMERICA

It was 6:00 A.M., time for reveille at the United States Military Academy, West Point, New York, on April 6, 1880, and the early hour showed in the faces of the still sleepy cadets. The usual morning chill was in the air, but when the order to "fall in" was given, the cadets had to ignore the 42° temperature. The roll call echoed on the West Point plain, and it was soon discovered that one cadet was missing; Cadet Johnson Chesnut Whittaker was not in formation.

Undoubtedly there was a stir among the assembled cadets and perhaps some happy feeling of anticipation. Whittaker, the most disliked cadet at West Point, was in trouble now, and few of the other cadets would feel any sense of grief at the punishment he might receive. Whittaker had not specifically gone out of his way to become unpopular, nor was he a bully or a troublemaker; his fault, as viewed

I

by his fellow cadets, was simply that he was a Negro. He was, in April 1880, the only black cadet at West Point.

Learning that Cadet Whittaker was absent, the officer-in-charge, Major Alexander Piper, immediately directed George R. Burnett, the Cadet Officer of the day, to go to the black cadet's room in the Fifth Division Building to see if he had overslept. Burnett moved quickly up the flights of barracks stairs and approached Whittaker's fourth-floor door immediately off the landing. He called out: "Mr. Whittaker." Receiving no answer, Burnett opened the door, stepped inside the room, and repeated his call. There was still no response. He moved toward the alcove where Whittaker's bed was located and called even louder. For the third time he heard nothing, but now he saw Whittaker lying on the floor, looking as though he had fallen out of bed. Coming closer, Burnett saw that Whittaker's legs were tied to his bed and that he was covered with blood. The room showed signs of mayhem. Burnett left the black cadet undisturbed and ran to get the officer of the day. As he started out of the room, he ran into Cadet Frederick G. Hodgson, one of the occupants of the room directly across the hall. "Look, look here," he said. "Wait here until I go for the officer-in-charge." Hodgson looked in and exclaimed, "I believe he is dead!"[1]

The United States in the year 1880 was made up of over 50,000,000 people. Bustling with activity and full of energy, the nation, over a hundred years old, confidently looked to the future after the terrible experience of a civil war. Gaping holes had been torn in the body politic, but these wounds seemed to be healing. Bitter sectional hatred seemed to be breaking down as Northerners and Southerners increasingly saw more advantages in reconciliation than in waving the bloody shirt or refighting old battles. All was not settled, but the air was filled with confidence that a solution was possible.

Trapped in the crossfire of this preoccupation with sectional reconciliation and a return to normality were six and a half million American Negroes. Their plight was becoming lost in talk of trusts, tariffs, money, civil service, Sitting Bull, and reconciliation.

When the Civil War ended in 1865 the black man, in America since 1619, found himself a citizen for the first time. According to the newly enacted Thirteenth, Fourteenth, and Fifteenth amendments, he was a free man and had constitutional protection against violations of his "privileges and immunities" as a citizen. The long period of bondage and subservience seemed over.

Unfortunately, dried ink on paper proved little guarantee of rights. In short order the freed black found his voting rights abridged and his very life controlled by restrictive custom and law. His hopes were raised during the period of so-called "Radical Reconstruction" in the late 1860's and early 1870's, but even then he enjoyed few of the rights of citizenship. The Ku Klux Klan, the Knights of the White Camellia, and sundry other organizations proved to be effective instruments in keeping him submerged. Nowhere in the reconstructed South did he have a truly effective voice; the political offices he managed to obtain tended to be symbolic and/or temporary. A number of blacks served in the House of Representatives and two were Senators, but none wielded any real power. White America was not ready for black citizens, let alone black political leaders.

In all fairness it must be said that Reconstruction was a period of transition. The nation as a whole and the South in particular were unsure of the role in American society that should be assigned to freed blacks. Segregation was present during this period, but total Jim Crowism lay in the future.[2] There was still a flame of hope burning in black breasts, although the winds of repression were already causing it to flicker.

The Gilded Age, the time of Presidents Rutherford B. Hayes, James A. Garfield, Chester A. Arthur, Grover Cleveland, and Benjamin Harrison, was an era of con-

3

tinued decline for black people. Southerners stripped away black voting rights and then equal access to public accommodations. Soon the two races were completely separated, and Jim Crow reigned supreme. Northerners, even liberals, abandoned blacks in the hope of material, political, or national gain. In short, Northern and Southern race feeling merged; it had never been as far apart as has sometimes been believed. North and South agreed that blacks were inferior to whites intellectually, emotionally, and even physically. The black race was an inferior race, and Africa was a dark continent that had never produced anything worth noting. Consequently, it was argued, American blacks were of inferior stock and not really able to fulfill the rights of citizenship. Their disenfranchisement might actually prove to be a national blessing. It would take from the voting rolls a mass of ignorant voters and protect the stability of the nation. Most importantly, it would pave the way for peace between the sections.

Not all Americans felt this way, of course, but the vast majority did. One need only read the leading Northern newspapers and magazines to see how widespread was the belief in innate black inferiority. The black man was depicted as lazy, shiftless, childlike, thieving, and apparently without any virtue. There was little, if any, press protest made against discrimination, and, more often than not, new restrictions were envisioned as good.[3]

Even those who considered themselves willing to give the black man a chance were checked by the all-encompassing doctrine of Social Darwinism. According to this science of the day, the black race held a position on the bottom of the ladder of human evolution, far below the dominant Anglo-Saxon race. Thus, science buttressed years of prejudice and provided a rational justification for believing that blacks were inferior and were destined to remain so unless eons of time brought about adaptation and change.

Faced with such impressive "evidence," even the most

sympathetic person found it difficult to argue for Negro rights. Since most Americans knew blacks only as slaves or as holders of the most menial positions in society, they felt constrained to believe that science was correct. It seemed useless to try to help Negroes personally or pressure the government to aid them. It would accomplish nothing. Darwinians such as William Graham Sumner even warned that any meddling with evolution would actually cause retrogression by disturbing evolutionary progress.[4] The best that could be done for black people was to let them live as second-class citizens. The more important task of political and economic life could then be considered without racial interruption.

Nevertheless, many Americans, particularly Republicans, felt a sense of responsibility toward the black man. As the party of Lincoln, the Great Emancipator, Republicans, particularly of the radical stripe, believed that the Negro should have political equality; some went so far as to include social equality. However, as the years moved on, many Radicals died off; others left office or lost interest in guaranteeing black rights. By 1876 the Republican party was beginning to re-evaluate its policy toward the freedman. Disappointed that they had not been able to build a solid party in the South based on the black vote, Republicans began to look toward their more natural allies—the former Southern Whigs, the upper-class whites. They saw the need to make their party more truly national and debated over how this could best be done: allying themselves with Southern whites or blacks. Most saw their only true hope in an alliance with whites. Industry would be a connecting link between North and South.

Yet they did not see this as an abandonment of the Negro. They still saw themselves as the black man's only friend and their program of sectional unity as his only hope. When Rutherford B. Hayes thought he had lost the election of 1876, for example, he was reported to have said that he did not care for himself but was concerned "for the poor colored man in the South." Despite such protestations, Hayes and his successors in the presidency did little for the black man.

The black man protested, but his cries went unheeded. He felt betrayed and talked of abandoning the Republican party. But where could he go? Nowhere else on the political scene was there a friendly face. So he stayed in the party of Lincoln and continued to hope for a fairer shake. He continued to be disappointed and remained nothing more than a weak pawn in the Republican game of political chess.

Throughout the Gilded Age conditions for blacks continued to worsen, and proscription increased. With the arrival of the 1890's the Republican party eliminated even its token support. Fearing that any bloody shirt waving, any concern for black voting rights would disrupt the business alliance between the North and South, Republicans simply gave up trying to build an effective organization in the South, leaving their black allies to the mercy of rising demagogues. The black man was now truly alone. His abandonment by American society was complete.[5]

Americans of the 1870's and 1880's solemnly remembered the Civil War and held the soldiers and leaders on both sides in veritable reverence. A military organization, the powerful Grand Army of the Republic (G.A.R.), was a leading pressure group listened to with great attention by Congress, President, and common man alike. Scores of other military organizations, North and South, were important focuses of social life for many Americans. Yet the active army during this period was a skeleton force, at times fearful for its very existence. General of the Army William T. Sherman often complained of Congressional cutbacks in money and army size and felt that the nation was ungrateful for the military sacrifices of the past war.[6]

This reverence for past exploits and neglect of the present was not the paradox it appears. While the influence makers of the Gilded Age—the businessmen, financiers, and leading intellectuals—might revel in past glories, they thought future wars virtually impossible and considered a large standing army an anachronistic waste.[7] They were indifferent to the Army and unconcerned with its maintenance. Many Southerners resented the Army's role during Reconstruction, and most radical Republicans never forgot the wave of resignations by Southerners that swept the Army at the start of the Civil War. In short, the Army's position in society was a perilous one despite the nation's general satisfaction with Civil War performance.

Without public interest and support the Army languished, living a hand-to-mouth existence dependent on the whim of Congress. Occasionally the public would become concerned when a Custer was annihilated or an Army outpost in the West was overrun. It might follow with interest the long political hassle over the Civil War Fitz John Porter court-martial or enjoy hearing about General Sherman's latest after-dinner speech. But for the most part the public paid scant attention to its Army.

At the United States Military Academy, the Army's training ground for officers, matters were fundamentally different in some respects. The nation might be pleased with its Civil War memories and its reunification, but West Point was still uncomfortable. Instead of looking back to the Civil War, the Military Academy tried to forget it. The late war was not a source of glory; it was a festering sore yet to be healed. The prewar sectional controversies which had split the Academy and its cadets remained a source of dispute, with Northern and Southern cadets trading blows over secession late into the nineteenth century.

This basic discord and the attacks from without made the Academy turn in on itself and revert to the past—to the era of founder Sylvanus Thayer. Here at a time when sectional discord was absent, the Academy hoped to find a purpose for its existence and a philosophy for the future.

This is not to conclude, as some authors have, that the

Gilded Age was a period of stagnation for the Academy. It would be fairer to call this period an age of uncertainty. Some successful attempts were made to change curriculum and make other adjustments, but many other attempts were defeated in Washington or blocked by feelings of uncertainty. West Point saw the need for improvement but was unsure how to achieve it. And as attacks on it grew, it tended to become more and more defensive.[8]

West Point's most persistent and powerful critic during the period was John A. Logan, the successful citizen-general of the Civil War and later leading Republican politician and founder of the G.A.R. During a Civil War battle Logan had prevented a disaster by rallying a segment of Sherman's army when the death of General McPherson had left it leaderless. Because of his valor and previous service he expected to retain command of the Army of the Tennessee, which he had so nobly rallied. When General Sherman appointed West Point graduate O. O. Howard to the post, Logan ascribed the slight to what he felt was the West Point clique's refusal to let a non-West Pointer have a position of authority. Despite Sherman's repeated disavowals, then and in later years, Logan maintained his belief throughout his political career and was a constant thorn in West Point's side.

In a book published after his death, *The Volunteer Soldier of America*, Logan called for the abolition of West Point and its replacement by military courses at the state universities. If it did survive, its only role might be as a graduate school of military science. He considered the Academy a danger to American democracy because it taught military skills to only a very few, giving them the ability to overthrow the government. The large number of West Point defections to the Confederacy in the late war showed yet another deficiency in the Academy, as did what Logan considered the general level of incompetence among its graduates.[9] Fortunately for West Point, the book had little real effect. Its tedious and drawn-out style made reading it a chore: com-

8

ing out as it did after Logan's death, it did not have his active push behind it.

Such criticisms only tended to make West Point draw into itself even more and increased its sense of uncertainty. The Academic Board, alumni, and others associated with the Academy critically examined the institution in private and in the pages of the *Journal of Military Service Institution.* But their uncertainty was evident. As Professor George L. Andrews put it: "It is not to be denied that the course at the Academy is susceptible of improvement; but precisely what changes should be made, it is not easy to say." As a result, substantial reform did not come during the Gilded Age. Those changes that came "were incremental rather than sweeping."[10]

Life itself at the Military Academy reflected this parochialism. During the 1870's and 1880's the average cadet's lot was a difficult one, not simply because of the strenuous military program but also because of a lack of diversion. There were few ways for a cadet to let off steam, to relax from the strain of day-to-day Academy life. There was little organized recreation and entertainment, and opportunities for individual relaxation were few. Cadets were almost forced to turn to illegal pranks.

A young man became part of the Academy by means of a Congressional appointment and by the successful completion of physical and academic examinations. The academic year began on September 1, but there was also camp the summer before where upper-classmen drilled the incoming plebes in military arts. This summer camp was a period of intense harassment. Some cadets were not able to arrive until late August and avoided this experience. They began their careers in September and were given the name Seps.[11]

New cadets or plebes arrived at the Academy armed with little more than their personal effects and a previously received circular of West Point rules and regulations. They were quickly given a thorough physical examination to check for any disqualifying defects and were weighed, measured, and asked if they smoked. Once over this hurdle, they were given an entrance examination in arithmetic, English grammar, descriptive geometry, and history. They were expected to be able to work with fractions, decimals, and proportions, to parse sentences, have a thorough knowledge of grammar, read with the "proper intonation and pauses," and write correctly. They had to display a knowledge of American and world geography and be able to explain the "periods of discovery and settlement," "rise and progress," and "successive wars and political administrations" of the United States. Having passed these examinations and having survived "Beast Barracks" orientation, they became West Point cadets.[12]

The successful completion of the next four years was another matter. According to the West Point circular, the "essential qualifications" for graduation were "sound body and constitution, a fixed degree of preparation, good natural capacity, an aptitude for study, industrious habits, perseverance, an obedient and orderly disposition, and a correct moral deportment."[13] Some cadets did not possess a requisite amount of these qualities, and their West Point careers were terminated before four years were up. Most, however, graduated.

The method of instruction had changed little over the years. Cadets were placed according to their grades in small sections of approximately twelve men. Each subject had its separate phalanx of sections. The better students were in the first sections, the weaker ones in the lowest. Here they recited each day. The cadet simply went up to the desk, recited the problem assigned him, and was given a grade. The instructor did little more than listen and evaluate. He did practically no teaching *per se*. The emphasis in all classes was on memorization, with understanding a tangential bonus. Performance in these recitations and in the January and June comprehensive examinations determined a cadet's academic standing.[14]

The perpetuation of the status quo resulted mainly from the sameness of the faculty. One need only look at the *Army Register* for any year during this period to see the inbreeding that went on. Almost without exception the faculty was composed of West Point graduates. The professors, all with long service at the Academy, often kept their best students on as assistant professors.[15] This tended to discourage academic change, since anyone wanting an appointment could hardly be an innovator.

Cadet living quarters added to the pressure of life at the Academy. As in any military institution, emphasis was placed on cleanliness and orderliness. Cadets lived in two-man rooms, containing only essential furniture. To add an element of privacy, a divider ran partway down the center of the room. This plus the exterior walls of the room and curtains formed two alcoves, each containing one cadet bed. The rest of the room, the larger part, contained two tables and chairs, a washstand, slop bucket, clothes presses, and gun racks. A door, a window with curtains, heating pipes, a wooden floor, and a gaslight completed the picture. There were rules and regulations of the usual military type governing how a cadet's clothes, books, and other personal effects were to be placed in his room and rules regulating the use and location of the furniture.[16] "Everything in its place, and a place for everything."

While in the classroom a cadet was under the direct command of the instructor. Outside the classroom he was part of a cadet company under the supervision of cadet officers and staff tactical officers. Over-all control of cadet non-academic life was in the hands of a commandant of cadets who was directly answerable to the Superintendent. Cadets walked tours of duty and punishment, stood guard either as cadet officers of the day or as guards, and performed all their other responsibilities. Their movements, while not on official duty, were closely monitored. There were places where they could and could not go and specific times when they might be permitted to do something

II

which they were forbidden at another time. For example, on Sunday afternoons they were generally free, and their rooms were not subject to sudden inspection. At this time they had more freedom and could take walks, play games, read, or even sleep if they so desired. Regulations permitted them to leave their bed mattresses unfolded and gave them the chance to get some extra sleep.

There were also other periods during the week when a cadet had opportunity for relaxation. The problem was that there was so little to do. Sports were a favorite pastime, as was walking, especially to Flirtation Walk with a young lady. There were no cadet organizations worth speaking of except for the ineffective Dialectic Society. The traditional Hundredth Night celebration, commemorating the fact that there were only 100 days left to graduation and the end of the term, was a yearly interlude in the drabness. The celebration consisted mainly of jokes, songs, and plays, most of which poked fun at Academy life, officers, and teachers. The Class Rush, the custom of running to meet the returning furlough class, also served as a tension release. Officers always felt the Rush was undignified but were never able to prevent it.[17]

Faced with an austere military life, restriction to the Academy except during their furlough summer, and a paucity of recreational opportunity, cadets turned to more adventuresome outlets. Drinking was frowned on by West Point officials but was nonetheless a favorite source of release. The almost legendary Benny Havens', a favorite gathering place for cadets of an earlier period, was gone by this time, but Philip Ryan's tavern helped to fill the void. Many a cadet availed himself of Ryan's services and not always according to regulations. Cadets would often go to Ryan's, change into civilian clothes, and then go out for a night on the town, reversing the process before returning to the Academy.[18]

Another favorite diversion was the prank—a way of demonstrating bravado as well as of breaking the Academy monotony. In the 1850's a cadet named John Schofield, who ironically in the late 1870's was appointed Superintendent of West Point, was perhaps the leading prankster. In his memoirs he tells how one night after Taps when all lights were to be out, he and a group of other cadets became involved in a spirited discussion. With a blanket over the window preventing their detection, they began to discuss the possibility of going to New York City and coming back without being detected by any officers. One thing led to another, and soon Schofield found himself challenged to make the trip. He had no real desire to go to New York, but the wager and the challenge "overcame any scruple." The following day he went to New York between the two compulsory roll calls. On the way down Benny Havens rowed him across the Hudson River to catch the train, and a ferryman got him back on his return. He arrived a few minutes before the evening parade, calmly walked across the plain in full view of the assembled officers and ladies, and appeared in ranks for roll call "as innocent as anybody." The only bad part of the whole affair, as far as he was concerned, was his failure ever to collect the bet![19]

Probably the most famous example of a cadet prank was the New Year's Eve maneuver of 1879-1880. A number of members of the corps of cadets decided that the Military Academy should welcome in the new year with the proper style and flourish. They therefore smuggled various kinds of fireworks onto the plain and finally into the barracks, planning to shoot them off at the stroke of midnight. But first some obstacles had to be neutralized.

A cadet hop was scheduled for New Year's Eve, but it would be over before midnight. However, the usual guard detail was to be mounted, and a cadet officer of the day would be on duty. The assigned cadet for the night in question was Cadet Captain George W. Goethals of later Panama Canal fame.

During Christmas week another first-classman, Hewitt by name, approached Goethals. In the course of commiserating with him because of Goethals' New Year's Eve guard duty, Hewitt added, "But the guardhouse is a nice place for the O.D. to sit and bone. Burn the gas and sit there and read, right up to midnight—if you want to, Goat." Goethals, nicknamed Goat, asked no questions, and Hewitt offered no further explanation. The word spread among the conspirators that the cadet officer of the day had been had.

That night Goethals sat in the guardhouse and listened to the music coming from the hop. About eleven o'clock the music ended, cadets returned to their rooms, and Taps sounded. The plain was silent. Goethals heard a slight noise and looked up to see a cadet peering in at him. The cadet, whom Goethals knew, said nothing but quickly slinked away. Goethals now was certain something was up but did nothing.

As the clock struck midnight Goethals' suspicions were verified. The quiet was overwhelmed by a tremendous series of explosions and noises. A yell went up from the barracks, "Yeh-eh-eh! Happy New Year!" Roman candles, fireworks of all sorts, and cannons lighted up the sky and filled the winter air with sound. Goethals and the now aroused tactical officer of the day ran in the direction of the pyrotechnics, only to find themselves under fire. They managed to make it to the barracks door but found it bolted and had to stand helplessly by while a cadet leaned out one of the windows and displayed his vocabulary of vulgarity. Frustration increased because the yelling cadet could not be identified. Like all the conspirators, he was wearing a mask made of torn sheets.

All the cadet officers were also locked in their rooms. The quickly ordered formation and subsequent investigation did not discover the culprits. What was perhaps the greatest prank in West Point history remained a mystery to all but the cadets.[20]

Pranks of the magnitude of the 1879-1880 New Year's Eve affair were rare of course. A more common method of blowing off steam was "hazing." Originally hazing had been confined almost completely to summer camp and had consisted mainly of practical jokes and pranks, but by the 1870's and 1880's it took on a more vicious form. It was now done throughout the year and consisted of humiliations, which at times approached physical and mental torture. Most of the time hazing was simply a form of harassment of plebes by upper-classmen or retaliation toward overzealous upper-classmen by the first-year men. Plebes might band together and, in the dead of the night, fall upon a particularly unmerciful upper-classman to repay his harassment with some of their own. Mostly, however, it was the "devilling" of plebes: making them brace, drink objectionable liquid, or perform equally unpleasant tasks such as countless deep knee bends.[21]

Hazing was a constant thorn in the side of West Point officials during the late nineteenth century. Several Congressional investigations were conducted, but no solution was found. The basic problem was that, while the Superintendent and Congress might want to eliminate the practice, the officers on duty, the alumni, and the cadets themselves did not really oppose it. William T. Sherman, as General of the Army, rescinded punishment for a number of cadets found guilty of hazing. Henry O. Flipper, West Point's first black graduate, said he did not want to defend hazing but felt it was "indispensable" for the Academy. It would be impossible "to mould and polish the social amalgamation at West Point without it." It was the best way, he said, for plebes to learn that regulations were there to be obeyed. Cadet Douglas MacArthur apparently felt the same way. While a cadet he was forced to do so many knee bends he lost control of his muscles and collapsed. Still he refused to speak out against hazing before a Congressional committee. Even the Academy Board of Visitors was ambivalent. In 1881, for example, their report called hazing "a vicious and unmanly practice" but also rationalized that it was "probably as old as the formation of colleges."[22]

With such feelings there was little hope that the hazing system would ever be completely eliminated. It was one element of spice in the drab cadet fare and had become too much part of the mix to be removed easily. Hazing seemed to be as much a part of West Point as the Academy's Hudson River Plain itself.

Another unpleasant part of West Point life was the practice of social ostracism. The strong morality of the day, reinforced by the class system at the isolated Academy, made the cadets harsh judges of their peers. If a cadet was considered to be ungentlemanly or cowardly or a believer in an idea that the Corps found repugnant, he was "cut." No one would have anything to do with him except on official business. He would, in effect, cease to exist as far as the other cadets were concerned. He could go for weeks, months, perhaps even his entire West Point career without anyone speaking to him. Considering the loneliness and pressure of cadet life and the cadets' need for friendship and an interchange of ideas both for social and academic reasons, this was a cruel punishment. It was a form of hazing, far worse than the physical variety.

Commonly, all plebes suffered ostracism until they were accepted as part of the Corps. Bad as this was, they at least had their fellow plebes to share the suffering. The man who was ostracized for some specific reason had no such mitigating factors; he was completely alone.

There are countless examples of ostracism, some involving names that later became famous. In the 1850's General O. O. Howard was ostracized because his peers considered him an abolitionist, because he associated with "cut" cadets and made friends with and visited enlisted men; furthermore it was suspected that he joined the Bible class to influence the ethics professor. Upon the unofficial advice of a tactical officer he began to "knock some . . . [people] down," and this pugnacious attitude slowly ended most of the ostracism by the time of his graduation. Just before the Civil War the military theoretician Emory Upton was ostracized because he announced he was an abolitionist. From that time on he was either avoided or insulted. This continued until a cadet made some remarks Upton found particularly offensive, and a fight ensued. After that, his situation improved, although he continued to experience some ostracism throughout his entire cadet days.[23]

One of the most tragic examples of social ostracism involved a cadet named Boyd, who, after Civil War service, had come to West Point in 1863. In 1865 some money was repeatedly stolen from a cadet company. The entire Corps, furious, appointed themselves amateur detectives to find the culprit. The investigation settled on Boyd. At parade one evening a sign labeled "Thief" was pinned to his back and he was drummed out of the Corps. After this humiliation the cadets en masse proceeded to beat him up. An official investigation produced no proof of guilt, but the cadets remained convinced Boyd was the culprit, and they ostracized him for the rest of his cadet and Army career. It was not until much later that the truth came out. Boyd had been framed by his roommate, the real culprit.[24]

A cadet never knew when he might be the next one to suffer the fate of being isolated by his peers. A chance remark, an indication of cowardice, or a host of other possibilities could place him on the outside. Most cadets, however, did not suffer slights; they were the slighters. In their conspiracy of silence they found some common purpose, a feeling of coming together. Though the target might suffer, those who were dishing out the punishment probably received some perverse satisfaction. Cadets who found the matter distasteful could do little. If they protested too loudly, they would soon find themselves on the receiving end. Ostracism was part and parcel of cadet life.

There was a group of cadets who were snubbed from the moment they stepped onto West Point property, even before any personal evaluation could be made of them. Black cadets were ostracized as a matter of course. Their color was considered reason enough for them to be "cut."

They lived their entire West Point careers in total isolation.

In the antebellum period there had been no blacks at West Point. The war, the emancipation of the slaves, and the new citizen status of black people caused a change. Very quickly the question came up: How and when was the first black man to be admitted? How would the cadets, particularly the Southerners, react to a black man among them? If blacks were indeed inferior, as many believed, could a black man make it through the Academy? No one had any easy answers. The obvious solution was to enroll a Negro and have him begin his course of study. Some naturally disagreed and suggested that the answer to the problem was simply to keep blacks out.

The leaders in the movement to enroll a black cadet were the radical Republicans. These Senators and Congressmen already viewed the Academy with suspicion because of the defection of cadets to the Confederacy. Though they were skeptical about West Point's reaction to the admission of a black cadet, they were firm in believing that someone would have to break the barrier. They hoped all would go well once a black man was in. The country did not share their enthusiasm, but the Republicans saw it as a duty and as a political necessity.

It was felt at first that the initial black cadet would have to possess extraordinary qualities. Led by abolitionist general-politician Benjamin F. Butler and by the president of Oberlin College, a search for the superman needed to fill the job was begun. No one could be found to meet the qualifications. Nevertheless, Butler appointed a Charles S. Wilson of Massachusetts. But Wilson was found to be underage and never entered the Academy.

The first real appointments were made in a more routine manner, by Southern carpetbagger Congressmen. In

1870 the first two blacks appeared at West Point to take the long walk up from the train landing to the plain—Michael Howard of Mississippi and James Webster Smith of South Carolina. They were followed in the 1870's and 1880's by twenty others. Of these twenty-three blacks, only three graduated: Henry O. Flipper in 1877, John H. Alexander in 1887, and Charles Denton Young in 1889. The latter rose to colonel and had the distinction of being the highest-ranking black officer in World War I.[25]

Obviously, twenty-three is not a large number, considering the span of years in question and the number of blacks in the nation. West Point could not, however, be blamed for this small number. As one historian of West Point put it, the explanation was more probably found in "the social system of the nation, the poor educational facilities available, and the system of Congressional appointment."[26] He might have added that the nation's indifference also played a part.

West Point was not responsible for the paucity of black cadets, but it was responsible for the hostile greeting they received when they arrived. Officially, officers and professors presented no opposition to the admission of black cadets, and, legally, they gave the black cadets their rights. But that was the extent of it. In no way did they attempt to prepare the institution for the friction that was inevitable, and in no way did they try to ensure that the new black cadets would be made part of Academy life. They secretly approved of the ostracism of blacks that was practiced by the Corps.

This can be seen most clearly in reading contemporary discussions of the problem, among them the writings by two of West Point's most esteemed professors, Peter S. Michie and George L. Andrews. Michie in an 1880 *North American Review* article defended the cadet practice of ostracizing black cadets by attributing its origin to "*the fact* that, in any altercation, where a colored cadet was a party, punishment of the white cadet was more certain, more severe and speedy." It was a fear of getting in trouble, Michie argued, that caused whites to stay away from blacks. This ostracism Michie asserted, "has nothing of hatred in it," the evidence being the fact that no black cadet had ever been hazed. West Point was not, in any case, responsible for white feelings of repugnance; cadets brought them from home. It was not fair, considering West Point's proud heritage, to accuse it of being responsible for something that was accepted practice throughout the country. In any case, the problem could be easily solved: "Let the authorities send here some young colored men who in ability are at least equal to the average white cadet, and possessed of manly qualities and no matter how dark be the color of the skin, they will settle the question here as it must be settled in the country at large, on the basis of human intelligence and human sympathy."[27]

Professor Andrews came to the same conclusion, though his argument was even more revealing. He described the superior quality of the Military Academy, buttressing his description with quotes from several non-West Pointers. The treatment of black cadets, he said, was related to this general pattern of excellence. West Point was doing its duty toward blacks despite the inferior quality of the black candidates it was receiving. Considering the close relationship necessary between cadets, the poor quality of the blacks, and the anti-black feelings brought in from home by the white cadets, the resulting ostracism was not unexpected.

Furthermore, how could social acceptance of blacks be expected of West Point since it was not being practiced in the nation? The argument that black cadets did not want full social acceptance but merely wished to be treated with civility and not total exclusion, Professor Andrews felt, was fallacious. "Where should the line be drawn?" he asked. "If the colored race may claim as a right some part of social equality, on what principle may they be deprived of any part?" In any case, Academy authorities neither "interfered to prevent or hinder" social intercourse, nor did they enforce it. It was up to the cadets. Any white cadet was free to associate with a black cadet at any time. "If he honestly does so from principle, and his general conduct is consistent, he will command the respect of those who differ with him. But if his object be to make himself conspicuous and show his superiority to others—if his motive be vanity rather than principle—his comrades will be quick to perceive it, and he may expect what he so well merits."[28]

The point seems obvious. Michie and Andrews saw nothing wrong in the ostracism of black cadets; if anything, they viewed the situation as natural and inevitable. Since they approved of the practice, they did not lift a finger to modify or eliminate it; nor did any other faculty member. Consequently ostracism of black cadets became standard operating procedure at West Point. Any incoming black cadet had this extra impediment to add to the normal cadet pressures. His chances for survival were even more limited than might ordinarily have been the case.

Black cadets reacted to the feelings and actions of their white colleagues in varying ways. James Webster Smith, one of the first blacks to enter the Academy, tried to meet the opposition head on. He failed but not without a battle that brought the Academy unwanted notoriety and increased in it the suspicion that blacks were being sent there as part of a political plan to undermine it.

On arriving at West Point, Smith and another black, Michael Howard, were quickly welcomed one midnight. They were baptized in their sleep with the contents of a slop bucket. Later they were involved in a pushing match at the bootblack shop, which, according to one account, resulted in both blacks attempting to make the incident appear more serious than it was. In any case, Howard failed the entrance examination and went home. Smith entered the Academy alone. His Academy career continued stormy. Every day seemed to bring some new problem. He became discouraged and wanted to quit, but his benefactor, a white Northern educator, encouraged him not to give up. Smith stayed on and continued using the *lex taliones* and gave an eye for an eye, a tooth for a tooth. At one point he broke a water dipper over a white cadet's head during an argument. For this he and his opponent in what came to be known as "the battle of the dipper" were given extra punishment tours. President Grant, however, stepped in and voided the punishment, saying it was too mild, but neither he nor the Secretary of War had the authority to increase it.

Later in his West Point career Smith was court-martialed for lying. He had been reported for "inattention in ranks," but he insisted that what was really going on was that he was trying to keep another cadet from stepping on his toes. The other cadets denied this; and so Smith was court-martialed for lying and sentenced to dismissal. Again President Grant stepped in and had the charge changed to a year's suspension.

West Pointers were now convinced that Smith would be saved by the politicians no matter what he did. They hated Negroes and politicians anyway. Smith's belligerent attitude, his loud and constant demands for his rights both at the Academy and in the outside press, and his apparent political influence made him intensely hated. Professor Andrews called him "malicious, vindictive, and untruthful." He was ostracized not only because he was black but also because his attitude was disliked. A white cadet of similar personality, Professor Andrews said, would have been not only ostracized but physically ill-treated. One wonders, however, if any white cadet had ever been called upon to fight the enormous odds Smith faced. All of his troubles were the result of race. As one author put it, he was "separated from the corps by a wall of prejudice." He may be criticized for some of his actions, but then so must West Point.

The upshot of the whole matter was that Smith returned from his suspension and took up his West Point career but never graduated. He was dismissed for academic reasons before he received his commission, though he had spent four years at the Academy. He went on to become commandant of cadets at the all-black South Carolina Agricultural Institute at Orangeburg until his death in 1876.[29]

During Smith's later years another black cadet entered West Point, a young Georgian who would become the first black graduate of the Academy. Henry Ossian Flipper came to West Point in 1873 at a time when Smith's difficulties were rather well known. Flipper, who never had much respect for the peripatetic Smith, was a completely different personality. Rather than appeal to newspapers or politicians or belligerently fight for his rights, Flipper apparently fought his ostracism and the surrounding hostility with quiet strength and determination. He stood up for his official rights but did not try to intrude in other matters. He had the amazing internal fortitude to be able to withstand four years of isolation and insults and he graduated in 1877.[30]

Upon his graduation Flipper published a book about his life at the Academy, graphically describing the terribly difficult life of the black cadet and viewing ostracism through the eyes of the victim. Flipper told how hard his life was and how discouraged he became at times. He had no one to talk to, male or female. Friends from the outside were able to visit him only during favorable weather, but during the long winter he was completely alone except for a few black workers at the Academy. Holidays were particularly difficult. On these occasions when other cadets were skating, rowing, or simply visiting, he had nowhere to go. He could either walk around the grounds alone or stay in his room. On these occasions, with the barracks empty, he would become "so lonely and melancholy," he "wouldn't know what to do."

Even during class days no one had anything but official conversation with him. What's more, the cadets veritably tripped over themselves to avoid him even on these occasions. During his third year, when he had the right to fall in the front rank at formation, he was asked "to instead fall in on the right of the rear rank, to keep down trouble, and to avoid any show of presumption or forwardness." This he did. One person still had to stand next to him, however. Therefore a roster of plebes was kept, and each week a different first-year man was detailed to stand next to him. To make matters worse, absolutely no effort was made to conceal this plan from him.

Another pressure Flipper and all black cadets faced came from the fact that they were a constant source of curiosity. No matter where they went, people stared at them and whispered behind their backs. Flipper tells how he and Smith once took two young ladies for a stroll on Flirtation Walk. They had found some seats and were enjoying their conversation when they noticed cadets and picnickers passing by and staring. Flipper said it looked as though the four blacks were "the greatest natural wonder in existence." Another time while on a solitary walk he was noticed by a young girl who excitedly exclaimed to all around her, "The colored cadet! The colored cadet! I'm going to tell mama I've seen the colored cadet."

All these occurrences were nuisances and insulting, but the only time Flipper really became upset was during the annual examination. He would take the floor to begin his recitation and hear and see the whispering and surprise among the lady visitors observing the ceremony. "All this tended to confuse" him, he wrote, and "it was only by determined effort" that he was able to maintain "any degree of coolness."

Flipper's book is replete with examples of turning the other cheek. At times his usual ability to look at the bright side of everything is broken and he expresses bitterness at his isolation, but the bitterness is quickly replaced with a characteristically conciliatory statement. Flipper points out that he really did not know how the cadets felt about him; he did not have enough contact with them to have an accurate idea. In rare nighttime conversations with white cadets he gained some notion that his total ostracism was more the result of white fear of being treated similarly than of universal hatred.

Despite Academy disclaimers, Flipper felt that his isolation was organized. It was not simply the result of prejudices brought in from the outside. Certain elements among the cadets, "from the very lowest classes," "uncouth and rough in appearance," with "only a rudimentary education," "little or no knowledge of courtesy," as Flipper described them, "ruled the corps by fear." Flipper consoled himself with the belief that some cadets would have befriended him had they had the chance. When he had first come to the Academy, the plebes had not snubbed him. His ostracism came at a later time. The few furtive conversations with white cadets showed they were willing to talk with him as long as no one else knew about it. One even borrowed a book but then mutilated it to prevent anyone else from recognizing it as Flipper's.[31]

And there would seem to be little reason to question Flipper's conclusion that his ostracism was indeed a conspiracy. A white cadet who might feel inclined to befriend a black was kept from doing so by fear of repercussions. One wonders, then, what the situation might have been if West Point officials had simply let it be known that ostracism would not be tolerated. Had they viewed black entrance into the Academy with favor and acted accordingly, there seems little reason not to believe that the impressionable young men under them would have followed suit.

Perhaps this is asking too much. Perhaps West Point was too much a reflection of American society to be able to do this. American society was not opening itself to black people, and the Academy simply followed suit. Whether from fear of subversion or as a reflection of society's aversion to the black race, West Point did not react with honor to the introduction of blacks into her midst. The life of the black cadet was a hard one, requiring almost herculean qualities. Only the truly superior had any hope of graduation.

Chapter 2

FROM SLAVE TO CADET

August 23, 1858, dawned on the Camden, South Carolina, plantation of the senior James Chesnut. The massive house of twelve bedrooms was abustle with activity in preparation for breakfast at 7:00 A.M. The house slaves scurried about cooking, cleaning, and polishing, while the field hands had already begun their long day in the sun. It was the start of another hot August day at "Mulberry."[1] This day, however, was to be different in one respect. Maria J. Whitaker, a house slave, the wife of freedman James Whitaker and the mother of eleven-month-old Edward, gave birth to twin sons, Johnson and Alex.[2]

Johnson Chesnut Whittaker (in later years he spelled his name with two t's) was born into slavery bearing the names of three of the most important white families in the Camden area—the Johnsons, the Chesnuts, and the Whitakers. Colonel James Chesnut, his owner, had long played a leading role in the history of South Carolina. James Jr., before

27

the war, was a United States Senator and later a Confederate general and aide to Jefferson Davis. He played an important part in the Confederate war effort. But it was daughter-in-law, Mary Boykin, the wife of the younger Chesnut, who was to give the family its truest historical significance. Her famous *Diary from Dixie* brilliantly chronicled the life of the Confederacy[3] and unknowingly also chronicled the lives of Maria and her children.

Upon her arrival at Mulberry in 1861, Mary Chesnut was immediately attended by her father-in-law's servants, including Maria Whitaker. The slave and the master's daughter-in-law had known each other from previous visits, so the conversation came easily. Mrs. Chesnut, watching Maria's face in her mirror as the slave stood brushing her hair, saw Maria's eyes filling with tears. Thinking that all the war talk had frightened the servant, Mary Chesnut tried to comfort her. "Now listen, let the war end either way and you will be free. We will have to free you before we get out of this thing." Maria waved this off, saying that, while the young master might feel that way, the older Chesnut had no such thoughts. In any case this was not the cause of her sorrow.

"Now, Miss Mary, you see me married to Jeems Whitaker yourself. I was a good and faithful wife to him, and we were comfortable everyway, good house, everything. He had no cause of complaint. But he has left me." Mary Chesnut, surprised, asked why. "Because I had twins," Maria answered. "He says they are not his, because nobody named Whitaker ever had twins." Bespeaking the slaveowner's mentality, Mary Chesnut tried to console her slave materially. "Come now, Maria! Never mind, your old Missis and Marster are so good to you. Now let us look up something for the twins." Musing further in her diary, Mary Chesnut wrote that Maria "deserved a better fate in her honest matrimonial attempt" because she was "one of the good colored women." But she did have "a trying temper." Apparently "Jeems was tried, and he failed to stand the trial." In November 1861 he was still adamant, and there is no record of his ever looking after his family.[4]

During most of the war, life on the Chesnut plantation changed little; it was almost as if there was no war going on. In fact, Mr. Chesnut reproached his wife for this sort of attitude. "This is no time for junketing and merry-making," he told her. "There is a positive want of proper feeling in the life you lead." She promised to change but as late as December 1864 compared herself and her circle to "outsiders at the time of the flood. We eat, drink, laugh, dance, in lightness of heart."[5]

Even old Mr. Chesnut seemed oblivious to the war. Mary Chesnut told how, in January 1862, he was making yet another will and telling each of his slaves to whom he intended to leave them. He did this, said Mary Chesnut, "as if there were no Yankees." Life moved blissfully undisturbed on the Chesnut plantation.[6]

And Mulberry was a beautiful place to forget the war. Proud oaks, holly trees, flower-laden drives and walks, gardens, beds of strawberries and raspberries surrounded the massive house. A large kitchen building, the smokehouse, and the dairy were also nearby. The brick cottages of the house servants, where Maria and her children probably lived, were located in a grove north of the house. South of the mansion was the so-called "Old Yard" area, where the field hands lived in less adequate but, by the hard standard of the times, still serviceable slave cottages. In a shady clump of trees nearby was the chapel where once a month a traveling Southern Methodist minister held services.

Life on Mulberry was an orderly existence presided over by the invalid Mrs. Chesnut and by the often cranky but basically kind master. Breakfast was served at seven during the warm seasons and at eight during winter. Dinner was at three, while tea and bread or biscuits were taken at seven in the evening. By the time breakfast was on the table, the house was cleaned and the master ready to make his rounds on horseback.[7] The slave, of course, was largely responsible for ensuring the efficient operation of the plantation. The Chesnuts were kind to their slaves and expected loyalty in return. Mary Chesnut often lamented the burdens of the institution of slavery and, like many other whites, expressed a desire to see it end. She, her father-in-law, and others, perhaps to convince themselves, argued that the slaves were the real beneficiaries of the institution, a happy carefree people, with no responsibility and all the real benefits.

Yet, despite the basic unconcern with the war and the confident belief that the slaves were living the good life, one question kept intruding into the sedate plantation existence. Just how loyal were the slaves? The murder of a Chesnut cousin in September 1861 "by her own people, her negroes," served only to highlight this question. Mary Chesnut wondered whether the same thing might not happen to her. "Why should they treat me any better?" she pondered. She and another cousin stayed up one entire night discussing the problem and came to no solution. Most disturbing, according to Mrs. Chesnut, was the fact that the slaves' "faces . . . [were] as unreadable as the Sphinx." Even at the approach of Sherman she felt she could not tell what they were thinking. "These sphinxes give no sign, unless it be increased diligence, and absolute silence. They are as certain in their actions and as noiseless as a law of nature —when we are in the house!"[8]

In truth, the Chesnuts had little to fear. Their slaves, unlike many others, remained loyal throughout the war even in the face of Sherman's march. Almost to a person they remained at their tasks. In 1862 some of them even offered to fight for their master if he armed them. Like the whites around them, they showed little interest in the war and carried on as if nothing had changed. In February 1864, for example, Lawrence, the body servant of the young Mr. Chesnut, transported $600 in pay over a long distance to Mary Chesnut. She told him that this proved his loyalty. To her consternation "he grinned, but said nothing."[9]

Examples of such devotion only served to convince Mary Chesnut how well off and "spoiled" the slaves were. It was with no small measure of satisfaction that she quoted the words of Jefferson Davis' slave Stephen: "Why Missis, your niggers down here are well off. I call this Mulberry place Heaven, plenty to eat, little to do, a warm house to sleep in, a good church and a good preacher all here right at hand."[10]

It was under this system that young Johnson Whittaker grew up. From an early age he was doubtless given light tasks around the plantation house. He and his brothers played with the white children. Members of the upper echelon of slave society under a mild regime, with a free mulatto father and a light-skinned mother, they suffered less in their slavery than the sons of darker field hands did. They had, in all probability, the best that the American system of enslavement permitted. Unlike the field workers, their lives were not physically hard. Still they suffered psychologically; they were never allowed to forget their station. They were slaves, considered inferior to the master whites. As long as they remembered this and did their work, they were not treated harshly. But they suffered anyway; Maria Whitaker, for example, never learned how to read or write, even after she was freed.[11]

Perhaps in no way was this superior-inferior attitude more obvious in Mrs. Chesnut's account of life at Mulberry than when she discussed the slaves in church. She told how Manning Brown, a white Methodist minister, preached to the "well dressed" black congregation on the horrors of sin and hell. One can picture the women house slaves, Maria Whitaker included, "in white aprons and white turbans," listening attentively to the torrent of words. When driver Jim Nelson was asked to lead in prayer, Maria probably joined in the sobbing and clapping and, like others, used her apron to dry her tears of religious fervor. Mary Chesnut was moved to shout but felt it beneath her dignity, and remained silent. Though she herself was caught up in the emotion of the religious ceremony she was describing, her account shows her condescending attitude toward the slaves and their worship.

Later in her diary Mary Chesnut described the visit of the circuit rider, a Mr. Shuford. She saw the slave wedding that took place after the service and described what she considered to be the hilarity of some of the attendant activity. Maria Whitaker was again present; that evening as she combed Mary Chesnut's hair, she discussed the event, refusing to accept notions of black inferiority, yet implicitly connecting whiteness and virtue as she compared the two preachers. She liked Brown a great deal more. "He is old Marster's nephew, a gentleman born, and he preaches to black and white just the same. There ain't but one gospel for all. He tells us 'bout keeping the Sabbath holy, honoring our fathers and mothers, and loving our neighbors as ourselves." Preacher Shuford, on the other hand, insulted his audience: "Mr. Shuford he goes for low life things, hurting people's feelings. 'Don't you tell lies! Don't you steal!' Worse things, real indecent. Before God, we are as white as he is, and in the pulpit he no need to make us feel we are servants." Mary Chesnut disagreed and defended Shuford. Her diary does not indicate if she convinced the strong-willed Maria.[12]

The two biggest events to occur at Mulberry during the Civil War were the death of old Mrs. Chesnut in March 1864 and the coming of Sherman's army early in 1865. Mrs. Chesnut had directed the work of the house slaves and was apparently kind to them. Maria Whitaker and her sons probably shared in the sorrow over her death, and their lives were affected by the depression of their bereaved master. Sherman's coming caused a far greater upheaval. Mary Chesnut stayed away from Mulberry and the Camden area while the Federal troops marched through, but she learned what had happened from Maria Whitaker. One can picture Maria with her sons clinging to her skirts watching the arrival of the Union army.

Elements of Sherman's force moved onto Mulberry in late February 1865 and began destroying the plantation house. Working systematically as the frightened inhabitants and slaves watched, they began to tear the house and its contents apart, until a general, possibly Sherman himself, rode up to survey the scene. "He said it was a shame," Maria recounted, "and he stopped them; he said it was a sin to destroy a fine old house like this, whose owner was over ninety years old. He would not have done it for the world. It was wanton mischief." Perhaps nodding to the assembled people and by chance noticing the Whittaker twins, the general rode on. His men stopped their work and departed, carrying off the Chesnut horses. After all the soldiers were gone, the onlookers were surprised to find that one side of the house was a wreck, while the other was perfectly intact.[13]

Later, in April, the Camden area recoiled from another raid, this one conducted by about 2,700 Negro troops led by General Edward T. Potter. According to Mary Chesnut, this raid caused more damage than Sherman's and left nothing "but bare land, and debts." In Camden, a mass meeting of blacks was held, and some slaves followed the troops when they left for Charleston. The Chesnut slaves ignored the talk of freedom and stayed by their masters as they had during Sherman's incursion.[14]

The war ended with Mulberry a scarred shadow of its former self and its slaves, freedmen, uncertain about their future. The elder Chesnut died in 1866, and the young Chesnuts lived at Mulberry until 1873. The new freedmen were, for the most part, on their own, though some stayed on as laborers. How Maria Whitaker, husbandless and with three young children, viewed the uncertain future is unknown.

The end of the Civil War in South Carolina, as in the rest of the South, caused a revolution in life. The black population was free and society's basic problem was defining the role to be played by this newly emancipated people. What should the relationship be between whites and blacks? What rights would the freedmen have? Could the two races live in peace together? There were no easy answers to these complicated questions. Until recently history has focused on the whites, sympathizing with their suffering under what was considered a harsh regime of reconstruction. However, it was black people, individuals like Maria Whitaker and her children, who suffered the most. It was they who had to find their place in the new society and adapt to a life of freedom after generations of slavery and in the face of determined white opposition.

Historians have debated the extent of segregation in the South during this period.[15] But perhaps the physical separation of the races was not so important as the mental one. Both races saw themselves as separate and reacted accordingly. Whites accepted without question the idea of black inferiority. In many ways this was a carry-over of the old antebellum argument in support of slavery with its religious and scientific underpinning. The white was convinced that, for the good of society, the newly freed black must be kept in his inferior status.

For the most part, blacks in South Carolina did not enjoy the luxury of such certitude. As might be expected, considering the rapid change from slavery to freedom, most blacks in South Carolina did not know intuitively what their role should be. Generations of slavery and brainwashing had convinced many of their inferiority. Black was not considered beautiful; it was a mark of subservience. There was, consequently, much confusion. Should blacks attempt to become part of white society and expose themselves to slights and humiliations or should they withdraw into themselves and build their own communities?

Particularly confused were people like Maria and her children, the mulattoes, persons with both white and black blood in their veins. In 1870 they represented about 7 percent of the black population in South Carolina. Though they were proud of their white blood, which had usually resulted from "stable liaisons," they did not reject their blackness. They were, after all, members of both races, similar to both, yet distinct. Theoretically, they should have been able to enter either society or form one of their own. In actuality they were rejected by white society. They themselves quickly rejected the alternative of a separate society and thus entered the black community and became an important part of it.[16]

Blacks like Maria who had been house servants generally took similar positions with white families after emancipation. Now, however, they were paid a salary. Maria Whitaker, for example, worked for the family of the prosperous Chesnut relative W. C. Reynolds in Camden. She apparently worked as a domestic, doing much the same work she had performed as a slave. Her sons were also employed at various times by this Camden family. The Whitakers owned a 66-by-264-foot plot of property adjacent to the "Methodist Episcopal Church (colored)" fronting on DeKalb Street in Camden and approximately 300 acres along the Wateree River outside the town. The circumstances of the DeKalb Street property acquisition are uncertain, although it is known that the purchase was made in 1876 from the church for the appreciable sum of $150. The Wateree property was sold to James Whitaker by John Kershaw, the receiver of a deceased white plantation owner named L. L. Whitaker. James Whitaker was a creditor of the estate, and the 1873 purchase price was $895.[17] Apparently on his death in 1883 James willed the land to the wife whom he had abandoned so long before.

From this fragmentary evidence it would appear that Maria and her children were spared the hard life of many of their fellow freedmen. In a society where property was a mark of wealth, the ownership of land by a former slave indicated a high standing in the black community. Maria still had to work hard for her existence, but she was not destitute.

Life for a husbandless woman with three boys is never simple, of course, and it was not made easier when a tragedy hit the family. On November 10, 1871, Johnson's twin brother, Alex, died from complications caused by jamming an acorn into his nose.[18] For Johnson, the loss of his twin brother must have been a particularly hard blow.

During the years immediately after the war, Johnson and his brothers, in addition to working and playing with the children of pioneer black Camden Baptist minister Monroe Boykin, attended a freedmen's school in Camden. It is unknown when they began, but, in Johnson's case, it was no later than October 1869. His teacher, Angelina Ball, later remembered first meeting young Whittaker that month. The teacher, a native of Massachusetts who may have brought her belongings South in a carpetbag, taught Johnson for five years and during this time she also employed him to some extent as a laborer.[19]

Religion played an important part in the young Johnson Whittaker's life. The family belonged to the Methodist Episcopal Church, which was located next to their DeKalb Street property, and became friendly with the church's minister, Edward M. Pinkney, who helped teach Johnson when the Camden public school closed. When the announcement of a competitive examination for entrance into the University of South Carolina was made, Whittaker came to Pinkney's house for instruction. He worked for an uncle in the morning as a hod carrier and mason's helper and studied in Pinkney's library in the afternoon. The black minister tutored him in arithmetic, algebra, geography, grammar, history, and Latin. Pinkney's own knowledge was limited, but when the scholarship examination was given in July 1874 Whittaker met it successfully. He was scheduled to enter the university in the fall of 1874.[20]

In many ways the University of South Carolina was a battleground for the clash of rival philosophies of education and race. Radicals and blacks generally felt that freedmen who had no suitable school of their own should be able to enter as students, while conservatives wanted at all costs to keep the school white. The resulting clash came to a head in 1873 and saw a wave of faculty and student resignations over the medical school registration of the first black student. A new faculty was recruited, and students of both races were welcomed. Only a few whites accepted the invitation. Professors came from all over the country. William Main, the professor of chemistry, was a University of Pennsylvania graduate. Fisk P. Brewer had been lecturer at the radical-controlled University of North Carolina until it had closed in 1870. He became professor of ancient languages and literature. Most importantly, a man who was to play a leading role in Whittaker's life, Richard T. Greener, Harvard's first black graduate, became professor of mental and moral philosophy.

At first the radical university faced the same problem the conservative one had—lack of students. To try to overcome this problem the state legislature passed a law in February 1874 providing for 124 scholarships to be awarded on the basis of competitive examination each July in the county seats. In order to fill the university immediately, the first examination took place on March 22, 1874. When the first winners arrived, in April, the faculty was shocked to learn that many of them could not meet the minimum admission standards for the freshman year. As a result, a so-called "sub-freshman" class was established and the deficient scholarship winners placed there. Still, enrollment was small.

Johnson C. Whittaker took his examination in July 1874 and, in the fall of that year, arrived in Columbia to begin his college work. He was quickly found insufficiently prepared. On October 5, 1874, after considering the report of the State Board of Examiners, the faculty placed Whittaker in the sub-freshmen class.[21]

During the two years he attended the university Whittaker did well scholastically. He quickly worked his way out of the sub-freshmen class to the full classical course and

37

ranked near the head of his class. His over-all yearly average in both 1875 and 1876 was 86 percent and in his work for January 1875 he scored 100 percent. His professors later remembered him as an outstanding student of determination and hard-working spirit with, as one noted, "excellent scholarship in languages." Apparently, Whittaker made the most of his educational opportunity.[22]

At the university Whittaker rubbed elbows with a number of future black leaders in South Carolina, among them men who were to become members of the House of Representatives (George Washington Murray and Thomas E. Miller), state senators, college presidents, newspapermen, ministers, and a future associate justice of the supreme court of Liberia.[23]

One of his acquaintances became a fast friend and adviser, black professor Richard T. Greener. It was through Greener's efforts that he left the university in 1876 for further education. In that year Greener selected him as the student most capable of receiving a Congressional appointment to the United States Military Academy at West Point. Within a year of Whittaker's departure, the university returned to conservative control, admitting only whites. Interestingly, many of the curriculum reforms adopted by the radical faculty remained unchanged.[24]

Johnson Chesnut Whittaker arrived at West Point on his birthday, August 23, 1876. He had been nominated by carpetbagger Congressman S. L. Hoge to fill the place vacated by black cadet James Webster Smith and by several unsuccessful white candidates. Whittaker was at that time eighteen years old and, according to his physical examination report, five feet eight inches tall and 110 pounds in weight. He had 20/20 vision, had been vaccinated, and used no tobacco. His various body measurements were appropriate for his height and weight; he was very slight, light-skinned, and he had freckles.

Whittaker passed the physical and academic examinations that took place during his first several days at West Point and began his military career as a member of the plebe class.[25] Since he had not arrived in June, he had missed the summer camp with its hazing and harassment of first-year cadets.

Very early in his career Whittaker ran into trouble. An Alabama cadet, J. B. McDonald, struck him in the face because of some disagreement. No doubt because of the influence of his black roommate, Henry O. Flipper, Whittaker did not fight back as Smith would have done but simply reported the incident to West Point authorities. McDonald was court-martialed and suspended for more than six months, thus being forced to repeat the year.[26] West Pointers, who had despised Smith for being too belligerent, now despised Whittaker for being unbelligerent. They tabbed him a coward.

The rest of the plebe year was quite uneventful. Rooming with a black first-class man, Whittaker was able to benefit from both his academic and social advice. There is no evidence of any further untoward occurrences that year. Whittaker received the usual cadet demerits for such offenses as slowness in doing the manual of arms or looking around in ranks, but his total of penalty marks was very low. He was, in fact, a leader in this respect throughout his West Point career. Along with many other cadets, he was, as of November 30, 1876, excused from all but the essential formations and allowed "to walk on public lands between reveille and tattoo."[27] This, of course, gave him and the other cadets a great deal more freedom and the chance to expand their confined worlds a little. It also indicated that their disciplinary status was acceptable.

Academically Whittaker's performance was far from spectacular, but he was in no danger of dismissal. He was transferred from section to section, as were all the cadets, and finished the first year near the bottom of his class. He did best in French, where he received middle ranking.[28]

In June 1877 Whittaker's roommate, Henry O. Flipper,

39

became the first black man to graduate from the military academy. Certainly this must have been a time of mixed feelings for Whittaker. He shared Flipper's joy and must have been encouraged to think that if one black man had made it he could make it too. At the same time, however, he must have been saddened to think that now he would be alone, the only black man left at West Point. It is uncertain just what the exact relationship between Whittaker and Flipper was that year, because Flipper makes only passing mention to his roommate in his autobiography, and Whittaker left no record. But their mutual dislike for Smith's actions and the fact that they were the only two blacks at the Academy probably made them close. Logically, the older, more experienced Flipper had a great influence on his younger colleague. Throughout his career, in fact, Whittaker turned the other cheek, yet stood on his rights just as Flipper had done.

Fortunately for Whittaker, when the next academic year arrived another black cadet did too, Charles A. Minnie. Whittaker again had a black roommate, though now he was the elder of the two and looked to for advice. Things seemed to be going well at first, and Whittaker was even the beneficiary of an unnamed tactical officer's concern. Several times during that fall this officer enforced Whittaker's rights against several cadets who tried to abridge them. But Minnie was a problem. He refused to study his mathematics despite Whittaker's constant advice, failed his January examination, and was dismissed. Whittaker said this was all done *"fairly and squarely,"* and Minnie knew it; on his departure, he acknowledged it and wished he could have had another opportunity to redeem himself. But there was no second chance, and, in January 1878, Whittaker was left alone.[29]

He finished that year successfully but the following January ran into difficulty. He failed an examination and was slated for dismissal. Fortunately for him the Superintendent, General John M. Schofield, gave him and two white cadets the opportunity to repeat the year rather than be dismissed. In Whittaker's case, Schofield said he was influenced by Whittaker's hard-working determination and the fact that he was the only black cadet at the Academy. Consequently, the academic year 1879–1880 found Whittaker repeating his second-class (junior) year instead of being a member of the graduating class.[30]

In summary, Whittaker could be described as a quiet young man with average academic achievement. Even though he was repeating subjects in 1879–1880, he remained in the bottom half of his class. In March 1880 he dropped into the sixth, or last, section in the nineteenth-century equivalent of physics, natural and experimental philosophy. But, according to later statements of his philosophy professor, he was in no danger of failure. Peter Michie called him a "very studious and very attentive" student whose memory was "excellent." His over-all average for the repeated year was about 83 percent.[31]

The real problem of Whittaker's life was not academic. It was the fact that, like the black cadets who had come before him, he was completely ostracized by the cadets and staff at West Point. No one spoke to him except on official business and then as briefly and usually as curtly as possible. Cadets reproached him if he tried to sit next to them at the mess table or if he tried to fall in next to them at formation. It was reported that one cadet was willing to give up his corporal stripes rather than stand in formation next to the black cadet. On one occasion another cadet, George Burnett, took a command which was supposed to be Whittaker's. A cadet named Blake got into an argument with Whittaker when Whittaker took his hat by mistake after a meal. No one would room with the black cadet, so, once Flipper and Minnie were gone, Whittaker had to himself a room normally occupied by two cadets.[32]

In short, Whittaker was completely on his own—academically, militarily, and socially. He never had the benefit of discussing a difficult problem; he was never invited to take part in cadet recreation; no one ever visited his room, nor was he ever invited to visit anyone else's. He was not hazed, but occasionally cadets would play pranks on him, as when in 1879 someone sent him a threatening note. In 1878 one of the poems in the unofficial cadet publication *West Point Tic Tacs* contained an insulting poem entitled "Nigger Jim." This was obviously a reference to Smith, but since Whittaker was the only black cadet at the time, its publication expressed, graphically, cadet disdain for him because of his race.[33]

Whittaker, for his part, was a naturally shy person and made no determined effort to break out of this enforced isolation and become an integral part of West Point cadet life. As a member of a race which had been constantly told that it was inferior and unworthy of associating with whites on an equal basis and having the same privileges, it is understandable why Whittaker "kept his place." All his life he had experienced the unwillingness of whites to mingle with blacks. Perhaps he felt that if he were not too forward, as time went on, the other cadets would accept him. Whatever the case, Whittaker seemed to accept his ostracism with stoicism, though internally, as shown in a brief Fall 1878 journal and in a number of letters, he was aware of all the snubs and bitter over them.[34]

Though no cadets would have anything to do with him, Whittaker did have a few fellow blacks in the area to converse with even if only on occasion. There were two black servants on the post, Louis Simpson and Walter Mitchell, with whom he sometimes talked. There was a colony of blacks located in nearby Highland Falls, and, on rare occasions, he visited them. During two vacation periods he visited a friend, Moses Wester, a janitor in New York, and another time he went to Washington to stay with his former South Carolina professor, Richard T. Greener. Wester visited him at least once in August or September 1879.[35]

For the most part, however, he kept to himself, studied, wrote letters to his mother or friends, and faithfully read a Bible. A perusal of this Bible gives a good indication just how alone Whittaker was at West Point and how much his religion served as a refuge from his loneliness. On the front leaf of this brown leather Bible, Whittaker, on April 21, 1878, had written, "Try never to injure another by word, by action. . . . Forgive as soon as you are injured and forget as soon as you forgive." On New Year's Day, 1879, he wrote that he would always try "to do his duty to God and man" and never do anything that would "make his mother blush." He promised to do right no matter how difficult it was.

In the text of the Bible, Whittaker underlined passages and wrote his own commentaries. All the underlined passages were concerned with loneliness. To cite only two examples, he underlined the sixteenth chapter, thirty-second verse of St. John: "Yet I am not alone because the Father is with me." In the margin he wrote in pencil: "I in my dreary solitude surrounded by none but enemies can say that I am not destitute of friends for God is near me." Verse 14 of the 27th Psalm was also underlined: "Wait on the Lord: be of good courage and he shall strengthen thy heart: Wait, I say, on the Lord." In the margin he wrote: "a world of comfort for sad souls is locked in this 14th verse, XXVII chapter." Throughout the Bible were pressed flowers and paper clippings and poems all dealing with loneliness, mother, God, and being away from home.[36]

Little is actually known of the day-to-day life of Johnson C. Whittaker other than what is cited above and the fact that he was on leave several times, including Christmastime, in 1879.[37] Basically he lived the drab life of the ordinary cadet, a life made more drab by his isolation, with little to distinguish one day from the next. This drabness was all changed on April 6, 1880. The unknown black cadet, the outcast, became a national celebrity. He was the principal in an incident that shook the Academy to its very foundations and changed his entire life.

Chapter 3

THE ATTACK
AND THE BEGINNING
OF A MYSTERY

JOHNSON C. Whittaker lay bleeding and unconscious on the floor.[1] One cadet, Burnett, ran for help while two others, Frederick G. Hodgson and Louis Ostheim, watched over the prostrate form. No effort was made to approach Whittaker, the two onlookers hesitating to take action until the arrival of a superior officer. They simply stood at the threshold, watched and waited, surveying a chaotic scene.

Whittaker, dressed only in his underclothes, was lying partially on his back, partially on his right side, with the right side of his face on a comforter topped by a pillow. His body formed a parallel line with the iron bed to which his feet were tied at a 25-degree angle. His right foot was touching the side rail of the bed, while his left foot, the outside one, was tied a bit higher than the right one. Both feet were tied to the bed with cut-down cadet belting, about an inch and a quarter wide (normal cadet belting was about two and a half inches wide). One band tied the two feet together at the ankles, while another one tied them to the bed, circling the bedrail one or two times. The knot was located between the feet.

Similar bands bound the black cadet's arms in front of his body. The insides of his wrists were pressed together, and the belting was wound tightly around them. The fingers were left free. The extreme tightness of the binding was evident in the fact that hours later that evening marks were visible on the wrists and ankles.

Whittaker was all covered with blood. There was blood on his face, his neck, his ears, on one of his feet, on the shoulders of his undershirt, and on his drawers above the knees. There was also blood on the center of the mattress, on the wall above the middle of the bed, and on the floor. Some of the material found on the floor near Whittaker was stained, as was the doorjamb. The pillow was soaked with blood.

Whittaker's right ear was slashed across the lobe, causing a wound five-eighths of an inch long, with a slighter cut just above the first. The left ear had a small piece of the lobe cut off. There were two five-eighths-inch parallel cuts on the little toe of his foot and a scratch and a non-bleeding abrasion on his left hand.

Articles littered the floor. At the foot of the bed was a blood-marked blanket and comforter. Near the table outside the alcove was an Indian club with spots of blood near the knob, at a point where an ordinary hand could not grip it. Within the alcove between the partition and the black cadet's feet lay a broken one-foot-square hand mirror face down, a wet sock, and burned pieces of paper with small pools of water on and around them. In a semicircle around the mirror were bunches of hair cut from the back of Whittaker's head. A riding jacket, a pair of pants, and a civilian necktie were lying on the floor near the partition. Near Whittaker's head were found an unspotted white-handled pocket knife, with one blade open, and a blood-soaked handkerchief with a 1½-by-2½-inch rounded rectangular hole cut out at a spot where a name tag might be located. On the table outside the alcove could be seen an opened philosophy book, a checkbook with an order written out, and miscellaneous papers. Later discovered was a small pair of black scissors with one-third-inch pieces of hair in them. The gaslight was only partially on and gave little illumination. The curtain of the alcove showed no signs of having been closed, but the window curtains were closed tightly.

Whittaker's room was sparsely furnished. At the head of the alcove dividing wall was a washstand and bucket. Along the wall opposite the door stood a gun rack, the mantel, chimney, and steam heater. A table and chair, a gas jet, some pegs for hanging clothes, and a doorless set of shelves completed the furnishings. The shelves served the purpose of a clothes press, holding, according to regulation, unused bedding and articles of clothing such as handkerchiefs, underwear, and toilet articles.

In addition to the door and accompanying transom, a window looked out on the barracks area, and a ventilator made of "slats of slanting direction" and a small wooden door pierced the twelve inches of stone wall into the hall. A fireplace flue passed through the ceiling onto the roof above, while steam pipes, with about an inch between them and approximately that much around them, came into the room from below. The combined thickness of the floor and the ceiling below it was eighteen inches. Whittaker's room was in a building of solid construction.[2]

While Hodgson and Ostheim waited for Burnett to return, other curious cadets looked in. Hodgson noticed Whittaker's toe twitch, indicating life, but no one made any move to aid the black cadet. The only conversation consisted of mutual denials that any cadet could have done such a deed. In the meantime, Burnett had run down the four flights of stairs and reported to the officer of the day at the guardhouse near the barracks. "There seems to be something wrong with Cadet Whittaker," Burnett blurted

46

out to Major Alexander Piper. "He is lying on the floor of his room and does not answer when spoken to."

Piper, thinking that Whittaker had probably overslept and then in suddenly jumping up had fainted, hurried to his room. Piper, his orderly, and Burnett arrived about 6:10 A.M. Walking into the room, Piper exclaimed, "Is he dead? Poor boy! He has been murdered." He immediately checked Whittaker's pulse, found it beating normally, and heard Hodgson report that Whittaker's toe had moved.

Burnett threw open the window curtains, then walked toward Whittaker, stopping to pick up the broken mirror and noticing that there was some blood on it. Thinking, according to what he said later, that Whittaker's throat had been cut, he took his head in his hand and turned it over. From this inspection he discovered that blood was still flowing from one of the ear cuts. He checked Whittaker's pulse again and felt that it was beating rapidly but then slowed down. He later opined that his own excitement may have caused this apparent change of pulse rate.

Hodgson, on Piper's order, had in the meantime started to loosen Whittaker's legs from the bed. Having difficulty with the knots, he asked for a knife, but then stepped aside when Burnett said he would do it. Burnett had untied the first half knot on the bands when he was handed a pair of scissors. Cadet Ostheim, having noticed Hodgson's difficulty, had brought a pair from across the hall. He had noticed Whittaker's scissors but had decided they were too dull to cut through the bands.

Using the scissors, Burnett cut Whittaker's feet loose while Hodgson freed his hands. The tightness of the bands around Whittaker's wrists made this latter operation difficult. In order to do the cutting, the scissors had to be slipped between the wrists and the bands, but the tautness and the secure knot made this a hard job. After some effort, however, the cutting was accomplished. The black cadet was free. He lay flat on the floor. He still showed no signs of consciousness.

Immediately, Major Piper sent his orderly to get the Academy surgeon, Dr. Charles T. Alexander. The orderly found Dr. Alexander at the cadet dispensary and within ten minutes the doctor was at Whittaker's side.

While they were waiting for the physician, the persons in the room were busy. Whittaker shivered from the 42-degree temperature, yet no attempt was made to revive him. Burnett simply threw a blanket and quilt over him for warmth. Piper told the cadets in the room, by this time about eight in number, to survey the scene carefully and to call in other witnesses to do likewise. Describing the situation to those who had just arrived, he said, "Of course you didn't see; but this is the way he was tied to the bed."

Piper also did some investigating himself, checking the bands for a name or initials. He found none. He feared that the entire back of Whittaker's head had been cut or bashed in and nervously awaited the appearance of the doctor; he went out into the hall several times to see if he was coming. When Cadet Ostheim left the room to go to breakfast, Dr. Alexander was coming up the stairs. The two men passed each other in silence.

Dr. Alexander, who was later remembered in one former cadet's diary as a stern judge of suspected goldbrickers,[3] walked quickly into the room. He said nothing to anyone but immediately went over to Whittaker. Taking the black cadet's arm, he checked his pulse and quickly reported that it was beating very regularly for a man in an unconscious state. "There is something wrong here," Alexander said. He checked for head injuries and made a quick perusal of the extent of the wounds. "What is the matter with you, Whittaker?" he asked. "Tell me what is the matter with you. I want to know what to do for you." Whittaker, still not opening his eyes, weakly responded, "Please don't cut me." "We are not going to hurt you," Alexander replied. "What is the matter with you?" "Please don't cut me," Whittaker persisted in a weak voice. "I never injured you."

48

Every time the doctor spoke to him, the black cadet responded in this fashion.

Not having been successful with words alone, Alexander tried shaking and pinching Whittaker, but the cadet remained insensible. Alexander now checked for a concussion by lifting Whittaker's left eyelid and looking at his eye. He later reported that he encountered a "slight muscular resistance." When he had opened the eyelid, the eye seemed to be turned up; the white part, looking very bloodshot, was visible. Cadet Burnett, kneeling at Whittaker's head throughout the examination, on noting the condition of the eye, blurted out, "I think this thing is a hoax." Alexander ignored Burnett and shook and pinched Whittaker again, saying, "Let me see your eyes. I want to see what is the matter with you." Whittaker made no response, but his pupil became visible. Alexander opened and closed the eyelid several times to check the effect of the light on the pupil and noticed a slight trembling in Whittaker's other eyelid.

Dr. Alexander also tapped Whittaker's breast during the examination, and the black cadet gave some indication of pain. This and a slight sliding motion with his head on the pillow were the only movements he exhibited.

This entire medical examination took about five minutes. Though he had not revived Whittaker, Dr. Alexander stood up and went out into the hall to await the appearance of General John M. Schofield, the West Point Superintendent, a Civil War luminary and later General in Chief of the Army. During the examination Piper had alerted Schofield and Lieutenant Colonel Henry M. Lazelle, the Commandant of Cadets.

Dr. Alexander, impatient for Schofield's appearance, started down the stairs and ran into Lazelle on the second floor. He told the commandant he believed Whittaker was faking unconsciousness. He also said that he thought Whittaker was "not so badly hurt as he tried to make out." Lazelle made no recorded reply but accompanied Alexander up the stairs back into Whittaker's room. Walking into the alcove, Lazelle commanded, "Mr. Whittaker, get up, be a man." Whittaker made no response. Going right up to the black cadet, Lazelle said even more forcefully, "Get up, Mr. Whittaker, get up, sir. Open your eyes." At the same time Dr. Alexander was again shaking him. The combined efforts were successful. Whittaker opened his eyes and became conscious.

Within a few seconds Whittaker was sitting up. On orders from Dr. Alexander, he stood up and walked stiffly and with a slight limp to the washstand. He put his hands to his eyes as if he were still dazed, complained of a pain in the side but otherwise seemed all right. He began to wash the blood from his face and with assistance took off his soiled underclothes and replaced them with fresh ones. All the time Whittaker was washing, Dr. Alexander was dressing his wounds, causing him to bleed again. At the same time, the doctor was interrogating the patient. Everyone in the room listened as Whittaker explained what had happened.

On the previous evening, after a day of no unusual activity, Whittaker had, according to his report, studied, read his Bible as usual, and gone to bed a little after midnight. Sometime during the night, perhaps around 2:00 A.M., he was awakened by a noise that sounded like the movement of the latch on his door. He groggily raised his head to listen, and then quickly fell back to sleep when it appeared that the noise was probably caused by the wind rattling the window.

Sometime later he was more rudely awakened. He felt someone jump on top of him and awoke to see three masked men, two dressed in dark clothing and the third in a gray suit. Fighting to overcome sleep, he tried to struggle against the assailants but with little success. He was seized by the throat until his breath almost left him and was struck on the temple and given a bloody nose. An assailant warned, "Speak now and you are a dead man." He was then forced to the floor, and one of the men whispered, "Let us shave his head," while another said, "Let us mark him as we mark hogs down south." The trio proceeded to slash Whittaker's ear lobes, probably with a knife. Blood flowed. Whittaker threw up his hands to prevent the mutilation and received wounds on his left hand for his effort. One of the three men took out a pair of scissors and cut Whittaker's hair, gouging out big chunks of it with each snip.

Throughout all this Whittaker continued to struggle, he insisted, so the trio knotted his arms very tightly in front of his body. Almost immediately they brought a looking glass and forced the captive to see himself. To add to the mockery, they struck him in the forehead, causing the glass to break. Finally the attackers tied the stunned cadet's ankles and legs to the bed railing at a 25-degree angle.

While all this was going on one of the three men, the shortest, stood at the foot of the bed not actually taking part in the attack. In fact he seemed to be almost reluctant to be there. He noticed how much Whittaker's nose and wounds were bleeding and, fearing too great a loss of blood, said, "Look out, don't hurt him. See how much he bleeds. Take my handkerchief and put it around his wounds." A handkerchief was placed under the black cadet's ears.

Whittaker, apparently feeling faint, asked his assailants to place a pillow under his head. They did. Before the masked trio slipped silently out of the room they warned the black cadet, "Cry out, or speak of this affair, and you are a dead man." The last words Whittaker said he heard were "Then he will leave."

After he was sure they had gone Whittaker unsuccessfully tried to loosen his tied hands with his teeth. He called for help but in a voice too weak to carry outside his room. He wanted to cry out louder, he said, but he was afraid that his attackers would return if they heard him and carry out their threats. He also had no confidence that his fellow cadets would come to his aid even if they did hear his cries. So he lay there on the floor, exhausted, terrified, and confused, trying to decide what to do. Before he could collect his senses he fell asleep or, more probably, lapsed into unconsciousness, not to come to, he said, until almost the present moment.[4]

Dr. Alexander displayed open skepticism. Why, he asked, hadn't Whittaker given an alarm; how exactly had he been held down; and so on? Whittaker answered clearly and carefully. Alexander stopped the questions and began looking around the alcove. He picked up the pillow, an open pen knife, and the bloody handkerchief, and asked Whittaker if the knife was his. The black cadet looked at it and responded that he did not think so; he thought his knife was on the table. But when Major Piper looked there, no knife was in evidence. Those in the room suspected that Whittaker had told a lie.

Dr. Alexander continued administering to Whittaker, while Major Piper made yet another trip to the hall in anticipation of General Schofield. The Superintendent, who had been roused from sleep about thirty minutes after reveille with a report that Whittaker had been hurt and perhaps killed, finally appeared in the hall. Major Piper greeted him and quickly put to rest the story Whittaker was dead or even severely wounded. "It is not as bad as we thought," Piper reported. Schofield, feeling relieved, walked into the room, surveyed the scene, briefly inquired about the severity of the wounds, and left within several minutes. In the corridor he ordered Colonel Lazelle to investigate the entire incident and to present him with a report as quickly as possible. By this time it was about 7:00 A.M.

Schofield walked down the stairs and was met by several cadet leaders. They offered their help in unearthing the culprit and emphasized their certitude that no cadet was capable of such an act. Because it looked at the time as though three cadets had committed the act, this cadet offer of help made quite an impression on Schofield.

Meanwhile, Dr. Alexander continued his ministration,

and Whittaker continued his task of cleaning up. As the black cadet washed and dressed, Colonel Lazelle peppered him with questions. Later, Lazelle said, he left the room believing in Whittaker's story. Before leaving, Lazelle unaccountably ordered that the room be put in order and all the soiled clothes be washed. It was a strange way to begin an investigation.

About this time, around 7:40, cadets returning from breakfast were gathering in little groups in the cadet wash-rooms, discussing the already famous incident and expressing indignation that such a thing could happen at West Point. They were confident, it was reported, that no cadet had attacked Whittaker. In the barracks, Dr. Alexander ordered Whittaker to report to the hospital for further treatment. Whittaker walked down the stairs and out into the barracks area. He encountered Louis Simpson, a black bathroom attendant, standing at the entrance to the boiler room. Seeing a friendly face, Whittaker went over and said, "You see that they tried to kill me." "Yes," said Simpson, "but I am glad it is not as bad as had been reported." Whittaker told Simpson what had happened and reported that he was on his way to the hospital. Simpson, noting the limp and what he called a "distressed appearance" on the cadet's face, told Whittaker to take care of himself. Whittaker made no reply and continued on his way, limping through the barracks area. He arrived at the hospital and was talking to the hospital steward when Dr. Alexander walked through the door. Meanwhile, back in Whittaker's room, a janitor was cleaning up and attempting to restore the room to normal.

At the hospital Dr. Alexander did nothing more than change the plaster on Whittaker's ears and ask him again what had happened. Whittaker told the same story with only minor changes of detail, standing throughout and exhibiting no signs of weakness or depression. Once Alexander was finished with the dressing, he noticed that it was too late for breakfast, so he told the steward to provide the cadet with something to eat. While Whittaker ate he and Dr. Alexander talked a bit more, but little new information was revealed. Alexander excused Whittaker from military duties because of the cut toe but told him that he should report for his classes.

Whittaker left the hospital and on his way to his room ran into Walter Mitchell, another of his black friends. "Hello, Mitch," he said. Mitchell replied, "I was just going down to see you. I heard you were very badly hurt." "No, I am not hurt much," Whittaker answered. "They only played a little trick upon me." "I am very glad," Mitchell said, and the two men went their separate ways. Whittaker limped along the pavement holding a handkerchief behind the back of his head.

During all this time a meeting had been taking place among Major Piper, Lieutenant William H. Coffin, Whittaker's tactical officer, and Colonel Lazelle. On the commandant's order Coffin had gone to Whittaker's room about 8:00 A.M. to make another investigation. After he had entered the room Cadet Dickenson came in and gave him some charred scraps of paper which he and another cadet, named Cornish, had found on the floor. He had placed the paper scraps first on the mantelpiece and then later in an envelope in his desk drawer. Unaccountably Dickenson had somehow thrown out one of the pieces with the trash. This piece, according to Cornish, revealed the words "tantly shrinking." Other papers showed the words "Dear Mother," "I," and "West Point NY, April" [sic] clearly visible. Dickenson was convinced that the papers consisted of old guard lists and a part of a Bible.

About 8:30 Whittaker walked in and in the course of conversation told Coffin that he felt "very well." He also told Coffin about a note he had received the day before the attack. Whittaker had returned to his room from dinner and had found a small envelope addressed to "Cadet Whittaker." Inside was the following note:

Sunday April 5

Mr. Whittaker

You will be fixed. Better keep awake.

A Friend

This was the second threatening note Whittaker had received during his West Point career, so he was not sure what to make of it. Should he consider it another prank or was it a threat serious enough to be shown to the Superintendent or some other officer? Perhaps remembering the adverse reaction when he had turned in the cadet who struck him, Whittaker was unsure what to do. He mulled the matter over in his mind and even asked the opinion of the black attendant of the bathhouse, Louis Simpson. Simpson warned Whittaker that if he showed the note to anyone in authority, he would only be laughed at. However, the next day Whittaker wrote to his mother that he was planning to show the note to the Superintendent. Obviously he had mixed emotions about the whole matter. In the excitement immediately after the attack Whittaker had, he told Coffin, forgotten about the note. It was only now that he remembered it. When Coffin asked to see the note, Whittaker immediately produced it. Coffin took it, looked it over, and later gave it to Colonel Lazelle.

Whittaker willingly answered every question Coffin put to him. He could, however, offer no clue to the perpetrators of the attack. When Whittaker left for class, Dickenson pointed out a pair of scissors on the desk with several small pieces of hair in them. Coffin confiscated these scissors.

Later in the morning Major Piper visited Whittaker's room. Finding Whittaker's Bible in the clothes press, he glanced through it and concluded that a section of Revelations had been torn out and burned. Some of the burned paper seemed to him to be a portion from Revelations. However, Piper made no real inspection of the room or, for that matter, of the entire Bible.

At four o'clock that afternoon Colonel Lazelle visited

Whittaker's room and inspected, he reported later, the cadet's Bible. He asked Whittaker for permission to check the papers in his room. Whittaker agreed, but unaccountably Lazelle did not follow up this opportunity immediately. However, Lazelle, or another one of the visitors, did give the black cadet demerits for not having his bedding properly "piled."[5]

Sometime between five and six-thirty that evening, on General Schofield's orders, Whittaker was again put through a physical examination, this time at the hands of the assistant post surgeon, Dr. Henry Lippencott. Colonel Lazelle was also present. Superintendent Schofield arrived soon after the examination began and asked Whittaker if he had been struck in the nose. When Whittaker said yes, Schofield called this to the surgeon's attention. Dr. Lippencott took Whittaker to the window, bent him backward, and looked into his nose. He found no evidence of any blood. (Later he admitted that there might have been some in the upper area of the nose, accessible only with the use of instruments.) When Whittaker complained of a pain in his side, Schofield asked Lippencott about it. The doctor answered, "I have examined him carefully and he has not received any injury in the side." Furthermore, Lippencott said he found no swelling or inflammation to indicate any recent blow, though later Whittaker pointed out the general area of a scar or scab on his forehead and claimed that it marked the place he had been struck. Lippencott did notice, however, that there were marks around Whittaker's wrists and ankles, the results of the tight bands tying his arms and legs. He also concluded that the black cadet's ears had probably been cut with a knife, resulting in a loss of one or two ounces (two or four tablespoons) of blood.

During this medical examination Lazelle said nothing. Afterward, however, he took a close look at the cuts in Whittaker's hair and concluded that the cadet had done the cutting himself. Despite this, Lazelle later argued, he had not yet made up his mind that Whittaker was a liar. "I regarded him as a very manly boy," he insisted.

On this day and on the next several days, Lieutenant Coffin, on Lazelle's orders, repeatedly visited Whittaker's room. At various times he confiscated fragments of burned paper, a black necktie, scissors, Bible, and pen knife. He gave all these things to Colonel Lazelle. Even Whittaker's mail was checked. Lazelle told Coffin one day, "I wish you would go up to Mr. Whittaker's room and inspect all his private letters and effects. Mr. Whittaker has consented to this." Coffin went to the black cadet's fourth-floor room and confronted him: "Mr. Whittaker, I have orders to inspect your private letters." Whittaker made no protest and quite willingly went to his desk drawer and handed his private correspondence to his tactical officer.

Wednesday morning, a day and a half after Whittaker had been found, Lazelle was apparently satisfied that he had uncovered all the available information. He personally delivered his completed report to General Schofield. In essence, the report accused Whittaker of writing the note of warning, mutilating himself, and then faking unconsciousness. All the evidence, Lazelle contended, pointed to this conclusion; there was no other possibility. His investigation and the professional opinion of Dr. Alexander, presented in a separate quasi-medical report, left no doubt of Whittaker's guilt. The lack of evidence against other cadets and their professions of innocence when questioned sealed the matter.

> I do not believe it possible that three Cadets can be found in the Corps who would so utterly falsify as they must have done in the total denial of all knowledge of the outrage on Cadet Whittaker, had they taken part in it; prompted to such a thing, as they must have been if at all, by the spirit of mere mischief.

I respectfully recommend that Cadet Whittaker
be given the choice of resignation, or asking for a
Court of Inquiry, or of a Court-Martial.[6]

Schofield received the report, apparently discussed it
with Lazelle, and at noon called Whittaker to his office. The
ground outside was covered with snow, following a heavy
flurry that day. In the presence of the commandant and
several other officers, Schofield told Whittaker, "It appears
from the report of the commandant, from the investigation
that he has made, that you did this thing yourself." The
report asserted that there was evidence of neither a blow
nor a nosebleed. There was no sign on Whittaker's forehead that he had been hit there by the mirror and no evidence of any injury to his side. If the attack had indeed
taken place several hours before reveille, Dr. Alexander
said the bleeding would have been stopped by the time of
discovery. There was no reason to justify a state of unconsciousness, yet Whittaker was found unconscious. The
material used to tie him had been flimsy, and he might have
freed himself with a "vigorous kick or two." Even more
than that, there was no reason why he could not have
untied himself. He had not been gagged, yet he had made
no sound, and, though the transom and ventilator were
open, no one in any of the surrounding rooms had heard
anything of the attack. Whittaker's hair looked as though
it had been self-cut, not barbered by someone else. The
handkerchief used in the affair matched his and he was not
able to account for all six he had previously purchased.
Whittaker had said he knew nothing about the burned
paper, yet some of it was from his Bible. The handwriting
on the note of warning also resembled his. Finally, there
was no reason to believe that the "uniformly tolerant" past
attitude of the cadets had changed.[7]

Whittaker listened to this catalogue of his supposed
transgressions silently, but when Schofield asked him to
respond he quickly and openly denied the report's conclu-

sions. As Schofield later remembered it, Whittaker expressed "just indignation at the imputation cast upon his honor in being thus accused of the crime which others had perpetrated upon him." He immediately asked for a court of inquiry. Schofield, somewhat stung at the reply, answered, "Mr. Whittaker, you are perfectly right in feeling as you do, under the state of the facts as you state them. You are entitled to a court of inquiry. And you shall certainly have one."[8]

Chapter 4

THE COURT OF INQUIRY
BEGINS AMID
NATIONAL PUBLICITY

ON April 8, 1880, General Schofield issued Special Order
#55 establishing a court of inquiry "to examine into and
investigate the facts and circumstances connected with the
assault upon Cadet Whittaker and the imputation cast
upon his character thereto." Four officers were appointed
to carry on this investigation. Major Alfred Mordecai, an
instructor in the department of ordnance and gunnery
since 1874, was the senior officer. It was said of him by a
former student that, because of a lisp, his "enunciation was
so perplexing" the cadets "could understand him better
when he was silent." Captain Charles W. Raymond, an
instructor in the department of practical engineering, military signaling and telegraphy, was the second man on the
panel. He had been at West Point since 1872. The third
member was First Lieutenant Samuel Tillman, assistant
professor of chemistry, mineralogy and geology and a
faculty power until 1911. The fourth member of the panel

and the recorder for the court of inquiry was First Lieutenant Clinton B. Sears. Lieutenant Sears, who had been appointed to the Academy as a cadet from Sherman's army during the Civil War, was assistant professor of natural and experimental philosophy. He had been on the West Point faculty since 1876 and was promoted to captain the day the inquiry began.

As recorder, Sears was to play the key role in the inquiry, being in effect prosecutor, investigator, and supervisor of the official record. He was, in many ways, the keeper of West Point's reputation. His handling of the inquiry would go a long way toward determining public reaction.

General Schofield, though he kept in the background, conferred on many occasions with Sears and the entire court. He took an active role in the inquiry, and his hand was always present. He never pressured or attempted to force a particular decision, but he did suggest directions for the investigation to take. And when a general as powerful as Schofield makes suggestions to lower-ranking officers, such as the members of the court, he is listened to. Thus Schofield's presence, whether he is mentioned or not, must always be kept in mind.

Representing Whittaker in these proceedings was First Lieutenant John G. D. Knight, assistant professor of mathematics, a West Point faculty member since 1874, and a man "of somewhat nervous disposition." Whittaker had requested his services, apparently considering Knight the officer most friendly to him. Next to Sears, Knight had the most crucial role to play in the inquiry. Like Sears, he must have found himself, in many ways, caught in the middle. He knew about Lazelle's report (although the court itself did not officially see it until late in the inquiry) and also knew about Dr. Alexander's findings. He knew that most West Pointers felt Whittaker was guilty and considered his mutilation an attack on the Academy. As defense counsel, his task was to protect Whittaker's interests; yet he himself was a West Pointer who had to live and work with his colleagues in the future. There is no evidence to indicate how this situation affected Knight, but it is clear that his defense was not the strongest possible one. He did not play as vital a role as he might have. Whether this was the result of reticence or incompetence is uncertain.[1] But in all fairness it must be noted that both the recorder and the defense counsel possessed approximately equal credentials. Neither was a lawyer and both had been at the Academy for approximately the same number of years.

According to the convening order, the first session of the court of inquiry was scheduled to meet on Friday, April 9. Even before it convened, however, it had already gained national prominence. The Whittaker case had become more than a simple internal matter. Americans—from the President, to Congress, to the newspapers, to the average man on the street—knew about the attack on the black cadet. The incident was front-page news and remained a topic of newspaper coverage and analysis throughout the prolonged inquiry. It could not be kept quiet. It almost immediately became not simply the story of one cadet's plight but the account of West Point's treatment of black cadets in general. Whittaker's treatment was used as a point of reference for a consideration of the entire question of blacks at West Point and, by extension, of the role of the black race in American society.

Aside from the press accounts, the chief source for sensationalizing this entire affair was General Schofield. On the day of the assault he followed correct military procedure and informed the War Department of the development. In a rather detailed telegram to the Adjutant General of the Army, he described what had happened. He reported that, contrary to initial appearances, Whittaker was not seriously hurt. He promised a thorough investigation and lauded the cadets for their cooperation. It was not yet known, he said, if any other cadet had been involved in the incident. The next day Schofield sent a follow-up telegram emphasizing the superficiality of Whittaker's wounds and the cadets' disclaimer that any of them had been involved.[2] Schofield also wrote to his long-time commander and friend, General of the Army William T. Sherman. He called the affair "a perplexing mystery" and one which might drag on for a long time. The only certainty was the cadets' candidness about their innocence. The next day, in answer to a query from Sherman, he wrote that assaults like this could not be prevented. Even a substantial increase in guard details would do little, and that would cut into the cadets' study time. He hoped, he added, "that all the world will see these things in their true light."[3]

Apparently Schofield decided to help the world, because he quickly granted a number of newspaper interviews in which he commented on the affair. In these interviews, broadcast to the nation by the press, the West Point Superintendent did not exhibit the sort of uncertainty he showed in his communiqués to his superiors. In New York City at the St. James Hotel, where he was attending a meeting of the Military Order of the Loyal Legion of the United States, Schofield faced the press. At first he protested that he could not say anything because the court of inquiry had sole responsibility in the matter. Then he volunteered the opinion that the cadets were innocent of any complicity; there was no evidence against them. Warming to his theme, Schofield then discussed Dr. Alexander's report in some detail and cited "three distinct points on which it is proved that he [Whittaker] has testified falsely." No one heard the attack take place despite the closeness of the quarters; Whittaker gave no alarm; and his hands were tied so loosely that, had he wished, he could have untied himself. Furthermore, the writing in the note of warning resembled Whittaker's handwriting.

As Schofield talked, reporters took notes feverishly. They must have recognized the significance of what was being said. The West Point Superintendent was, in effect, trying the black cadet in public. He was accusing the victim of being the perpetrator. Perhaps Schofield realized what he was doing, because he hastened to add, "None of the points I have mentioned can have the least bearing on the reputation of Cadet Whittaker." It was the court of inquiry's job to make a determination, and he was sure it would make the right one. Of one thing Schofield was certain, however, and that was the innocence of the cadets —the white cadets, that is. As for Whittaker, if he had indeed committed the act, he had probably done it to avoid the June examination or "to gain a commission in the Army without graduating."

Later, speaking to other reporters both at West Point and in New York, Schofield elaborated on his story and in some cases contradicted himself. He again left the clear impression that the person responsible for the night assault on Whittaker was the black cadet himself.[4] In essence, then, on the eve of the West Point inquiry to determine responsibility for the outrage, the Academy's commanding officer had already publicly assigned guilt to Johnson C. Whittaker.

All during this time the victim, now the accused, was facing the crisis alone, with no communication except through the mail. His ostracism remained in effect. He wrote to his mother, telling her not to worry because he was feeling fine. He expressed confidence that unnamed "friends in Washington" would look out for him and ended by asking for her prayers. He reminded her that he was being guided "by one who sees when even a sparrow falls and will not forsake those who trust in him."

Other letters were not so confident. Writing to his friend and former teacher Richard T. Greener, dean of the law school at Howard University, Whittaker seemed almost desperate. He asked Greener to come to West Point because the whole affair was a "heinous plot engaged in by no others than cadets" and apparently "sanctioned by the authorities." In a letter to Moses Wester, his friend in New York, he said he was "troubled" and his "heart" seemed "drooping and distressed." His depression and loneliness were obvious. He saw himself as having no friend but God at West Point and lamented the treatment the cadets had given him since his first day there. He hoped for justice but had little confidence he would receive it.[5]

The press, meantime, was keeping the entire matter before the public eye. In addition to the reporters' accounts, newspapers quickly began to take editorial stands. While many ostensibly took Whittaker's side, their statements in reality could give him little comfort. The Charleston *News and Courier,* for example, said it found the accusation that Whittaker had mutilated himself "rather hard to swallow" because there was "not usually as much nerve or as much sensitiveness among persons of his class." They wished to see a full investigation but were sure no Southerner had committed the act. Southerners had "no harsh feelings toward the negro." They believed in the necessity of white supremacy for free institutions but would not ill-treat a black person who had taken advantage of an opportunity presented to him by whites. The New York *Times* lamented the fact that Whittaker was "as much alone in the Military Academy of the United States as if he had been on a desert island" but said little else. The New York *Tribune* seemed convinced of Whittaker's guilt but showed friendliness toward his race.

> It is painful to know that the one representative of the colored race among the cadets, who had such an opportunity to do credit to his people, should have made such a dismal failure. But the quick indignation of the public over the first story was such a demonstration of honorable feeling that it almost reconciles us to the hoax.

Not all newspapers were even this favorable to Whittaker. The New York *Herald* and the *Army and Navy Journal* tended to be pro-West Point. Sherman sent Schofield some favorable clippings, as did the editor of the Cincinnati *Commercial.* But in all, the press, though not overwhelmingly pro-Whittaker, at least leaned in his direction. If nothing else, they felt some sympathy for him. Not surprisingly, a black newspaper, the Charleston *New Era*, was the most forthright. It called the incident "one of the most brutal, malicious and cowardly crimes, that has ever been recorded in the annals of time."[6]

On Friday, April 9, 1880, at 10:00 A.M., when the court of inquiry met, much had already happened. The case was a national *cause célèbre*, and West Point's handling of it would therefore be closely watched. In many minds Whittaker's guilt was already established, and the court would merely confirm it. Others saw the affair as much more significant than the case itself and viewed it as a symbol of West Point's treatment of black cadets. In short, it was the kind of case that could have no winners—only losers.

The sessions of the court of inquiry were held in the impressive Academy Library at the southeast corner of the West Point plain. The room was wood-paneled, and all around were hung oil paintings of famous generals. The three-man tribunal sat at a table in one corner of the room, and the recorder and Whittaker's counsel sat at desks on either side. The first day a blackboard with a sketch of Whittaker's room was set in front of the witness stand, and beneath it stood an iron cadet bedstead. Later other materials were brought in and exhibited as the court required. The blackboard was there for most of the trial.

Every day that the court of inquiry was in session the room was filled with spectators. More than thirty ladies from the Academy and its surrounding area were regular viewers. They sat in the alcoves of the library with their fancy work, their novels, and their newspapers. When the testimony became dull, they would keep themselves busy with these diversions until excitement picked up again. Officers dropped in when they were free, and their uniforms added color to the occasion. General Schofield was present almost every day and often conferred with the court before or after the official sessions. Professor Richard T. Greener was also there, on the first day of the trial, as was Reverend Justin D. Fulton of Brooklyn, who told reporters he was there to show Whittaker that at least one white man sympathized with him.[7] In many ways the court of inquiry took on a carnival atmosphere. But to Whittaker and to West Point it was no laughing matter. Whittaker's career, and the role of the black cadet at West Point and even the future of the Academy, were at stake.

The court's first session set the tone for the entire two months' proceedings; it completely revolved around Johnson C. Whittaker. He was the victim, the only witness to the event, and, in many minds, the perpetrator.

The first actual order of business was the reading of the convening Special Order #55 and making certain all the principals were present. Then Whittaker was asked if he objected to anyone involved in the inquiry. He replied that he did not. The recorder swore in the court and was in turn sworn in by Major Mordecai, the court's presiding officer. The official reporter, Corporal Edward Henry, was sworn in, and Sears explained his function, emphasizing that, though Henry would be taking everything down in shorthand, he, as recorder, still had ultimate responsibility for the accuracy of the longhand record. Following an explanation that both sides could recall witnesses and the surprising disclosure that the defense had waived the right to cross-examine witnesses, the inquiry proper began; Cadet Johnson C. Whittaker was called to the stand.

Whittaker, who had been sitting impassively next to his counsel throughout the opening formalities, stood up on hearing his name called. With a slight limp he moved in front of the assembled officers of the court and reported. He saluted smartly, was sworn in, and told to take his seat. All eyes were on him—a twenty-one-year-old mulatto—and it was evident that in a parade or at a distance his race would have been difficult to notice. His hair was not kinky and his light-skinned face was covered with freckles. He was probably no more than one quarter black.

As soon as Whittaker had taken his seat, Captain Sears,

the recorder, asked him to tell the court exactly what had happened. Whittaker, in a clear and steady voice, belying the discouragement his correspondence showed he felt, related again the story of his night of horror. He spoke clearly, though at times quickly, and poured out the tale of masked attackers, slashed earlobes, and cut hair. His still evident wounds gave his tale a ghostly reality.

The court listened carefully. When Whittaker had finished, the reporter began a series of questions intended to give more exact details of the attack: where had he been grabbed; had he been struck with a fist or something else; exactly where had each man stood? Whittaker answered that he had been grabbed around the throat; that he wasn't sure what had been used to strike him; and that he was unsure as to the exact location of all three men during the attack.

Q: "During this affair, did you continue to struggle throughout?"

A: "I did, sir."

Q: "Did you make your best effort physically to prevent their touching you?"

A: "I did, sir."

How had his ears been cut? He thought with a single blade. Had the rope covered his fingers? No. Had he tried to free his legs by kicking? He had. Was he now limping from the affair? Yes, the wound on his toe and the pain resulting from the pressure of the rope was causing a limping or halting in his step. Had he recognized any of the voices? He had not.

When had he received the note of warning? He had found it when he had returned from supper, Sunday night. This was the second note he had received at West Point. The previous fall he had been sent a note with the words "Look Out." Recently he had had no particular troubles, though he had twice been struck while at West Point. Had the attackers been civilians or cadets? He didn't know. How did he feel about getting through West Point? He had

always felt confident about his chances. The recent letter
to his mother indicating he might resign was occasioned by
worry over her inability to pay her rent, not Academy
problems. When some friends promised to take care of the
rent, he no longer worried about it.

Q: "Have you any cause to suppose that there is any
prejudice against you in the minds of your instructors due
to which it would be more difficult for you to graduate than
other cadets against whom such prejudice did not exist?"

A: "No cause to think so from their action toward me in
the least."

Q: "Has your social isolation had any effect on you in
the progression of your studies?"

A: "It has, sir."

Here, for the first time, the issue of prejudice was raised.
Several other times that first day and the following one
during Whittaker's long testimony this question was mentioned, and each time Whittaker denied being unfairly
treated. He repeatedly spoke of prejudice at West Point in
his letters, and there is no doubt he believed it existed.
However, it was not until later that he was willing to say
so publicly. Apparently he felt that accusing West Point of
racial prejudice at this time would only make things more
difficult for him. So he technically perjured himself to a-
void problems. In reality, however, this stand caused him
more trouble. When his letters were confiscated and he
later changed his story, the inconsistency was pointed to as
proof of his basic untruthfulness.

Whittaker was kept on the stand all that first day until
4:40 P.M. No one else was questioned, though Lieutenant
Knight did take a piece of belting which had been used to
bind Whittaker and tied it to a chair to show how much of
an effort it took to break it. The next day, at 10:00 A.M.,
Whittaker was recalled and again asked a series of questions
on the various details of the attack. The recorder then asked
the key question:

You are aware that the opinion is held by some that this assault is entirely an imaginary one and that you were alone concerned in it; now for your own benefit I have here this Bible which you state you are accustomed to read, which has been in your possession for some years, in whose sacredness I presume you have every belief, and I want you to put your hand upon that Bible and take an oath that you are in no way cognizant of nor were in any way a free agent, nor had any knowledge of or connivance with your assailants.

As Captain Sears asked this grammatically garbled sentence, Whittaker bowed his head and for one of the few times during the court of inquiry sessions displayed the inner torment he was feeling. When the recorder had finished his question, Whittaker affirmed his innocence by placing his hand on the Bible and clearly saying, "I do, sir." A newspaper correspondent present at this tense moment reported that the assembled ladies "drew long breaths, looked at each other and said 'Ah!' and 'Oh!' in a tone that implied anything but implicit belief in the accused['s] veracity."[8]

With this dramatic scene over, to the excited buzz of the courtroom, Whittaker was excused for the present. He had told his story well, he had stood up under the pressure of long hours of interrogation, and he finished his testimony by swearing to it on his cherished Bible. He made a favorable impression on spectators and court alike. Whether they believed he was telling the truth or not, all seemed impressed with his bearing and manner.

The next witnesses called that second day were two barbers, Max and Charles W. Rappenhagen. At Lazelle's request both had examined Whittaker's hair. Both were questioned about the still visible cuts in the black cadet's hair. Despite attempts to shake them, both men remained convinced that the cuts in Whittaker's hair could not have been made with the scissors found in Whittaker's room.[9] This, of course, was important testimony because it seemed to call into question the West Point theory that Whittaker had committed the outrage to himself. If what the barbers said was true, there was nothing in Whittaker's room that he could have used to cut his hair. The cutting must have been done by an outside agent who brought his own instrument. Whether or not this testimony was accepted, a fundamental doubt was presented.

The next witness buttressed the case against Whittaker, however, overshadowing the barbers' testimony with his own. Cadet George R. Burnett, the cadet officer of the day, testified at length about his findings when entering Whittaker's room the morning of the sixth. He displayed unusual eagerness to unearth evidence to damn Whittaker, and the answers he presented pointed to Whittaker as the sole perpetrator of the act. The fact that Burnett had had a run-in with the black cadet earlier in their West Point careers and that he was later pointed out as one of the cadets Whittaker suspected of attacking him must be borne in mind in evaluating his testimony. He might simply have been eager to do his duty, but ulterior motives must not be overlooked.

Describing his actions on the morning of the sixth, Burnett told the court how he entered Whittaker's room, found the bleeding cadet, and summoned authorities. When describing Dr. Alexander's examination of the black cadet's eye, Burnett asked if he should tell the court his "impressions" at this time, but Sears told him to stick to the facts. When asked how Whittaker was tied, Burnett proceeded to lie down on the floor and demonstrate, graphically, the position of the body, belting, and knots. In the afternoon he again conducted a demonstration and showed how Whittaker could have tied himself. He also showed that Whittaker could easily have broken the straps used to tie him by tying his own hands and then breaking loose. Later he tied himself to the iron bedstead located in the court-

71

room and showed how easy it was for him to reach his feet and his hands. The obvious inference was that Whittaker could easily have committed the entire act himself; tied to the bed, he could have reached all the instruments needed for self-mutilation. Burnett's testimony, then, displayed in the flesh the reasonableness of West Point's case against Whittaker.[10]

Another important development that second day was the decision that Whittaker would not be present during the court hearings. After the testimony of the barbers but before Burnett came on the stand, Captain Sears announced to the court that Whittaker's counsel, Lieutenant Knight, considered it "better for him to withdraw during the rest of the testimony." Sears said he agreed to this, and if the court had no objections, Whittaker would be withdrawn until it was felt his presence was "necessary." There were no objections, and Whittaker returned to class. By Schofield's orders he was excused from all military duties. No more was said, and the testimony continued. It was not until three days later that the reasoning for this move was justified. Captain Sears, answering newspaper criticism of the black cadet's absence at his own inquiry, presented an explanation. He said it was felt that "as a matter of fairness" Whittaker should not be in daily attendance. His "standing in his class," Sears said, was "not such that he ... [could] afford to lose time from his studies." In any case, it really was not necessary for a person before a court of inquiry to be present at each of the sessions so long as he was being represented by a counsel who was in attendance. Whittaker would be recalled when needed; his continual presence would serve no real purpose.

At least one newspaper did not buy this reasoning. The New York *Times* wondered out loud what might have happened had Whittaker been present to confront Burnett during the exhibition with straps and bed. Might not Whittaker have been able to point out mistakes in Burnett's dramatization which would have helped his case?

At the same time that he felt called upon to justify the absence of the black cadet, Sears also explained why he had used the word "accused" in reference to Whittaker. He said that, press and public opinion notwithstanding, it was proper to use this term in a court of inquiry. The only accusation against Whittaker was the imputation on his character spelled out in the convening order. "Furthermore," he emphasized, "I would like to say that personally I have no opinion whatever on this case, nor any personal theory to support."[11]

While the inquiry was being conducted in the library there was a great deal of activity in other parts of the Academy. By order of the Secretary of War, Major Thomas F. Barr of the Judge Advocate's Corps came to West Point to confer with Schofield. Richard T. Greener, Whittaker's former South Carolina professor, also came, with Secretary Ramsey's blessing, to aid the black cadet. The day these two men arrived, the Academy Adjutant, Colonel William Wherry, left for New York to acquire the services of a detective to help investigate the case. The move had been suggested to Schofield by the Adjutant General, E. D. Townsend. On April 12 James Gayler, the Superintendent of City Delivery of the New York Post Office, the first of five "handwriting experts" retained by West Point, began his investigation of the note of warning.

The arrival of Barr was particularly significant. A judge advocate, Barr was instructed by Alexander Ramsey, the Secretary of War, to discuss the entire matter with Schofield and discover what added powers might be needed to arrive at the truth. "This is a matter of too much importance," Ramsey told Barr, "to admit of any measure being omitted to discover the true history of the case."

Upon his arrival from Washington on April 9, Barr immediately went to see Schofield. The West Point Superintendent discussed the entire case with him, showed him Alexander's report and the note of warning. Barr, in comparing the note with specimens of Whittaker's handwrit-

73

ing, "at once noticed the great resemblance." He also suggested the theory that the note might have been "written by two persons." Schofield explained that he had not sent Alexander's report to the War Department because it stated that Whittaker was guilty. Should Whittaker be found innocent, this would look bad. But he wanted it made clear that the material was available to the War Department anytime it was wanted. Barr listened, attended the afternoon session of the court, and then returned to make his report as Ramsey had ordered.[12]

The highest circles of American government were becoming involved in the inquiry into the guilt or innocence of the black cadet. And nowhere was this more evident than in the United States Congress.

On April 7, the day after the discovery of the outrage, Representative Anson G. McCook of New York asked for unanimous consent to introduce "a resolution of inquiry into the alleged outrage at West Point." Representatives S. S. Cox and James A. Garfield, both of Ohio, agreed that the resolution should be read. The Clerk of the House then read McCook's resolution stating that since it had been reported that Whittaker had been "visited in his room at night-time by a number of his fellow cadets and subjected to a most shocking and barbarous treatment," it be resolved:

> That the Secretary of War be directed to furnish
> this House with all the information he may have
> in regard to the alleged outrage perpetrated upon
> Cadet Whittaker, and also what steps, if any, have
> been taken in relation thereto.

Since, according to House rules, resolutions like this needed unanimous support to be promulgated, only one objection would kill it. Representative D. Wyatt Aiken from South Carolina immediately raised such an objection. He said that, since he represented Whittaker's district, he felt "competent" to ensure that the black cadet would be

74

"thoroughly protected." Besides, West Point was investigating the entire matter, and it seemed wiser to wait for their verdict instead of jumping to conclusions based on press reports.

There is no evidence that Aiken offered any help to Whittaker throughout his ordeal and much evidence to indicate the opposite. His only action was to write to General Schofield offering the Superintendent his full support. As a Redeemer elected to the House on the same ticket with Governor Wade Hampton, little else could be expected. Over the opposition of fellow Democrats, Aiken blocked the House from taking action by promising he would protect Whittaker's interests and then simply ignored the black cadet's plight. The House Military Committee skirted him by setting up a special subcommittee consisting of Representatives William Sparks of Illinois, former Confederate general Joseph E. Johnston of Virginia, and Thomas M. Brown of Indiana to investigate the attack. Nothing of significance came from their efforts.

On the Senate side, the sound and fury was even greater, but again little of a concrete nature resulted. John A. Logan, West Point's persistent critic, introduced a resolution on April 9 directing the Secretary of War to furnish the upper house with all available information on the case. Senators William Eaton of Connecticut and Samuel B. Maxey of Texas responded that the resolution was premature because the West Point investigation was still going on. Senator Daniel W. Voorhees of Indiana disagreed. He called for every possible investigation of West Point, "a system of brutality and barbarism" which drove even whites away. He believed everything possible should be done "to humanize, and civilize, if not possibly Christianize West Point," and if this was impossible, it "ought to be abolished." The report that Whittaker had mutilated himself was "absurd, ridiculous" and only served to document his contention. The resolution should be adopted.

Senator Ambrose Burnside, the former Civil War general and a West Point graduate, disagreed with Voorhees that West Point was any worse than any other college when it came to hazing. However, he too felt that a thorough investigation over and above that conducted by the court of inquiry was needed.

Senator Blanche K. Bruce, the black Mississippi Senator, rose to support his Indiana colleague. He said the Senate had been recently involved in the necessary work of adopting a bill to civilize and Christianize the Indians. He thought it would be well for the Senate also to "devote a little time to the civilization of West Point." He expressed happiness that Senator Voorhees had not brought race into his discussion, because, like his Indiana colleague, he wished the issue to be decided on the questions of "humanity," "good order and efficiency." Whoever the guilty parties were, Bruce said, they should be punished.

In any case, the whole matter of hazing at West Point was difficult to understand in the first place. Bruce said he found it hard to believe that "hazing and other irregularities and personal indignities, could happen in a military institute with its exact and stringent discipline, unless there was a vice somewhere in the methods of governing the institution." An investigation like the one suggested by Senator Voorhees would have a "healthy influence" on West Point administrators, and he favored it.

Next to speak was George F. Hoar, the powerful Senator from Massachusetts. As one of the Senate's leading lights, his words were listened to carefully. He disagreed with Voorhees in the Indiana Senator's assertion that the Whittaker case was a typical example of West Point hazing. Instead he felt it was more representative of the treatment afforded black cadets in general. West Point ostracized black cadets to the degree that their "solitude" was "as complete . . . as Robinson Crusoe was on his desolate island." It was a shameful situation and one without justification. Hoar predicted, "This American Republic, with its four million colored citizens equal before the constitution and the law, will grind that institution to powder unless this abuse is cured." A week later Senator Bruce asked that the appropriation for West Point be delayed until it could be confirmed that Whittaker was getting fair treatment. However, no specific action was taken.[13]

The very fact that the case was the subject of debate in both houses was ominous for West Point. The talk of disbanding the Military Academy taken within the context of Congressional cutbacks in the Army as a whole did not augur well for West Point. Its handling of the case could be crucial to its very existence. Obviously the Whittaker case could no longer be considered the simple intramural controversy West Point insisted it was.

Cadets, officers, and all other West Pointers, perhaps yet unaware of the true significance of this case, were speaking freely to the press during the first several days of the inquiry. Their statements showed not only their opinions on the matter at hand but also their views of the black race. Most West Pointers were convinced Whittaker was guilty; a New York *Times* reporter estimated about "5/6" felt this way. There was little sympathy for Whittaker. When asked why they felt as they did, West Pointers answered, " 'Oh, it's just like a nigger, you know.' 'Just the sort of thing he would do to get sympathy and tide him over his examination.' " Even those who didn't blame Whittaker were adamant in their belief that no one at West Point committed the act. Outsiders were accused, but, over-all, little breath was wasted in considering other possibilities. Whittaker was the culprit. " 'Why, he's a nigger, and niggers are capable of anything.' "[14]

Although it is uncertain just when the entire theory developed, West Pointers, convinced of Whittaker's guilt, developed a complete story of self-mutilation to counteract Whittaker's story of masked attackers. Whittaker had not been attacked by three masked men; he had committed the act himself. According to this story Whittaker, mainly because of fear of academic failure but also to get back at West

Point for its ostracism of him, devised the whole affair in his mind. About a month before the event he began to prepare himself. He asked the barber to let his hair remain longer in the back, thus making it easier to cut himself. At a later time he prepared a note of warning, disguised his handwriting as best he could, and used the type of paper that he believed would be hard to trace.

The night of the event Whittaker took one of his handkerchiefs, again of a type owned by many cadets, and cut a hole in it at a place where a name might have been printed. He took the scrap of linen and burned it by using some old guard lists and a leaf from his Bible for kindling. He used his Bible to throw suspicion away from himself, feeling that no one would believe he could tear his own cherished sacred book. At the same time, by bringing his Bible into the act, he was able to call attention to the writings and holy cards in it, thus hoping to demonstrate that he was a religious person incapable of such an act. When the linen was burned Whittaker poured water on the fire to extinguish it. Burned papers and a wet floor only added to the chaotic scene and served his purpose. Then, West Pointers believed, Whittaker prepared the bands by splitting old cadet belting lengthwise, getting the idea from having seen such straps used for tying at the laundry. He placed on the floor a civilian-type tie, unwisely his own, and later put a few drops of blood on it to buttress his case that he had been attacked by persons in civilian dress.

Just before daybreak he arose from his bed, lit the gaslight, and adjusted it so it was bright enough for him to see by but not bright enough to be noticed by anyone else. He needed this light to tie himself, but once he was tied he could not turn it off and it was still on the next morning. He next sat on the floor with his back to the foot of the bed and toward the light, his legs straight out and the mirror upon them. He used his own scissors to cut his hair, forgetting to get all the hair out of them when he was finished. He took the cut hair and arranged it in bunches in a semi-

78

circle around the mirror to make it appear it had fallen that way when cut by the attackers. He broke the mirror and placed it on the floor. He threw some riding clothes down to add to the confusion and placed an Indian club in such a position that blood from his toe would get on it and add to the effect. A pillow and a white pillowcase were then readied for dramatic contrast with the red blood, and a blanket and comforter were placed nearby for use while waiting to be discovered.

Having prepared all this material, Whittaker was ready to begin the actual mutilation. First he tied his legs. Next he cut his toe and the back of his hand, these wounds providing enough blood to place on the tie and mirror and to smear the wall above the bed. Some of the blood dripped on the Indian club, which was then pushed toward the center of the room where it might more easily be seen. The wrists were tied and then the ears cut with his pocket knife. After the cutting was finished, the knife was carefully wiped with the handkerchief and left on the floor nearby. The handkerchief was then placed under the ears and the head moved around to make the blood flow even more. Having accomplished all this, Whittaker threw the comforter around himself and awaited reveille and discovery.

When discovered, Whittaker feigned unconsciousness, yet he uttered several clear statements. He pretended he was more hurt than he actually was and tried to make it appear that the attack had been inflicted by Southern cadets intent on driving him from the Military Academy. On his way to the hospital he let Louis Simpson know the plan was going well and later spoke lightly of the whole affair to another black man, Walter Mitchell.

The following day Whittaker wrote a detailed letter to Moses Wester, an intelligent and influential black man in New York, explicitly accusing the cadets of the attack and denouncing the Academy. He also wrote his mother and in this surprisingly brief letter said he would appeal to Congress for support. When asked to give up his private correspondence, he did so freely, feeling confident that there was nothing incriminatory in his letters.

In short, then, West Pointers came to the conclusion that the evidence discovered in the black cadet's room the morning after the attack pointed not to a hostile attack by three masked intruders but to a case of plotting and self-mutilation. Whittaker had committed the act himself and then concocted the story of masked attackers to save his academic skin and repay West Point for its treatment of him.[15]

The court of inquiry was faced with two contradictory stories—Whittaker's and West Point's. Its task was to find out which one was true.

Chapter 5

———————— ··•·⟨∞⟩·•·· ————————

THE COURT OF INQUIRY:
A LAWYER, A MILKMAN,
AND A TAVERNKEEPER

The court of inquiry, now a focal point of national attention, continued its hearings. On Monday, April 12, 1880,
the court met for the third time, and the gallery included
the entire nation. Captain Sears announced at the outset
that he was beginning an investigation to determine the
writer of the note of warning. He indicated that he had
prepared a list of twenty-five sheets each containing the
handwriting of a different cadet. This list and the warning
note would be submitted to New York mail superintendent
Gayler for his analysis and report. In this way, Sears
hoped, the culprit would be discovered.[1]

Cadet Burnett was recalled and continued his testimony.
Whereas on the previous day his "impressions" had not
been desired by the recorder, this day they were; and he
was happy to respond. He told the court he had begun to
believe that Whittaker had faked the whole affair when he
watched Dr. Alexander examine the allegedly unconscious

cadet's eye. He had thought an unconscious person had no control over his muscles, but that morning he noticed that Whittaker seemed to have control. When Alexander first opened Whittaker's eye only the white could be seen. After a few shakes and a command, the pupil came into view. This, to Burnett, was an indication that Whittaker was not truly unconscious but was merely feigning and he so told Dr. Alexander.

Burnett related other indications that had caused him to suspect Whittaker. It had seemed strange that Whittaker had not been gagged and that his hands had been tied in front of him and not in back. The blood drops on his knees seemed to have been dropped there while Whittaker was in a standing position. The hair seemed to have been cut by the black cadet himself because it was lying in bunches and was not scattered as it usually is at a barbershop. All this appeared very suspicious, Burnett concluded, causing him to doubt even more the veracity of Whittaker's story.[2]

In the afternoon Cadet Frederick G. Hodgson of Georgia took the stand. Hodgson, who had remained in the room during Burnett's search for the authorities the morning of the attack, corroborated Burnett's story in most essential facts, though he did not editorialize as Burnett had done.[3] In the midst of Hodgson's testimony Superintendent Gayler appeared in the courtroom and took the stand. He reported that he had examined the twenty-five samples of cadets' writing and seven other ones given him by the recorder and could find no comparison with any of them and the note of warning. This disclosure caused quite a reaction. Obviously one of the twenty-five specimens must have contained Whittaker's writing, yet Gayler exonerated it with the rest. Here was a West Point-appointed expert punching a hole in the conviction of Whittaker's guilt. Undeterred, Captain Sears handed Gayler seven more pieces of writing and asked for a further investigation. It was suspected that these additional specimens were all in

Whittaker's hand, though Sears, of course, said nothing to that effect at this time or later.

The next day, after Major Piper, who had been the officer of the day on the night of the outrage, had testified, Gayler returned to the stand and again shook West Pointers. He reported that he could find no resemblance between the note of warning and the specimens given by the recorder. There were similarities, but these were more than offset by the differences.[4] A point had apparently been scored in Whittaker's favor.

The black cadet and his supporters had little time to savor favorable developments, however. The tide quickly turned with the testimony of Dr. Charles T. Alexander. The post surgeon, who had treated Whittaker the morning of the assault and had later written a damning report, stuck by his story on the stand. In a word, he held that Whittaker was faking his condition. His pulse was too regular for someone supposedly unconscious, and the eyelid offered resistance when Alexander tried to examine the eye for evidence of a possible concussion. When Whittaker stood up he showed no ill effects of the attack, no yawning, no nausea. There was nothing in his physical condition, nothing in the cuts or blows, to account for a faint, though, Alexander submitted, fear might have caused it. As far as he could surmise, Whittaker's unconsciousness was purely put on.[5] Therefore, Whittaker had not been attacked, as he was insisting, but had committed the entire act himself. When this strong medical opinion sank in, the handwriting evidence declined in significance. The favorable turn had indeed been short-lived.

Events outside the court added still another volatile element to the already explosive mix. S. L. Woodford, the United States attorney for the Southern District of New York and later minister to Spain during the Spanish-American War, sent his assistant John Fiero to discover if the Whittaker assault might not be a crime punishable under civil law. Fiero arrived on April 13 and immediately began his investigation. He talked to Schofield, to Whittaker, and to a number of other cadets. He told a reporter that he found Whittaker's story quite plausible and saw in his isolation "an element of pathos . . . that would move a heart of adamant stone." "He looked me straight in the eye and stood by his story like a drum major," Fiero said. As the *Army and Navy Journal* was quick to point out, indicating truthfulness through the analogy of a drum major was rather strange; still, the essential fact was not the figure of speech but Fiero's belief in Whittaker's story. The black cadet had gained an important ally.[6]

Still another ally was on the way. Justin D. Fulton, the Brooklyn minister who had been present during the first day's session, wrote Alexander Ramsey urging the "best of legal talent" for Whittaker's defense. He feared what he called the inexperience and prejudice of the inquiry board. President Hayes's Cabinet met on the thirteenth and, whether influenced by Fulton or not, decided to have the Justice Department send someone to observe the court of inquiry. Martin I. Townsend, a former Congressman and presently the United States District Attorney for the Northern District of New York, was chosen. He was ordered to go to West Point "at the request of the *President* to furnish such aid as his professional skill and experience" suggested. He was also to "report and advise in the matter." He was the direct representative of the President and his Cabinet, their source of information. The case was growing in importance.[7]

Townsend's entrance into the case could not have been more dramatic nor disruptive. West Point authorities had been aware of his assignment because a telegram was received from him on April 13 announcing his arrival the next day.[8] Still, when Townsend arrived on the morning of April 14 his entrance into the case provoked the first real turmoil of the inquiry. He registered at his hotel and, upon being questioned by a reporter, expressed his opinion of

the entire affair. "I don't say the cadets did it; but if it was
not a hostile attack, then the world is a farce." Having
dropped this bombshell, he went to West Point and, instead
of presenting his credentials to General Schofield as proto-
col and common sense required, hurried directly to the
library, where the inquiry was being held. When he walked
in, Dr. Alexander was on the stand, having just stated that
the fact that the white of Whittaker's eye was showing had
little bearing on his belief in Whittaker's guilt; in sleep the
eye tended to move up or down a little. While Sears was
continuing the questioning Townsend approached him
from behind and tried to get his attention. He nudged
Sears's elbow and said something like "I would like a word
with you." Sears, preoccupied with the questioning,
glanced up but, not recognizing Townsend or noticing the
paper in his hand, replied, "I cannot interrupt the proceedings of the court to listen to you, sir." Townsend, taken
somewhat aback, replied sharply, "I am not in the habit of
being treated with incivility." Sears, now apparently angry, retorted something like "I call the attention of the
court to the manner of this gentleman."

The inquiry stopped and the attention of the entire
courtroom focused on the verbal battle between the
young recorder and the seventy-year-old attorney. The
court of inquiry was involved in the first of several
clashes. Townsend announced: "I came here at the direction of the Secretary of War, and all I did that was
uncivil to this gentleman was to say to him that I
wished to confer with him one moment. I just arrived,
as you have seen here, and I wish certainly to act in entire subordination in everything that could be desired,
but I desired a moment's conference with that gentleman."

RECORDER: "My answer was that I did not think that
anyone had a right to interfere during the proceedings
of the court. If that is uncivil then I want it spread
upon the record."

TOWNSEND: "If it be not so, but in my imperfect civil education I am unable to tell what is uncivil."

MAJOR MORDECAI: "I presume the recorder thought you were one of the audience."

TOWNSEND: "I am certainly not one of the audience. I am here against my will and I am here under the direction of the Secretary of War."

MORDECAI: "That is perfectly understood now."

RECORDER: "If any gentleman comes by authority, I should suppose it was customary first to name that fact and not take anyone at a disadvantage by first calling him out, saying that he wants to see him, and afterwards saying that he did it by authority."

TOWNSEND: "I asked him if I might speak a word with him."

MORDECAI: "A mere misunderstanding, I presume."

At the request of the recorder, the court then took a ten-minute recess. Sears, Townsend, and Schofield went into a side room and discussed the matter. The court then resumed its questioning of Dr. Alexander. Just before noon Sears finally announced who Townsend was and said he interpreted the attorney's orders to mean that he was "at the service" of both Whittaker and the court. Townsend then had a desk assigned to him next to the recorder. Schofield and Townsend sent the Secretary of War separate explanatory notes and the affair seemed over.[9]

The following day, April 15, Townsend was present during the inquiry. For his benefit most of the session was taken up with the reading of previous testimony, although Whittaker also testified again. On the following day Townsend's status in the court of inquiry was made official. General Schofield, after lecturing the attorney on the gravity of his courtroom encounter, established Townsend's position as "Assistant Counsel and Advisor to the Recorder, sent by the Honorable Secretary of War to represent the War Department, and to give the Court and Recorder the benefit of his experience and professional skill and knowledge."[10]

From the time of his controversial entrance Townsend played a turbulent role in the court of inquiry. After hearing Whittaker, on April 15, deny that he had ever expressed doubt to a New York *Times* reporter that he could receive justice at West Point, Townsend sent his initial impressions to Secretary of War Ramsey and Attorney General Charles Devens. He told Ramsey he believed in Whittaker's innocence but feared the subconscious prejudice of a few officers. For a time, he wrote Devens, it looked as though Whittaker would be convicted on the "construction" of evidence which a "man educated in another atmosphere" would consider "startlingly absurd." This had all changed, however. "He [Whittaker] had no motive to do such an act and could not have done it if he had wished to." "His real crime," as Townsend saw it, was to have "some indications of African blood" in his light features. But, Townsend said, Whittaker would have justice and "no effort . . . [would] be spared to save the credit of the Institution which had been and may be so useful if not perverted."[11]

No one would question Townsend's last statement about West Point's desire for survival, but many West Pointers questioned his belief in Whittaker's innocence. His actions in trying to ensure the justice that he was so confident Whittaker would receive made him unwelcome at the inquiry. West Pointers did not seem to realize the national implication of Townsend's presence. They saw him as an outsider, complicating a basically simple case. They considered the whole matter an open-and-shut case and resisted any efforts to take Whittaker off the spot.

When the April 15 issue of the New York *Times* hit the newsstands, the Whittaker case took a new turn. A story by Edward Z. Lewis was a bombshell that disrupted the well-laid West Point lines. Sears quickly called the reporter to the stand, but Lewis refused to speak until his lawyer had arrived.[12] The story, for the time, stood on its own.

In the April 15 article reporter Lewis contended that, at Highland Falls, a village a mile and a half away from West Point, it was generally known who had committed the Whittaker outrage. The morning of the attack a milkman on his rounds had told an unnamed tavernkeeper the news of the Whittaker attack. The tavernkeeper, learning of the incident for the first time, told the milkman and two others that the night before three cadets had been in his establishment talking about getting rid of the black cadet. When news of the statement spread, Lewis said, West Point officers had warned the tavernkeeper to remain quiet lest West Point be hurt. In fact, officers had visited this man every day since then, and two were seen "talking earnestly with him."[13]

Highland Falls housed many of the people who worked for the Military Academy and was the obvious rendezvous for cadets wishing to get away from military life. One of the favorite watering spots was the establishment of one Phil Ryan, the post-Civil War successor to the legendary Benny Havens. At Ryan's, cadets could find liquid refreshment and, it was sometimes whispered, pleasure of a different kind. Ryan's tavern was not the only such place in Highland Falls, but its location made it the most convenient of all for cadets. A cadet simply took the path that led from the "back road" of the Academy directly to Ryan's. The path began at a broken stone wall and ran through some scrub-pine woods littered with rocks and boulders. When the woods ended, a swamp began, its crossing expedited by carefully positioned steppingstones. A little farther along was a boulder painted with a red "M.A." Beyond this rock the path ran over some slightly hilly terrain, crossed through gaps in several stone fences and dropped into a grove of cedar trees about thirty to forty rods deep.

Continuing under the overhanging tree branches, the path led directly to Ryan's back door.

Because for most of the route a person was hidden from view, this path was a definite asset to Ryan's business. It was not used by all cadets, but it was a handy device for anyone wishing to avoid notice on a drinking spree. People living near the path were used to hearing and seeing cadets in uniform making their way, and littered pages torn from cadet textbooks were silent evidence to the cadet traffic.[14]

In his story Lewis made no mention of the tavern-keeper's name, but the following day it was reported that Highland Falls residents were convinced the place in question was Phil Ryan's. The tavern, in fact, was overrun by visitors, and the nervous host, suffering from consumption, was kept busy denying the whole story. He said cadets had visited his establishment a month before, but none had been there the night in question. Sometime previously two drunken sergeants had charged him with having a disorderly house, but they had gone away peacefully. Later he had threatened to have their stripes taken away, but this had been idle talk. He had spoken to a milkman the morning of the assault but had not said anything about three cadets.[15]

The entire matter shocked West Pointers, and though Lewis had refused to testify when first called, he was recalled by the court on April 17. He told the court that, on advice of counsel, he would discuss nothing in his articles except for nineteen innocuous lines. If the court required more, it would have to wait until Monday, when his lawyer, General McMahon, would be present. Any prior statement would constitute "a breach of confidence and the sacrifice of personal honor on his part."

The court was taken aback by Lewis' refusal and went into conference. After consultation, Major Mordecai, displaying obvious anger, retorted, "This witness has sworn to tell the truth, the whole truth, and nothing but the truth; but now he declines to give away information but what he deems politic. Under these circumstances, no importance will attach to any information which he may hereafter give to the press from this place. The court will report the facts to the Superintendent and let the matter drop."

Reporter Lewis left the stand without comment, but he soon returned to demand that his testimony be read back to him. He protested the court's statement and reiterated his right to remain silent. Captain Sears countered that the court's only aim was to discover the truth; that was the only reason Lewis had been called. The court did not wish to try him. The New York *Times,* predictably, lashed out at the court's handling of the entire matter. "The court has succeeded in making itself ridiculous." There the matter rested for the time being. It was not dead and would remain a dominant factor in the inquiry, despite Major Mordecai's statement and General Schofield's report to General Sherman that "there was nothing whatever" in Lewis' story.[16]

The court was upset by the excitement raised by the New York *Times* but carried on its deliberations nonetheless, hopefully aided by two reward offers of $1,000—one an anonymous donor announced by Townsend and another in response from the Corps of Cadets. On Friday, April 16, and Saturday, April 17, Lieutenant Colonel Lazelle, the commandant of cadets; Lieutenant William H. Coffin, Whittaker's company commander; Lieutenant Crozier, who slept near Whittaker's room; and Edward T. McEnearny, clerk of the quartermaster department, were all questioned. Lazelle, particularly, expressed disbelief in Whittaker's story and repeated the accusations found in his report. The two lieutenants stated that black cadets were not hazed but were simply left completely to themselves. The quartermaster clerk indicated that the handkerchief used to stop Whittaker's bleeding ears was like the ones purchased by probably fifty cadets. General Schofield also took the stand, and his testimony vied with that of the *Times* reporter. Schofield produced no startlingly new information; he simply described his actions on the morning of the attack. But his position as Superintendent caused even this brief testimony to be followed closely.[17]

Soon the real excitement was taking place outside the court with the arrival from Washington of Louis Simpson in the custody of a detective. Simpson, the forty-five-year-old son of the West Point bootblack, was in some circles, including Hayes's Cabinet, suspected as Whittaker's accomplice. His testimony might be important. For a time, West Pointers even considered locking him up to prevent escape. Some Army men postulated that Whittaker's assailants had not been cadets but young blacks jealous of Whittaker and of the appeal exerted by his uniform on neighboring girls. Simpson might be able to provide information about this too.[18] Simpson might also prove an effective deflector for the spotlight now trained on Highland Falls. Despite all these possibilities, however, Simpson was surprisingly not called until April 22.

Monday, April 19, with Townsend and Fiero both absent on other business, the court again examined Gayler, the New York mail superintendent. Though on two previous occasions Gayler had been unable to match the note of warning with other writing specimens, the court now gave him a new task. This time, Recorder Sears had given Gayler an example of the writing of every cadet at West Point, a total of 257 specimens. Out of these, Gayler selected several examples of writing, number "8," as resembling the writing of the note of warning. He also felt that flourishes had been added to some of the letters in the note in an attempt at disguise. Sears then gave Gayler the two pieces of paper found on Whittaker's floor the morning of the assault and a third specimen provided by Lieutenant Knight. Gayler retired to another room but quickly returned to state that one of the pieces, he believed, had been written by "No. 8." Only Captain Sears knew who No. 8 was, but he said nothing and simply called the next witness. No further reference to this startling piece of evidence was made until much later in the trial. The obvious suspicion was present, however.[19]

On Tuesday a long-awaited witness was put on the stand, the tavernkeeper Philip Ryan of Highland Falls. Very quickly Ryan put his head in a noose; he stated that no cadets had ever visited his place. The recorder, apparently unable to believe his ears, tried to give Ryan another chance. Learning that the tavernkeeper was a Catholic, he had Ryan resworn on a Catholic Bible and then gave him a chance to change his testimony. Ryan remained adamant. He insisted that no one he knew as a cadet had ever come into his establishment. Cadets, promised immunity, quickly testified to having visited the tavern in uniform, and Ryan was shown to be a perjurer by the very cadets he seemed to be trying to protect.

All cadets in the first class, in fact, were called to testify not simply about Ryan but about their actions on the night of the assault. They were all asked the same basic questions: Had they and their roommates been in their rooms "continuously" from Taps to reveille? Did they know of any cadet who had been missing during that period? Did they know who had written the note or who had been involved in the attack or if anyone had threatened any such act?

Having been granted immunity from punishment for absence after Taps that evening, a number of cadets admitted having been out on the night in question. But they all seemed able to explain their whereabouts. Several, including Burnett, admitted having been in Ryan's tavern in uniform on several occasions, but none admitted any knowledge of the assault.

The case had undergone a definite change. Ryan's perjury, the cadet admission of their ability to sneak out at night, and press disclosures of previous escapades caused a real shift in the inquiry. Before, Whittaker had been the sole target of speculation; now the entire corps of cadets joined him in this unenviable position.

Adding more fuel to the controversy, a suspended cadet, B. C. Welsh, testified that a candidate for the Military Academy by the name of Palmer had told him two days before the *Times* article that a milkman had told him the story about cadets planning to fix Whittaker.

The following day the second and third class were called before the court and the same questions were put to them. All denied any knowledge of the affair, with the exception of one cadet, H. R. Curtis, who testified that another cadet, Greble, had told him that three cadets had been at Highland Falls the night of the attack. Surprisingly neither Sears nor Townsend called on Greble to verify this statement.

During the questioning of an Indiana cadet, Frank B. Andrews, still another telling point was made. Townsend asked Andrews if it was true that he had refused to stand next to Whittaker in formation. Andrews said it was true. He felt so strongly about it, in fact, that he had asked permission to fall in in such a way that Whittaker could not stand next to him. Another cadet, he said, was willing to give up his corporal's stripe rather than stand next to the black cadet.[20]

This new testimony added little to the skidding reputation of the corps of cadets. The West Point cadet had previously been pictured in the press as a "vulgar snob rather than the brave and gentle gentleman," and the corps was entitled the "West Point Aristocracy." The last several days' testimony served only to emphasize these and other accusations. How trustworthy were the cadets if they continuously insisted on the strength of their honor yet habitually broke curfew and liquor laws and refused to have anything to do with another cadet simply because he was black? How valid were their protestations of innocence? *Puck* magazine, becoming momentarily serious, felt that "the fact ... [was] conclusively proved that they [the cadets] were entirely capable of the act."[21]

The Whittaker inquiry seemed to have gotten out of

hand. It was no longer simply a matter of corroborating the guilt of a single cadet. Now other members of the corps of cadets were under suspicion. West Pointers squirmed because of this unexpected turn of events and searched for a way out. On April 20 a delegation of cadets denounced the *Times* article before the press, but their denunciation swayed few reporters. General Schofield, who was present at most of the court sessions, apparently decided to rectify the situation in one grand sweep. During the afternoon dress parade and review of the corps, on April 21, Schofield issued a General Order. In it he said he wished "to assure the Corps of Cadets of his unshaken faith in their honor and integrity, and of his appreciation of their manly bearing under the grievous wrong and injustice which they have recently suffered." Because they had withstood the "insults and indignities" placed on them "with becoming dignity and confidence that justice would be done to all," he wished to express his appreciation by rescinding all the restrictions he had placed on them for the New Year's Eve escapade. He also established an all-night "police force of 2" in the barracks area.

In his official diary Schofield explained his reasoning for issuing this order in the midst of the court of inquiry. From the outset, he wrote, he and the cadets had suspected that no cadet had committed the outrage. After the cadets had sworn their innocence, no lingering doubt remained. Yet, he had still constituted a number of cadets as detectives to investigate further. The cadets had searched around, found nothing, "and the unanimous belief of the Corps . . . [was] that the alleged culprits were not cadets." He continued:

> Although anyone at all acquainted with the Corps knew that these statements upon honor could not possibly be changed under oath, all the Cadets were again undergoing the same examination under oath before the court of inquiry, as if their statements upon honor were doubted. Be-

94

sides this, they were publicly accused, from all parts of the country, of conspiring by falsehood to conceal the guilty. They appealed to me to know if something could not be done to defend them against such accusations.

I *know* that they were all innocent except possibly three or four.

Besides, he argued in this May 1 entry in his diary, he had evidence that the court would soon publish that proved Whittaker's guilt. "The order of April 21 was issued as a simple act of justice to the Corps of Cadets."[22]

Faced with attitudes and obvious contradictions like this, Whittaker's fate was sealed. His chance for exoneration was slim at best. Yet he kept his outward composure, kept going to class and following the day-to-day accounts of his trial. His reaction to Schofield's order was not revealed until later. The press, on the other hand, immediately responded with anger, finding the order a shocking response to the facts at issue. From this point on, press attacks on West Point began to focus on Schofield. He was seen as the chief perpetrator of the West Point plan to treat Whittaker unjustly. Schofield, however, began receiving letters of support; he saw himself as deserving censure only for "extending unusual kindness to one who was unworthy of it."[23]

The excitement over the General Order still lingered when another example of West Point touchiness unfolded in the courtroom. After the publication of Schofield's order and after hearing Phil Ryan's wife and daughter deny that any cadets had been present at the tavern on the night of the attack, Townsend was in the process of questioning Walter Mitchell, a black servant.

TOWNSEND: . . . Do you understand the rule requires a man [a cadet at West Point] to fight when he is struck?

MITCHELL: The rule don't require him to fight.

TOWNSEND:	It prohibits him, don't it?
MITCHELL:	It prohibits him, I think; I am sure of it.
TOWNSEND:	Except in the case of a colored cadet, it perhaps may—
MAJOR MORDECAI:	Does the assistant counsel desire these remarks made by him to go upon the record?
TOWNSEND:	No sir, sometimes I cannot quite avoid—
MORDECAI:	These remarks reflect upon the officers of the Academy.
TOWNSEND:	I am not reflecting upon anybody, I am only reflecting upon a pretense that—
MORDECAI:	The remarks of the assistant counsel that reflect upon the character of the officers of the Academy will be struck from the record.
TOWNSEND:	[in substance] I hope they don't go there. I am very careful, I don't want to get into trouble, and if I do, I hope I shall not be called a coward. I want you to understand that I am not afraid to strike back.

By this time the courtroom was in a turmoil, and Townsend, not fully understanding the uproar and given practically no chance even to finish a sentence, was stunned. The court went into an adjoining room to consult, and General Schofield rushed to confront Townsend. He was livid with anger over what he considered Townsend's intimation that a white cadet, when struck, would be protected by Academy officials and thus did not have to fight back, while a black cadet had to fend for himself. He said:

> If you think the rule is taught at West Point that
> a cadet is to tamely submit to a blow without
> returning it or defending himself you are greatly

mistaken. If you meant to say that any such rule as this is or ought to be enforced here, I must insist that your words be allowed to remain on the record. That rule may perhaps be taught in the Bible, but it is not taught here or anywhere else so far as I know.

Townsend, bewildered, began to answer, "I really don't understand what all this . . ." but Schofield cut him off by simply walking away and joining the court. Later Townsend was able to tell Schofield that his point had merely been to convey that the case should be conducted without insinuations that "this poor boy is a coward." Still reeling from this encounter, Townsend was then approached by Lieutenant Knight. Whittaker's counsel, "fairly quivering," said, "I don't think there is anything to justify your sitting here and insulting us officers. Pardon me for saying this to your gray hairs, but I will protest against it to anyone."

Schofield, still fuming, instructed the court that Townsend's remarks should remain on the record so that Washington would know exactly what had taken place in the inquiry. This was done, and two days later Sears and Townsend both indicated their acceptance of the written record. Schofield later confided to his official diary that he considered Townsend's whole attitude "extremely offensive and insulting to the officers of the Military Academy." The general felt that the visiting counselor was continually impugning West Pointers by doubting their "veracity" and by contending that, even if Whittaker had committed the act himself, he had been driven to it by his treatment at the Academy.[24] Schofield seemed to feel that preconceived notions were acceptable only on one side of the issue.

After this blast of excitement the court, still tense, returned to the investigation of witnesses. It heard Louis Simpson testify that he had told Whittaker not to expect justice at West Point because of officer prejudice. The court

97

heard this statement calmly, though it had reacted with agitation to Townsend's intimation. In fact, Simpson's entire testimony was received with repeated laughter. His humorously told account of rumors that officers were planning to put him into the penitentiary because they considered him the leader of a "gang of desperadoes at Highland Falls," and his admission that he had referred to Whittaker as a "nigger," had the court in stitches. Earlier whisperings that Simpson was Whittaker's accomplice had come to naught. Though Simpson again testified on the next day, April 23, it was obvious he had little to offer as evidence.[25] But he had helped to break the tension, and this was no small achievement.

The second witness on Friday, April 23, caused the sensation that had been expected from Simpson's testimony. Squire VanBuren, a well-to-do farmer and brickmaker of Fishkill Landing, New York, had, on April 22, sought out Townsend with information to impart. He told the assembled court that he had had a conversation on April 18 with John Dutcher, a brickmaker and the father of a cavalryman stationed at West Point. Dutcher had told him that Whittaker was a "damned black cuss" who would have to leave West Point soon. He said that he had visited the Academy in the early spring and had talked with a cadet by the name of "Brunnette," who reported that he was going to get Whittaker out of West Point one way or another. Dutcher said that he considered this cadet, "Brunnette or Barnett," to be a "damned bad egg."

As soon as VanBuren was finished, John Dutcher took the stand and with much nervous laughter tried to convince the court there had been a misunderstanding. He denied knowing Burnett and said that he had talked to VanBuren when he was "full of beer." He insisted with a nervous laugh that he was sober now. He moved around in his chair and seemed anxious to get off as quickly as possible. He seemed sorry he had ever become involved in the whole matter. Henry Dutcher, the cavalryman, testified that he had no idea where his father had gotten the idea about Burnett, but perhaps he had confused him with someone else. He personally had never heard anyone threaten to take care of Whittaker, neither Burnett nor any other cadet. On being recalled, VanBuren denied that Dutcher had been drunk during their conversation. His story was corroborated by Ernott Youmans of the New-burgh, Duchess and Connecticut Railroad, who told a Poughkeepsie *Eagle* reporter that he had overheard the con-versation in question.[26]

This new testimony "created the most profound sensa-tion" since the case had first begun. Burnett's name was on everyone's lips. The possibility of cadet collusion was again present. Adding to the effect was the testimony of a hand-writing expert, J. E. Paine, who could not match the note of warning with any of the slips of paper submitted to him. Affairs were again looking up for Whittaker.

The next several days the inquiry tried to follow up the VanBuren–Dutcher story by summoning a whole series of witnesses. Only two testimonies need be considered. Gov-ernor Kemble, a student at a school near West Point, said he had seen three men dressed in dark clothing and looking like cadets leaving West Point about 7:00 P.M. the evening of the attack. They looked suspicious and kept peering over their shoulders in the direction of the Academy. The milk-man, W. H. Haight, from whom many of the other wit-nesses said they had first heard the story of the three cadets, testified that Ryan had told him about the three cadets the morning of the outrage; but a few days later Ryan changed the story and claimed that he had been talking about three soldiers on an undisclosed night. That was about all the milkman cared to say about the incident.

Q: "Your story, saying positively there were three cadets there, went all over the country?"

A: "It seems so."

Q: "Then as far as you know there is not [sic] truth in the story?"

A: "None whatever."

To West Pointers, this last bit of testimony was conclusive. It indicated that the suspicion placed on the cadets was unfair. As the *Army and Navy Journal* put it, "The whole testimony of Haight shows that the three-cadet story was a bit of milkman's gossip, which is about as trustworthy as barber's gossip." To seal the issue, Phil Ryan was arrested for perjury and taken to New York to jail. He was released under $2,000 bail, and his trial was postponed until after the end of the inquiry to prevent any prejudicial impact.[27]

As far as West Point was concerned, the case now had settled down to its correct course. The focus was again on Whittaker. Yet one may question just how dead the New York *Times* three-cadet story really was. Was it simply the invention of a tavernkeeper, spread by a gossipy milkman, or was there more to it? Did the combination of circumstances require a more thorough investigation? The Van-Buren–Dutcher story and the Greble testimony both seemed to result from more than the influence of a milkman. Finally, had there really been three cadets at Ryan's the night of the attack?

Whatever the case, the story had produced revelations about cadet transgressions, about curfew violations, the consumption of liquor and hidden paths that enabled the cadets to sneak away from their quarters. Whether or not there were three cadets at Ryan's that night was not the only issue. Whether or not the deed actually had been done by cadets, it was amply clear now that it might have been done. Whittaker was not the sole suspect. Was it fair for West Point and the court of inquiry to accept the word of the cadets and not accept Whittaker's word? Was there not a double standard in existence, and could Whittaker truly hope for justice?

nson Whittaker at West Point. *Mrs. Cecil Whittaker McFadden*

Cadets in formation before marching to dinner. *U.S. Military Academy Archives (From the 1882 Album)*

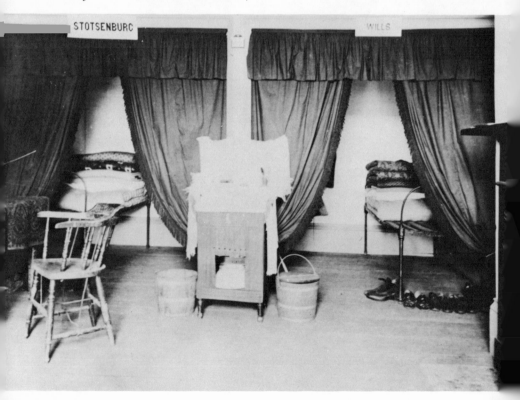

A typical room housing two cadets. *U.S. Military Academy Archives*

(Below) Cadets Frederick G. Hodgson *(left)* and George R. Burnett *(center)* discovered Whittaker on the morning of the attack. Cadet Walter M. Dickinson *(right)* found charred pieces of paper in Whittaker's room. *All three, U.S. Military Academy Archives*

West Point's inquiry into the Whittaker case took place in the imposing Library Room.
U.S. Military Academy Archives

Sunday   April 4th,

Mr Whittaker, You m
be 'fixed'   Better keep
awake

A friend

ut. Col. Henry Lazelle (*above*, *left*), the Commandant of Cadets, conducted the preliminary
estigation the day after the accident. Dr. Charles T. Alexander (*above*, *right*) the Post surgeon,
nined Whittaker's wounds. *Both, U.S. Military Academy Archives*

posite, below) The note of warning. *American Law Register, xxx, 1882*

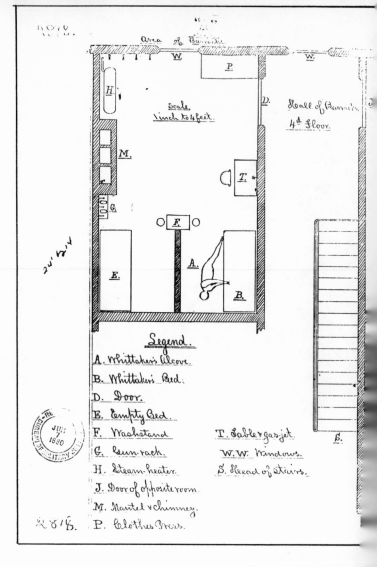

Area of Barracks

Scale
1 inch to 4 feet

Hall of Barracks
4^d Floor.

W.

P.

H.

D.

M.

G.

T.

F.

E.

A.

B.

Legend.

A. Whittaker's Alcove.
B. Whittaker's Bed.
D. Door.
E. Empty Bed.
F. Washstand.   T. Table & gas jet.
G. Gun-rack.   W.W. Windows.
H. Steam-heater.   S. Head of Stairs.
J. Door of opposite room.
M. Mantel & chimney.
P. Clothes Press.

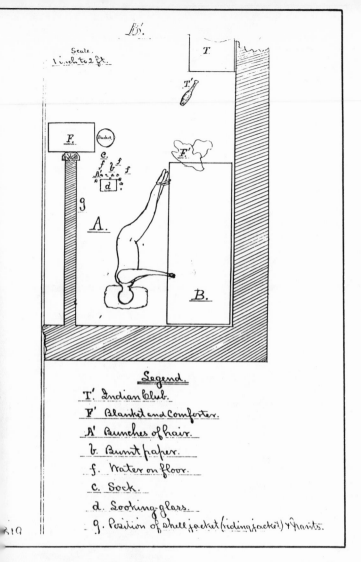

Scale.
1 inch to 2 ft.

Legend.

T'. Indian Club.

F'. Blanket and Comforter.

A'. Bunches of hair.

b. Burnt paper.

f. Water on floor.

c. Sock.

d. Looking-glass.

g. Position of shell jacket (riding jacket) & pants.

Charts *(above)*, from the official record of the court-martial show how Whittaker was discovered in his room. *National Archives*

John M. Schofield *(opposite)* was superintendent of West Point at the time of the incident. General O. O. Howard *(left)*, former head of the Freedmen's Bureau, frequently mentioned as an eventual successor to Schofield. *Both, U.S. Military Academy Archives*

107

A scene from the West Point inquiry, shown in *Harper's Weekly*. *Harper's Weekly*, May

(Above) Long after the court-martial, Johnson Whittaker *(far right)* posed with other member of the faculty of the Colored Normal, Industrial, Agricultural and Mechanical College South Carolina. *South Carolina State College*

(Right) Page Harrison Whittaker as a young girl. *Mrs. Cecil Whittaker McFadden*

World War I: Johnson C. Whittaker, Jr., as a soldier

World War II: Peter Whittaker (center), Whittaker's grandson, as a soldier, standing betw‹
Whittaker's two sons. *Both, Mrs. Cecil Whittaker McFadden*

Chapter 6

THE COURT OF INQUIRY:
HANDWRITING EXPERTS AND
THE DECISION

THE court of inquiry continued. More witnesses appeared,
and a number of diverse points were investigated. An attempt to discover any new leads on how Whittaker had
received the note of warning proved fruitless, but several
West Point professors provided some significant information. They agreed that Whittaker's chances for passing
were good, his recent drop into the sixth section in philosophy meaning little. All were also adamant in defending the
honor and integrity of the Corps and justifying Whittaker's
ostracism. In South Carolina, at the same time, the Republican state convention was passing a resolution supporting
Whittaker. This gesture had no impact on the inquiry and,
judging by a local newspaper, had little impact even in the
Palmetto state.[1]

The court of inquiry had come to an apparent standstill.
No new information was being produced, and now that the
Highland Falls controversy had seemingly been put to rest,

proceedings were dull. The only real activity centered about the note of warning. Several individuals were added to the parade of handwriting experts as it became increasingly evident that most of the court's future attention would be concentrated on the little scrap of paper.

On Friday, April 30, a new expert appeared. W. E. Hagan, who had been making a handwriting analysis with a microscope and other devices, reported a similarity between the note and a number of the specimens that had been given him. Hagan made no direct references to names or numbers, so the public did not know which specimens he meant or if they were the same ones indicated by Gayler. Only Sears knew and he was not saying. Suspicions against Whittaker were so prevalent, however, that when the court next assembled on May 4, Sears felt compelled to deny newspaper allegations that Hagan had indeed implicated the black cadet.[2]

On May 4, another expert discussed his findings. Daniel Ames, editor of the *Penman's Art Journal*, submitted a long report indicating a strong resemblance between the note of warning and the writing of specimen No. 23. He also warned of the strong possibility of forgery. This opened new avenues of investigation. Who was No. 23? Was he the same person as No. 8? Was either one or both Whittaker? Again no one but Sears knew, and he was maintaining his silence.[3]

On May 12, the last of the handwriting experts, A. G. Southworth, testified. He saw no forgery, but he believed that No. 27 had written the warning note. Sears heard his long testimony and then gave Southworth two sets of specimens and asked him to make another comparison with the note of warning.[4]

And so yet another confusing element had been added to the inquiry. Who was No. 27? Was he the same as No. 8 or No. 23? And why was it that when one expert, Hagan, had made his choice, his testimony had been allowed to stand while the other experts, after giving their opinions, were told to try again? Was the court of inquiry looking for corroboration for its predetermined conclusions?

The next several days the experts testified again about their new findings. Southworth, Ames, Gayler, and Paine, in separate testimony, agreed that a certain set of papers had been written by the same person who had written the note of warning. This time they were not asked for any further opinions.

Confusion was rampant. The technical nature of the testimony and the rapidly charging expert opinions made it difficult to follow what was happening. Affairs became even more chaotic when Whittaker's former teacher, Richard T. Greener, who had been in attendance at War Department request since the beginning of the inquiry, confronted one of the experts, Southworth, with the assertion that before Southworth's testimony Recorder Sears had shown Southworth a copy of the New York *Herald* containing another expert's opinon. Both Southworth and Sears denied any wrongdoing, but the obvious inference was certainly there.[5]

On May 12, the same day that Southworth testified, another confusing event occurred. The President's representative, Martin I. Townsend, did not attend the inquiry. There were newspaper rumors that he had quit the case. Sears tried to contact him to learn the truth. The only response he received was a terse telegram announcing that Townsend would not be present any more and had no further suggestions to make. The matter stood unresolved, and the court and recorder were puzzled, though doubtless pleased at the departure of their nemesis.

Townsend had indeed left for good. On May 5, 1880, he had sent the Secretary of War a full report of the case and a separate letter asking to be relieved. Perhaps he felt he had completed his duty and had no further responsibility toward Whittaker. Though obviously convinced of the black cadet's innocence and critical of West Point's handling of the case, he left before the decision had been rendered. He had from the first insisted he would not have to remain for the entire trial, and the Secretary of War had given him permission to leave when he felt Whittaker no longer needed him. But as it was, Whittaker lost his services just when he needed them most.

The *Army and Navy Journal,* for one, accepted Townsend's departure with no tears. "We fail . . . to see what new light Mr. Townsend has thrown on the case, or what of value he has contributed to it." Whittaker's reaction is unknown, but Greener wrote the Secretary of War asking permission to ask questions during the rest of the inquiry since Townsend's departure had left the black cadet "practically unrepresented." Permission was not granted.[6]

Meanwhile, General Schofield was neither silent nor forgotten. His General Order defending the cadets was still a topic of conversation. Letters from all over the country were being sent to the Secretary of War suggesting Schofield's removal, and elements of the press supported the idea. Schofield began to feel the pressure. When he read an editorial in the pro-West Point magazine, the *Nation,* criticizing his order, he wrote a defense and had his adjutant sign and send it. To Schofield's surprise, the *Nation* printed the letter and expressed its continued friendship for West Point; but the magazine insisted that Schofield's order had been a mistake, because it had provided excellent anti-West Point ammunition. Schofield's rebuttal had backfired. It was becoming obvious that his position was tenuous and that the court of inquiry's outcome would go far in determining his future status. He did get some support, however, from Vice President William A. Wheeler during a train trip when Wheeler expressed his agreement with West Point authorities.[7]

At the court of inquiry the Highland Falls story also came up once again. Assistant United States Attorney for the Southern District of New York John Fiero was placed on the stand. Most of his evidence, Fiero announced, belonged to the grand jury; nonetheless he would say what he could. Sears asked if there was any truth to the rumor that Fiero had been followed during his last visit to Highland Falls. Fiero answered affirmatively. On April 14, while on his way to check out a clue in the village, he saw two riders wearing "blue pants" following him. He sat down near a stone fence and began whittling, and the riders turned around. He then continued his trip. On his return, he saw two men wearing "blue pants" talking to Phil Ryan. A little bit later he met two inebriated soldiers who, on being questioned, admitted that officers did often go to Ryan's.

When Sears asked Fiero if he was sure he had been followed by officers, Fiero corrected the recorder. "I call them nothing more or less than blue pants." Abruptly Fiero's superior, Stewart Woodford, handed Sears a note indicating that neither he nor Fiero would say any more. Further information would be given only to the proper civil legal authorities. Sears could do nothing but agree.

Not to be outdone, Sears immediately summoned two lieutenants who, he said, had been the only two officers on horseback on the evening of April 14. These officers admitted their brief excursion but denied stopping at Ryan's. Further testimony by cadets and two Army sergeants seemed, to West Pointers at least, to put Fiero's story to rest. All Fiero had, Sears told the court, were "two idle rumors." Fiero's role in the Highland Falls story was a matter of "bad faith,"[8] and the story itself was equally baseless.

By May 15, despite all the previous excitement, the dullest evidence of all was taking on more and more significance. The decision of the handwriting experts would either corroborate or implicate the black cadet. The feeling was prevalent that the writer of the note of warning had been the perpetrator of the entire affair. Whoever the experts pointed to would be judged guilty.

At no time during the testimony of the experts had any person been cited by name. Only numbers had been mentioned, and no one but Captain Sears knew who the numbers represented. The obvious suspicion was there, of course; most persons associated with the inquiry suspected that Whittaker was the writer of the specimens chosen by the experts in their numerous investigations. Therefore, when Whittaker was called back to testify, on Saturday, May 15, "a rattle of expectation" swept through the crowded library. The presence of the ladies, a large number of officers, and General Schofield heightened the excitement.

Whittaker, dressed in regulation uniform with white gloves, advanced smartly toward the stand. As he approached, Professor Greener tried to have a word with him. Defense Counsel Knight, however, quickly stepped in front of the black professor and spoke to Whittaker instead. Once on the stand, Whittaker crossed his arms and calmly faced the recorder. He remained composed throughout his testimony, showing little physical effect from the April incident. His feelings can only be guessed at.

Captain Sears immediately began a series of specific questions. Did he suspect anyone? Yes, Whittaker answered, he suspected Cadets Blake and McDonald—two persons with whom he had had difficulties in the past. What about the letter Sears held in his hand? Was it his? Whittaker asked to look at it more closely. Sears refused. Lieutenant Knight stepped forward and said he would be responsible for it. Sears waved him off and said that had he known Whittaker had wanted to read the letter, he would have given it to him; but he would think Whittaker would know his own writing at a glance. Greener, sitting in the audience, interjected that Whittaker had a right to read the letter. Sears angrily asked the court to tell persons in the audience either to be silent or be removed. The court reiterated Sears's warning. In the meantime Whittaker read the letter held by Lieutenant Knight and said that it was one he had sent his friend, Moses Wester. However, he denied that its sharp attack on his treatment at West Point proved anything.

Sears then dropped the subject of the letter and moved to a wide range of other subjects. Did Whittaker know how hogs were cut in the South? Whittaker answered that he did not know but he had seen hogs running off with bloody ears. What about Ku Klux Klan outrages? Did he know what they were like? Whittaker answered that he had heard about them but had never seen one or known a black man to feign one. Was it true, Sears asked, that he was writing stories for publication, stories of a sensational nature? Yes, Whittaker planned to publish his writing. Did he feel he had any special mission at West Point? No, he simply wanted to do well.

Sears continued in this manner and even had Whittaker re-enact his now famous story on the blackboard. Throughout, Whittaker did not rattle. Finally, Sears launched his *coup de grâce*. He asked Whittaker if he had written the note of warning. Whittaker said he had not. Why, then, Sears retorted, had the experts agreed he had? Whittaker said he did not know; perhaps someone had forged his handwriting.

A buzz went through the courtroom as this information sank home. Sears immediately pressed his advantage by bringing out charts and describing in detail the experts' findings. He even showed that Southworth had matched the edges of the note of warning with the edges of Whittaker's letter to his mother and a requisition slip. This indicated, Sears said, that the three sheets had come from the same piece of paper. Whittaker sat silent.[9]

For all intents and purposes, the court of inquiry was over. The press, which had generally supported Whittaker, was taken aback by Sears's evidence but accepted what seemed to be the inevitable. Newspapers and magazines contented themselves with articles and editorials praising the poise and strength shown by the black cadet and blaming West Point ostracism for driving him to commit such an act. The Charleston *News and Courier* was one of the few papers to argue that it did not necessarily follow that Whittaker had committed the act because he had written the note. Yet it concluded its article with a condescending appraisal of the black personality. An editorial prophesied Northern disappointment until the North realized that blacks could not compete with whites at West Point or anywhere else.

Pro-West Point journals like the *Nation* and the *Army and Navy Journal* were practically ecstatic in their evaluation of the case. The former, for example, said the entire affair should not be considered simply "as a vulgar and unsuccessful attempt at imposture on the part of an audacious young rogue." It should be placed within the framework of the turbulent events of the past several years. Having seen a black man feign an incident in the North, Northerners should be more careful in condemning the South for so-called atrocities. Stories told by "a people with very low moral standards, and beset by very strong temptations to lie" should not be taken at face value. Besides, the whole question of black persecution was entirely overdone, the *Nation* insisted. The black man "has become the pet of a large and influential portion of the community" and had all sorts of special advantages. It was time for him to "stand fairly and squarely on his own feet and kill the prejudice against him in the only way that prejudice is killed—by quality and performance." As long as the public mind continued to look for such incidents as the Whittaker case, such incidents would happen. It was time for a change, the *Nation* concluded, but it feared that the "detection of one tricky rascal" would have little effect on those with closed minds on the subject.[10]

And so most Americans, whether they had been in favor of Whittaker or against him, were convinced of his guilt. West Pointers, however, wanted more; they wanted him to confess his wrongdoing. The two detectives who had been investigating the case from the beginning and had questioned him on countless occasions tried once more to get him to change his story. He continued as before to insist that he was innocent. General Schofield decided to try his luck and, after supper on the evening of Whittaker's testimony, summoned him to his chambers. He too was unsuccessful; Whittaker remained polite but firm. Schofield pointed out what he called the strong circumstantial evidence against him and urged a confession. Whittaker replied that if he were guilty he would own up to Schofield, whom he had always considered a "dear friend." Schofield responded that he wanted to continue these past good relations, so for Whittaker's good he was directing him to remain in his room and ordering the Corps not to show any unpleasant feelings toward him.[11]

Whittaker, though maintaining calm before the detectives, Schofield, and the rest of the Military Academy, poured out his true emotions in a letter to a friend, a Mrs. Ferndon. He insisted he was innocent and despaired at his prospects in the inquiry. He particularly worried about his mother.

> Oh! Mrs. F., how crushed I feel when I think how my *dear Mother* suffers from all that is put upon me, & I can't see *how* she bears it, for she knows I *never* committed an act at which she has ever had cause to blush, & with God's help I never shall.[12]

Important questions remained. Who was No. 23? Who was No. 27? Perhaps later testimony would clear this up. But on the following Monday, the detectives who were testifying never mentioned it, and neither did Captain Sears nor Lieutenant Knight. A black servant, Peter Mitchell, testified that he had ridden a cavalry horse to Highland Falls the night Fiero said he had been followed. Mitchell said that Ryan, the tavernkeeper, had told him that the now famous three cadets had in reality been three boisterous soldiers. The case was closed, with what the *Army and Navy Journal* called a "resonant rounding off."

To make matters worse for Whittaker, on May 25 a pair of dark civilian trousers were found hidden in his alcove.

Despite his disavowals he was charged with hiding them. He was again considered a liar.[13]

On May 28 excitement filled the air. The wood-paneled library was filled with the largest number of spectators yet assembled, many of them ladies from Highland Falls. They seemed so intent on not missing a word of these last days' summations that many had even brought their lunches. A host of West Point officers was also in attendance, including General Schofield, in full dress uniform. Whittaker sat at the side of his counsel, Lieutenant Knight, and listened intently to the summations that were deciding his destiny.[14]

Captain Sears, the recorder, was the first to present his final remarks. He told the court that he believed that the trial had been fair. He wished it understood that he personally had had no preconceived notions on the case. He was "without prejudice against the colored race as a race." He was in fact "a republican in sympathy and an original abolitionist in education." He personally liked Whittaker. He wished this remembered when in the course of his summation he might seem harsh toward the black cadet. His only interest was in doing his "official duty."

Sears said he felt that many people, ignorant of West Point procedures, had unfairly criticized the Academy for its handling of the case. Townsend, for example, had brought in many irrelevant facts which had forced the inquiry off its rightful path into wasteful and useless byways of investigation. The Dutcher and Ryan cases were examples of this waste. Both were brought to the surface by an "overzealous public official through the medium of a credulous and sensational newspaper correspondent, who failed to have the 'courage of his opinions' when placed upon the stand." As for Townsend, his activities in the trial indicated his basic untrustworthiness. He was "Assistant Counsel to the Recorder *de jure* but the virulent and partisan counsel for Cadet Whittaker *de facto.*"

Sears proceeded to reiterate yet again the basic facts of

the case. Following this, he argued that the attack on Whittaker was not an example of cadet hazing; black cadets were never hazed and those whites who were hazed rarely suffered physical harm. The fact of the matter was that white cadets left black cadets completely alone. This, of course, amounted to social ostracism, but some whites also suffered like treatment. Instead of discrimination, Sears contended, Whittaker had received special treatment. When, early in his West Point career, McDonald had hit him and Whittaker, for some unexplained reason, had not fought back, West Point authorities had expelled the attacker. This was certainly a more severe punishment than McDonald would have received had he attacked a white cadet. Then too, in 1879, Whittaker should have been academically dismissed but because of his race had been given another chance. Despite this, at the time of the mutilation he was near the bottom of his class in "an exceedingly dangerous place."

As for the attack itself, a number of theories had surfaced during the case and ought to be reviewed. One theory held that Whittaker had been attacked by cadets out of spite, or in order to get him to leave. This theory, Sears felt, was not tenable. It would have been too risky for cadets to have committed the crime; they had all sworn that none of them had done it. "Their characters for probity, honesty, veracity and integrity, have never been questioned," and there was no reason to begin now. John Dutcher's alleged accusation presented to the court by Squire VanBuren was simply an example of an "ignorant rustic getting things confused." There was "not an iota of evidence" to implicate any of the cadets. Besides, why should they try to get rid of Whittaker in such a bizarre manner? It would have been much simpler to have done it by official means, pinning demerits on him. Since Whittaker had one of the best demerit records, the essential fairness of the cadets seemed obvious. The cadets' offer of a $1,000 reward was yet another example of their attitude. They simply had not committed the act, and the theory that they had was invalid.

Another theory offered by some was that the cadets, after planning the act, had hired someone to commit it for them. Again, urged Sears, there was absolutely no proof to validate this theory. With little money left after taking care of necessities, the cadets could not have afforded to hire anyone. Besides, professional hirelings would have done a better job of it and afterward would have claimed the $1,000 reward by pleading state's evidence.

A third theory, as bogus as the first two, was the assertion that the whole matter was a political scheme perpetrated by Republican "stalwarts" with or without Whittaker's help to aid the Negro cause. This theory was based, Sears said, on the Republican outcry and the publications of the Republican press. But this theory made little sense since most cadets and officers were Republicans.

The fourth theory was that Whittaker had committed the act himself. This theory, Sears felt, explained the incident. "Besides the two strong circumstantial evidences afforded in the matter of the paper and the handwriting we have a multitude of minor circumstances, little incidents, none conflicting, all of which readily and completely fit into their appropriate places in this mosaic of stupid mendacity. This theory at once seems to cover the whole ground, is in every way supported by the evidence, and under it nothing is untenable or improbable." Whittaker was the guilty one; he and he alone had committed the act.

History, argued Sears, abounded with examples of individuals who had mutilated themselves. Significantly the wounds Whittaker had inflicted on himself were trivial, the cuts on the ears causing no more pain than a girl experienced in having her ears pierced. Slavery was particularly full of instances of self-mutilation. Unrequited love, which Whittaker apparently had experienced at the beginning of the year, had driven other men to similar actions and even to suicide. The argument that Whittaker's previous good character indicated his incapacity for such an act lacked force because of the many "painful examples of long

124

and continuously righteous and honest lives suddenly con-
taminated with some lapse from honor and rectitude."
Whittaker obviously saw himself as a martyr and thereby
convinced himself of the correctness of his act.

Whittaker's very testimony showed his guilt clearly. He
gave no motives for the attack, and in places his account
was absurd. His obstinacy gave a bad impression. Most
importantly, many trivial items in the testimony taken together pointed to his culpability.

To buttress this statement, Sears proceeded into a long
discussion of the inconsistencies and discrepancies he saw
in Whittaker's story. Despite Whittaker's insistence that he
had had a nosebleed, no evidence of one was found by the
doctors. Why had Whittaker not struggled? Why was it that
his hands were tied after and not before the assault? His
hair seemed to have been cut in a manner that indicated
self-barbering; there was no evidence of any cut hair on his
shirt. Why was it he could account for only four of his six
handkerchiefs? Why had the attackers not used a gag? Why
had Whittaker not freed himself after his attackers had left?
There was no physical reason for him to faint, and Dr.
Alexander was convinced that he was feigning unconsciousness.

Significantly, Sears said, Whittaker often contradicted
himself. He cited three different places where the attackers
supposedly put their hands on him. At first, he said he
suspected no one, then he named two cadets as suspects. He
seemed uncertain if his hands had been tied before or after
the attack. He was not sure if the gaslight had been ignited
or not. On and on, Sears continued, contradictions and
inconsistencies filled Whittaker's story. Even his manner of
testimony indicated his guilt. He constantly gave himself
the loophole of saying, "I think" or "it may have been." He
consistently evaded giving direct answers. He insisted
upon reading through letters when a glance was sufficient
to identify them. His calmness convinced many of his innocence; but it should be considered, Sears warned the court,

that "a dark complexion hides facial expression." On only one occasion did Whittaker show any emotion. When he was confronted with the conclusions of the handwriting experts, this evidence was so totally unexpected, Sears argued inconsistently, that Whittaker's "face by its sudden pallor betrayed that he knew that the game had been cornered."

But what were Whittaker's motives? Why had he mutilated himself?

> Cadet Whittaker, laboring perhaps under a diseased condition of mind, due to fear that he will not graduate, possibly lovesick on account of some girl, irritated at not having obtained the social recognition he desires, pining and brooding over it in an unmanly way, in a morbid and sentimental condition, concocts in the recesses of his own mind a scheme whereby he may either get into the hospital and avoid study for the time or gain the sympathy of his instructors and thus get through the approaching examination, may make a hero of himself in the eyes of his friends and may go out to the country as a martyr on account of his color, thus exciting a powerful action in his favor causing him to be retained through pressure of public opinion; or in default of accomplishing this result, raise up a host of friends to aid him hereafter in the battle of life.

In addition to the other circumstantial evidence, the main proof for Whittaker's guilt was contained, according to Sears, in the note of warning. Experts had not only agreed that he had penned the note but that it, the letter he wrote to his mother, and a requisition for stamps came from the same sheet of paper. The only other possibility was that the note was a forgery. This theory had too many difficulties to be considered seriously. The forger would have had to have sneaked into Whittaker's room, torn off a piece of paper, used or taken a model of Whittaker's handwriting, and then escaped. A crowded barracks made this improbable. In any case, the note itself showed no real signs of forgery; and only one expert even thought forgery a possibility. All experts agreed that Whittaker himself had written the note, and his authorship of it, in conjunction with the other evidence, was clear indication that he had staged the incident.

In conclusion, Sears said, there was "not a scrap of evidence ... adduced ... to show that any cadet save Whittaker was in any way connected with this assault." In fact no evidence was presented that anyone but Whittaker had a "reasonable *motive* for making such an assault." On the other hand there was much evidence to indicate that Whittaker had the only valid motive and was the sole perpetrator of the whole incident. Sears continued:

> I think I may fairly ask the Court to declare that Cadet Johnson C. Whittaker, United States Military Academy *has not* in any way cleared himself of the 'imputation cast upon his character' by the official reports of this matter, made by the Commandant of Cadets and the Post Surgeon; but, on the contrary, that the circumstantial evidence against him is so strong, that the merits of the case stringently demand that he be tried by a General Court Martial under Charges and Specifications, for Conduct unbecoming a Cadet and a Gentleman and for Perjury.[15]

With these final startling remarks, Sears rested his case. It was now up to Whittaker's counsel to present the black cadet's side. In contrast to Sears's detailed summation of more than a hundred pages, Lieutenant Knight's rebuttal took only eighteen pages. Knight presented a number of significant points, but he left a great deal unsaid and seemed to lack the confidence and certitude shown by Sears. For example, he left uncontested the prosecution's assertion that Whittaker was faking unconsciousness, and he made no use of the Phil Ryan and Dutcher incidents; he also accepted the idea that the black cadet was intellectually inferior.

At the outset Knight asked the court to put no stock in the idea that Whittaker's "brooding" had caused him to perpetrate the incident. This supposition was based only on a four-month journal written by Whittaker in 1879. Whittaker's drop into the last section of philosophy also meant little, since the most important part of the semester was still ahead. Finally, the court should not believe that Whittaker's mind had been "warped" by Bible reading. It was true that Whittaker's correspondents had done him much harm by emphasizing his isolation, but this was not sufficient to inspire him to thoughts of self-mutilation.

Aside from the testimony of the experts, Knight continued, there was nothing to cast doubt on Whittaker's testimony and, considering his character and manner, no reason to believe he was lying. In many instances his testimony was validated by others. He really had no motive to commit the act, and if a motive could be found, there were better ways to achieve his ends than by self-mutilation. As for his alleged inconsistencies, Knight argued, "I hardly think it is reasonable to consider that a man suddenly assaulted in the night, incident pressing incident in close and probably rapid succession, is to be held to a clear, complete and unerring statement of details, as generally shown impossible under circumstances more favorable in degree than these were unfavorable."

If Whittaker had indeed committed the act, why did he exhibit so much ignorance of important details—positions of legs, gaslight and so forth? Why had he not, if he had invented the story, made better use of materials at hand? Why hadn't he said he had been hit with the Indian club? Why had he reported that he had called for a pillow? Why didn't he leave his drawer open to suggest forced access?

Unlike Sears, Knight saw Whittaker's bearing on the

stand as an indication of innocence. Whittaker's class standing, Knight reminded the court, testified "to the slow crude workings of his mind, to the deficiency of his reasoning power." On the stand he was matched against very experienced persons. Yet he held his own. "Would not the contest have been unequal had not conscious innocence lent its sustaining power?"

The only strong evidence against Whittaker, Knight continued, revolved around the note of warning. He reminded the court that experts had been proved wrong before, including experts who had testified at the inquiry. Knight stated that the possibility of forgery was great. It was a relatively simple matter to enter any cadet's room, so it would be easy to tear off a slip of paper and imitate Whittaker's hand. Furthermore, there was so little writing on this small slip of paper that the experts had complained about the difficulty in evaluating it. The method used to get around this problem was to increase the number of specimens. This, however, did not rectify the basic situation; if anything, it "concentrate[d] the attention of the experts upon these [specimens] as the examination continued." Since even the experts agreed that analysis under these conditions was difficult, how much trust could be put in their findings? Knight concluded:

> With you I now leave it, convinced that should the opinion which you are to render be unfavorable to Cadet W., the mystery surrounding the cause of this investigation will yield to another equally great and involved in the question. What could make one at the very threshold of manhood, of Christian training and principles, apart from all contaminating influences, what could make such an one a wretch to whom perjury is as easy as the truth.[16]

With the summations completed, it did not take long to make a decision. The following day the report of the court of inquiry was promulgated. After presenting the "Facts" and "Investigation" sections, the board presented its "Conclusions" and "Opinions." It said that it could not believe Whittaker's "slight wounds" could have been inflicted by anyone else. It did not understand how Whittaker could have submitted to an assault without calling for help and stated that he could easily have released himself. Indeed, the board contended, Whittaker alone had a motive for the act, had written the note of warning, committed the mutilation, and feigned unconsciousness. Thus, he was not "ignorant of the person or persons engaged in the affair." "The imputation upon the character of Cadet Whittaker, referred to in the order convening the Court, and contained in the official reports of the Commandant of Cadets and the Post Surgeon, was fully sustained."[17] Whittaker and Whittaker alone was the culprit. West Point was vindicated, at least in its own eyes.

Reactions to the decisions varied. The New York *Tribune* felt that Whittaker's guilt was still a matter of doubt, because so many questions had been left unanswered. It particularly felt that Sears's attempt to prove Whittaker's guilt by citing unrequited love was "unworthy." The New York *Times*, on the other hand, felt that the handwriting evidence, when taken with the other facts, seemed to prove Whittaker's guilt. But, it insisted, while "the plan was his own, the suggestion originated in the Academy." The Charleston *News and Courier* felt the court could have come to no other conclusion but that Whittaker was "a storyteller and mean rascal generally." He should now be separated from the Academy immediately and all should recognize the impossibility of elevating blacks. *Scribner's Monthly* disagreed and concentrated its reaction on West Point. It might be "a very useful institution in its educational and military aspect," the magazine said, but until a black man could receive fair treatment there, it could "lay no valid claim to being a collection of gentlemen." The small-town Orangeburg, South Carolina, *Times*, was thankful that the incident had happened in the North. If it had occurred in the South, the paper stated, "what a flutter would have been given to the bloody shirt!" *Harper's Weekly* was worried that the Whittaker case had hurt the black race as a whole.[18]

General Schofield accepted the court's decision with little comment, except to put Whittaker under room arrest. General of the Army Sherman saw the decision as an obvious one; he felt that everyone had been bending over backward too long for the black cadet. Professor Richard Greener, who had left the trial about the middle of May and had not been present during the reading of the verdict, responded that he planned to take the entire matter to the Secretary of War. He felt Whittaker had been "tried in strict Star Chamber Style."[19]

The man found guilty by the court proceedings tried to maintain his outward calm, but perhaps he overcompensated. On May 28 he received demerits for "Continually smiling in ranks, at parade during and after the publication of an order placing him in arrest." In a letter to Professor Greener he let his true emotions pour out. The day after the decision he wrote his friend, "My heart droops in despair and life seems almost a burden." As he wrote, he said, tears were streaming down his face. He said he was being kept in close arrest, could not mail his own letters, and could not leave his room except for academic or military duties. He was so confused he did not know what to do, but had resolved to bear up. How though, could he ever study for the coming examinations? He asked Greener for advice about his next step and promised to do his best in his studies. His particular concern was for his mother; he just could not bear to tell her, fearing her reaction to the latest news. He thanked Greener for all his past kindnesses and then ended the letter because he felt "too despondent to write more." This letter and all the letters written by Whittaker during this period were intercepted by West Point authorities, read, and later used against him. Whittaker knew his mail was being read but could do nothing to prevent it.[20]

Chapter 7

BETWEEN THE COURTROOMS

THE court of inquiry was over, but the issue was not settled. West Pointers were disappointed to find that the completion of the investigation and the decision of the court
did not put the case to rest. Too many people believed that
the inquiry's conclusions were open to question and, most
importantly, saw Whittaker's actual guilt or innocence as
incidental to the main issue—the treatment of black cadets
at West Point. *Harper's Weekly*, for example, argued on May
1 that, whatever happened, the important fact was that
"with the tacit connivance" of the officers, Whittaker, because of his race, was "practically proscribed and avoided
and despised, like a leper or a pariah in a semi-civilized
community." Something had to be done to protect blacks
at the Military Academy. The New York *Tribune* and the
Washington *National Republican* took similar positions.
Professor Peter S. Michie, on behalf of the beleaguered
Academy, published a long defense of the status quo, but

it is doubtful that anyone's mind was changed. Even the New York *Herald*, which had generally supported the Academy, called the professor's article "premature" and described its own editorials as "the process of defending the Academy from its defender."[1] West Point remained suspect.

As a result, what had occurred in the paneled library was only the first battle in a long war. Few seemed willing to lay down their arms; the fighting escalated, and the casualties increased. But because of changed circumstances, most of the fighting took place away from the public eye, and only the casualties were seen.

Neither the nation nor West Point had much chance to give more than an initial reaction to the court of inquiry decision because their attention was preoccupied with other events. In the nation, the first week of June saw the beginning of the hotly contested Republican national convention; the Democratic meeting followed some weeks later. On the Hudson River plain, year-end examinations and graduation were the main preoccupation. Still, Whittaker was not forgotten. As people began to converge on West Point to take part in the year-end events, the black cadet was a constant topic of conversation and source of curiosity. It was reported in at least one newspaper that Whittaker was hard at work at his studies and that Lieutenant Knight felt he would pass his examination. But Whittaker was doing more than studying. On June 2 two Army officer members of the Academy Board of Visitors interviewed the now celebrated cadet and, after talking to him, seemed to go away impressed.[2] But mostly Whittaker stayed in his room in keeping with his confinement, studied, and hoped for success in his upcoming examinations.

In addition to the academic exercises, the intrusion of visiting dignitaries, the funeral of General Sherman's aide, and a cadet hop, excitement of another sort hit the Academy area during this period. In Highland Falls John G. Thompson, Jr., the son of the sergeant-at-arms of the

House of Representatives, was severely wounded by a young man named Beaumont Brick. Both youths were candidates for West Point and were prepping at a neighboring school. Brick shot Thompson in retaliation for some hazing, and, although particulars were not made public, Brick said he had been angered by the fact that some fellow students had entered his room after Taps to play a trick on him. He told the judge to whom he had surrendered that "the students had used him worse than a nigger."[3]

Since the two students in question were not yet West Pointers the Academy was not implicated. But a comparison must have been made between this incident and the still-debated Whittaker case. Whittaker claimed he had been attacked in the night; now a student in a school preparing students for West Point had shot someone as the result of a night attack. Were night attacks more common than previously believed? Was there more truth to Whittaker's story than the court of inquiry had judged?

During this time, too, the Board of Visitors assembled to hold their annual inspection and meetings. General Schofield took the opportunity to send them a long memorandum discussing, among other topics, the West Point attitude toward race. Schofield contended that West Point had done a great deal for black cadets and could do little more. It certainly could not interfere in the social relationships between whites and blacks. "Social recognition of colored cadets cannot be forced by official action. The Military Academy cannot be made the propagandist of political, religious or social theories. It can only keep pace with the public sentiment and practice of the Country."[4]

Schofield was obviously arguing that criticism aimed at the Academy during the inquiry had been unfair. The Visitors were not so sure. They set up a subcommittee, consisting of Senators Garland and Edmunds and Representatives Felton, Philips, and McKinley, which was to report to Congress about the Academy in December. Also they arranged to interview Whittaker several times.[5]

While the Visitors carried on their discussions, Schofield forwarded the court of inquiry records to Washington for further action. By separate order he sent Captain Sears to the nation's capital to present West Point's report in person. In case there might still be any question about his position, he also penned an explanatory letter. He recommended that Whittaker "be promptly separated from the Academy." Even if his "impossible" story could be believed, his "total lack of manly character" was sufficient cause for dismissal. "Exemption from the requirements of ordinary courage cannot be claimed for him on account of race, for many thousands of the colored race, to which he belongs to a small degree, have displayed commendable courage in circumstances far more trying than those in which he claims to have been placed."

Schofield also included a copy of the May 25 trouser charge against Whittaker, told of his confinement awaiting War Department action, and said Whittaker's inquiry had not interfered with his preparations for the upcoming examinations. If a court-martial was indeed decided upon, he recommended it be "appointed by the highest authority" and be made up of non-West Point officers.[6]

All of this was but the prelude to June 9, the first examination day for Whittaker. On that day, with a large crowd in attendance, including many of the visiting dignitaries, Whittaker made it through his first oral examination with no apparent difficulty. But his examination in his problem subject, philosophy, was not scheduled until June 11.

On the eleventh a large crowd was on hand again, with all eyes on Whittaker. Twelve cadets, including Whittaker, were examined in a group by Professor Michie and Captain Sears. Each cadet was allowed to draw his question from a pile on Captain Sears's table; then he went to his board, illustrated his problem, and waited to be called on. Several other cadets recited first. When Whittaker's turn came he answered the questions posed him by Professor Michie in what was described as "a clear distinct voice without the least show of trepidation and only now and then slight embarrassment." He stood erect with his pointer in his hand, illustrating his answer by means of his blackboard drawings. When he did not understand a question, he politely asked for clarification. While he spoke, the other cadets also watched him intently. After he had finished answering the drawn question he was told to advance to the center of the room, where Captain Sears peppered him with other questions. He was then allowed to take his seat but was soon recalled and asked another question. He took some time to think, then began, only to be stopped by Michie, who told him he was wrong and asked him once more to take his seat. Sears then announced that the examination for the section was over. Results would not be known for several days, but at least one officer in the crowd felt the black cadet had not done well. Whittaker's feelings are not known. One newspaper, with an observer at the scene, reported that he had performed admirably.[7]

Again, graduation excitement cut short speculation. With General Sherman, General Nelson A. Miles, and Secretary of War Alexander Ramsey on hand, the Corps passed in review and diplomas were distributed; this was the same day Whittaker was examined. Whether any of these dignitaries saw the black cadet recite is unknown. In any case, the exercises themselves provided a reminder of his plight.

The main address at the graduation exercises, delivered by General Miles, who had not been educated at West Point, consisted mainly of practical advice for the newly commissioned officers. General Sherman gave one of his typically humorous addresses which was received with great pleasure by the assembled crowd. Others also spoke, but the address of the Secretary of War attracted the most attention because of its obvious allusion to recent events. Secretary Alexander Ramsey told the cadets that it was their duty as "beneficiaries of all our people" to exhibit their belief in the equality of all men. He called it "an ignoble thing" "to make active exhibition" of feelings of superiority over the less fortunate. "A true manhood," he said, "dictates the extending of the helping hand to lift up the lowly and kind words of encouragement to those who are struggling to elevate themselves."

Ramsey's address was loudly applauded by the assembled cadets and audience; apparently his tough words were not resented enough to prevent an outward show of courtesy. More significantly, when the diplomas were being distributed, the Corps burst into its loudest applause for Burnett and the two other cadets mentioned by Whittaker as possible suspects. Thus Whittaker's original class was graduated, while he awaited his fate. West Point returned to normal. As Schofield saw it, everything about the examinations and graduation seemed about the same. The only difference had been a "somewhat increased public interest."[8]

But public interest quickly died away. With West Point settling into its summer hiatus, and with party convention excitement filling the press, little public attention remained for Whittaker. The New York *Times* did in an editorial express its wish to know the outcome of the entire matter, but the editorial also pointed to a more significant truth. The country had lost interest in Whittaker's case, and, as a result, Washington was apparently unwilling to let it become important again by an overt action. It seemed to make more sense to work out the entire matter behind the scenes. The *Army and Navy Journal* contented itself with printing a column of humorously insulting letters received by Captain Sears and Cadet McDonald during the inquiry.[9]

The court of inquiry records did not arrive at the War Department until June 17, and the examination report of the Academic Board was not officially received until June 22. Considering these delays, official action was not slow. On June 25, after Cabinet action, Schofield was informed that disposition of Whittaker's case had been suspended.

The black cadet was, in effect, placed in a state of limbo. Though the Academic Board had ruled he had failed his philosophy examination, his status was neither disqualification nor restoration. As it was explained to Schofield, suspension had been chosen as the action best suited to preserve Whittaker's "military status for trial by Court Martial" should a study of the inquiry records indicate this would be "necessary to enable him to vindicate his character."

Before the arrival of the records, the sympathetic Brooklyn minister Reverend J. D. Fulton had discussed the matter with President Hayes and had heard Senator James G. Blaine state that Whittaker should be returned to West Point forthwith. On June 11, Fulton had sent a letter to Judge Advocate General W. M. Dunn, beginning it, "Dear Brother" and saying, "Ever since I saw you I have been grateful that Whittaker's case is in your hands."[10] Fulton's confidence was misplaced. On June 30, 1880, Dunn presented an anti-Whittaker opinion. "After as minute and laborious a study of all the testimony" as he had the chance to make, Dunn said, he did not "hesitate to express" his "entire concurrence." He felt strongly that the evidence completely and obviously pointed to Whittaker's guilt. The black cadet's own testimony was "full of improbabilities and impossibilities." Dunn believed that "no rational being" could believe that Whittaker was not the sole perpetrator of the attack. "Whatever the motive," Dunn argued, "I can entertain no doubt that Whittaker himself devised the entire project . . . and that he has perjured himself at the cost of his honor and his conscience, and has adhered obstinately to a series of falsehoods through many weeks of investigation, in the vain hope of escaping the consequences of his stupid and criminal scheme."

Were Whittaker put on trial, found guilty, and sentenced, Dunn prophesied, no "just and fair-minded man" would protest that he had not received justice. But the Academic Board decision that he was deficient was yet another consideration. The answer, Dunn felt, was simply to disqualify him on the Academic Board's recommendations, for since Whittaker had already failed to vindicate his name at the court of inquiry, a court-martial would discover little new evidence. The best action would be simply to disqualify him and be done with it. Discharge Whittaker for deficiency

> or drop him summarily . . . as a person whose moral unfitness has been so conclusively made manifest as to justify a much severer and if possible more disgraceful penalty—which penalty however the Government, acting with its habitual clemency and from a feeling of humanity and pity for one whose mind has probably been impaired and his power to distinguish between right and wrong blunted by the isolation in which he has lived so long—does not deem it expedient to exact.[11]

The matter was not that simple. The Judge Advocate General could recommend the black cadet's dismissal in any manner convenient to the Army and government, but government and Army officials recognized the danger. Whittaker and his case had been at the center of public interest for several months, and though interest had now waned, any untoward act could cause its return. The longer nothing happened, the shorter the public memory would be. And so, publicly, all parties procrastinated. As the *Army and Navy Journal* expressed it: "The authorities at Washington seem as indisposed to disturb Cadet Whittaker as the inhabitants of the frontier were the Indian who had swallowed dynamite; his case is so full of political explosives that it must be handled gingerly."[12]

This is not to imply inactivity. Much was going on, but it was all behind the scenes. Whittaker's friend and former professor, Richard T. Greener, saw Secretary of War Ramsey in late June but received little satisfaction. Another friend of the black cadet, a Mrs. Ferndon, knew Mrs. Hayes and had already written her on Whittaker's behalf. She was contemplating another appeal. The wife of former Massachusetts Governor William Claflin knew Secretary Ramsey and was also thinking of writing. Republican politicians Benjamin Brewster and Emory Storrs offered aid to black Senator Bruce. Reverend Justin Fulton called on Whittaker at West Point and hinted to Schofield that he had some new information that might exonerate the black cadet. He did not say what this information was, and it never was mentioned again.[13] Whittaker, at least, had not been abandoned.

As events developed, Whittaker's fate became confused with several other matters. The hue and cry for Schofield's replacement at West Point by an officer more able to guarantee black rights increased in volume, and more and more the whole matter fell on the shoulders of President Hayes. On top of this, Hayes was also being pressured by friends to intervene in the case of another cadet who had just been academically dismissed from the Academy. Thus Hayes was faced with three separate yet interconnected questions: What should he do about Whittaker? Should a change be made at West Point? What action should he take concerning the academic disqualification of Cadet John C. Kilbreth, the son of some Cincinnati friends?

All these problems faced Hayes at about the same time, the summer and early fall of 1880—the very time when his attention, like the nation's, was distracted by the election battle between Garfield and Hancock and by an extended tour he was making of the Pacific Coast and the Western states.[14]

In all three cases, pressure was applied to Hayes in the form of letters and petitions. During the court of inquiry he had already begun receiving letters urging him to get rid of Schofield and replace him with someone like O. O. Howard of Freedman's Bureau fame. These letters continued. Senator George F. Hoar wrote that while he deferred to the "better judgment of the President," he felt the "constant breeding in & in" at West Point had to be stopped. He suggested a distinguished non-West Pointer like Nelson A. Miles for Superintendent. Elihu Washburne, U. S. Grant's close friend, had earlier written Secretary Ramsey demanding Schofield's removal and threatening that if the administrator did not act, there would be "justice in the air."

Most letter writers, were not so important as Hoar or Washburne, but they were even more certain in their views. They either called for Howard's appointment or asked that Whittaker be given justice in the form of a court-martial. As for Cadet Kilbreth, his parents and aunt asked that, though he had failed both French and mathematics, he be given another chance and reinstated by the Military Academy.[15]

Faced with such persistent pressure, Hayes wrestled with the problems, discussing them during at least five Cabinet meetings and writing several letters seeking advice. He wrote Schofield twice, telling him that Kilbreth was "a boy in whose welfare" he felt "a very great interest." If Schofield could "save him from dismissal," Hayes said, "I hope that it is done." Schofield responded that he had brought the matter before the Academic Board as requested in Hayes's earlier letter, but the board had "declined to make any favorable recommendation. I can only regret," Schofield added, "that it is not in my power to do what his very worthy friends so desire."

Hayes was not satisfied with this answer and asked the War Department to give an opinion on Schofield's plea of powerlessness. A study of the records indicated that, on several occasions, Schofield had overriden the Academic Board and restored deficient cadets. Even before he received this answer Hayes noted that he was determined to "get him [Kilbreth] back if practicable." And he did just that. At the West Point parade on August 23, 1880, ironically Whittaker's birthday, an order was read reinstating John C. Kilbreth.[16]

Thus Hayes solved one of his West Point problems. But the greater problems remained: What should he do about Whittaker, and, even more, what should he do about West Point? Again he sought advice. When General Casey, the man in charge of the construction of the Washington Monument, came to dinner, Hayes took the opportunity to discuss the issue with him. He wrote an old friend, General M. F. Force at Fort Leavenworth, Kansas, about "*whether* to, and *how* to reorganize West Point," which was not "on a satisfactory footing in several important respects." But considering that he had only six months left in his term, Hayes wondered if he should make any changes. Then, too, if he made the changes, who should he put in charge of West Point?

General Force's answer supported a change, because much of the country considered West Point's tone "un-American [and] unrepublican; the tone of clique, of caste." Whittaker's case only intensified this feeling. Leaving the question of Whittaker's guilt aside, "the tone of the entire proceeding was exasperating to the people." Schofield's order congratulating the cadets "was an arrogant defiance of the people." Something had to be done and done immediately to wipe away this bad feeling. Force could not think of anyone to recommend as a successor for Schofield.

Hayes agreed with Force completely—"You have hit the nail on the head in every point you make," he wrote. But, he complained, as in all governmental affairs, the matter came down to the same problem: "to find the right man." "Who?" Though Hayes said he did not know, actually he had made up his mind. On January 26, he had had his Secretary of War write a confidential letter to General Alfred H. Terry, Custer's former commander, offering him the West Point post.[17]

Meanwhile at West Point General Schofield was active himself. He recognized the fragility of his position and feared for the survival of his Army career. He kept in close contact with his old friend and long-time commander, William T. Sherman, and the two tried to work out their solution to the problem. Schofield remained very bitter about the Whittaker case; by July he saw it as nothing more than a conspiracy against the Army and against himself. He was upset by rumors of his removal and clung with tenacity to Sherman's support. He did not want to leave the Academy under pressure, he wrote Sherman, but would like the command of the Department of the Atlantic if "natural changes" put him in line for it. In any case, he did not wish to stay at the Academy "any longer than the general interest seems to require." In other words he wished both to remain and leave.

Sherman also found himself in a quandary. Should Schofield be moved from West Point the Army would have a surplus of major generals. There were only three major-general slots presently available, and Sheridan, McDowell, and Hancock already occupied them. Sherman could retire in 1882, let Sheridan move up, and thus open a position for Schofield; but this was a possible solution for the future. What about the present?

Faced with the problems, Sherman showed Schofield's two letters to Secretary of War Ramsey, who had just returned to Washington. Characteristically, he asked Ramsey point-blank if there were any plans to move Schofield. The Secretary of War answered yes; the President seemed to have made up his mind. Ramsey agreed with Sherman that the Whittaker case was not the best basis on which to move Schofield but said that the move had to be made to end public outrage at the ostracism of black cadets. Sherman defended Schofield, but the President's decision had been made, and Sherman ended up agreeing to tell Schofield that his days at West Point were at an end.

Sherman immediately wrote Schofield. He told him that apparently a decision had been made to dismiss Whittaker because of academic deficiency and to change superintendents as a concession to Whittaker's supporters. Though Sherman was confident Terry would not take the post, he would be "greatly embarrassed" to find a command for Schofield if any change was made. He was going to Columbus, Ohio, with the President the following day (where he was to make his famous "War is hell" statement) and said he would use the opportunity to discuss the entire matter. He promised to keep Schofield completely informed.

Shaken by this information, Schofield quickly decided to take stronger action to protect his position. He wrote the Secretary of State, William M. Evarts, and asked for help, claiming that the entire matter was mixed up with party politics and that no change should be made until the situation had cooled down. Evarts wrote back a month later saying the President was "existing under certain erroneous impressions." He offered his help, for which Schofield later thanked him, but the correspondence ended there.

Schofield wrote Sherman a very formal letter, from appearances a letter intended for publication. He reviewed the circumstances of his appointment to West Point and emphasized the promises made at that time granting him independence of movement and making him answerable only to the Secretary of War and the General of the Army. Those promises had generally been kept, he said, until April 6. Even then he had felt so much confidence in his superiors' support that when friends suggested the use of "a Democratic Congress to protect" himself "and the Military Academy against a Republican Administration," he ridiculed the suggestion. But, he said, he had come to realize that perhaps his "confidence was not altogether justified."

His "confidence" was shaken even further when on August 14 his rumored successor, General Terry, appeared at West Point. Fresh from duty in the West and from a meeting with Administration officials, Terry had come to sound out Schofield's attitude about a transfer; the Secretary of War, Terry said, was under the impression that Schofield wanted a change. Schofield emphatically stated that he would regard his removal "at this time and under the circumstances as an outrage." He quickly penned a plea to Sherman to correct the erroneous impression. He admitted having written a letter to the Adjutant General the previous December discussing the possibility of his transfer, but this request had been revoked a few days later in a letter to Sherman. He asked for Sherman's aid in correcting the misconception and again reiterated his opposition to being relieved while under fire. When Sherman reported the nebulous results of his discussion with President Hayes during the Columbus trip, Schofield responded that all he wanted was for everyone, especially the President, to know all the facts. He would be happy to come to Washington to settle the confusion once and for all.[18]

The issue thus seemed at an impasse. President Hayes was determined to make a change at West Point, but he did not have a definite replacement for Schofield; and Schofield was determined not to be pushed from office under a cloud. Sherman, as General of the Army, was concerned that, if Schofield was removed, he would have no position for him equal to his rank. And in the background, looming large as ever, stood the figure of Johnson C. Whittaker. Though apparently out of the main arena, he was in reality at the center of the entire controversy.

Suddenly a frontal attack was made on the impasse; the decision was made to bring Schofield to Washington to discuss the affair with Rutherford B. Hayes. The parallel lines now came into contact. The Hayes–Schofield meeting took place in the White House at 10:00 A.M., August 17, with Secretary of War Ramsey in attendance. Schofield had met with Sherman at Army headquarters earlier that morning, but the General-in-Chief was not present at the White House meeting. The only record of the conversation is Schofield's and this must be taken into account in evaluating what happened.

Schofield, in the company of the Secretary of War, went into the President's office, was greeted by the Chief Executive, and offered a chair. Immediately Hayes said that, for the good of the country, a decision had been reached to make changes at West Point to ensure the fair treatment of black cadets. The Secretary of War nodded in agreement. Then, Schofield responded, there was nothing for him to say. "No, no," the President said quickly, and he asked Schofield to speak up. Seizing the opening like the driving general he had always been, Schofield began. He did not know about the rest of the country, he said, but at West Point blacks enjoyed all their constitutional rights. In fact, black and white were closer there than anywhere else. Unfortunately, "this enforced association had the effect of increasing rather than diminishing pre-existing prejudice and hence of preventing rather than encouraging voluntary social intercourse." And, Schofield asked, what could be done to establish social relations between white and black cadets.

> Were the cadets, white and colored, without reference to character, antecedent or paternity or other things about which no one has any right to inquire, especially in the case of people recently emerged from a state of slavery in which lawful marriage was not recognized, are all such persons, without the usual social discrimination, to be introduced into officers' families, and that as an *official duty?*

Did not those who were opposed to mingling with blacks have the same rights as those who favored it? How could West Point force social intimacy when the rest of the country was opposed to it? As for Whittaker, he was ostracized not solely because of his race but because "he had provoked a difficulty with a white cadet, had tamely submitted to blows in the face: and then turned in his assailant, who was therefore court-martialed."

The President sat silently during this long soliloquy, then questioned Schofield. Should he be replaced as Superintendent? No, Schofield answered, because it would look like a political move. The President seemed disturbed by this answer, but continued. He expressed ignorance about details of the Whittaker case, saying he had not kept up with the newspaper reports or read the official transcript. From what he knew, however, he believed that Whittaker would have been more seriously hurt had the assailants been cadets. In any case, did Schofield believe a court-martial was in order? Schofield answered yes but cautioned that it should not be called until around December. If Whittaker was found innocent, he should be granted a commission despite his academic deficiency. But then again because his "cowardice . . . totally unfitted him for military service" he should receive no commission. "The only necessity," Schofield continued, was "to get him away from West Point where he does not belong." It was not right that a "convicted criminal" could sit between two white cadets and escape punishment. Whittaker should be given a leave of absence and sent away from West Point until his court-martial was convened. The President nodded in agreement, said he would discuss the matter further with the Secretary of War, and then turned to other less inflammatory topics.[19]

That very day, sometime after Schofield left, Hayes scribbled a quick note to the Secretary of War granting Whittaker a leave of absence "until further notice." Nothing was said about a court-martial, and Hayes in his preoccupation with his upcoming Pacific Coast tour probably did not give the idea much thought. It is true that Richard T. Greener, on August 14, 1880, sent a long legal letter to the Secretary of War showing that, because there was so much evidence to indicate that Whittaker had not received a fair shake during the inquiry, he ought to receive a furlough and a court-martial. There is no evidence that Hayes either saw this detailed letter or, if he did, that he was in any way influenced by it. It would seem that Hayes granted the leave of absence on Schofield's recommendation. Later events would show that he also paid heed to some of Schofield's other suggestions. Interestingly the *Army and Navy Journal* felt that Greener's "indulging in war talk" with Hayes over the Whittaker case brought about the furlough, but the *Journal* cited no evidence for this and made no mention of the Schofield–Hayes conversation. More importantly, it stated that had Whittaker been white, he would have long since been separated from the Academy.[20]

After Schofield left the President he talked to General Terry and, to his surprise, learned that Hayes had planned to offer him a mission to Austria in return for his departure from West Point. Both soldiers agreed that Hayes had not broached the subject as planned because he had come to realize that Schofield would never have accepted. That night Schofield dined with General Sherman and received yet another shock. Sherman told him that he would no longer express any opinion concerning Schofield's replacement unless specifically asked to. The stunned Schofield could respond only by writing in his official diary, "Thus 'had vanished into thin air' all his promises of support and protection." The only consolation Schofield had that day was to learn at 7:30 P.M. that Whittaker, the source of all his problems, had as he had suggested indeed been given an indefinite leave of absence.[21]

With the President on his tour of the West, accompanied by, among others, General Sherman and the Secretary of War, and with the presidential election campaign swinging into high gear, Whittaker again faded into the background. He visited his mother and family in South Carolina, spent some time in Washington, apparently with Greener, and on one occasion addressed the Young Men's Colored Republican Club in New York on an unknown but non-West Point topic. In late December, along with Reverend Justin Fulton, he addressed an interracial audience in Tremont Temple, Boston. He expressed gratitude for the "noble kind words" Secretary Ramsey had said at the West Point commencement which represented the feelings of "noble citizens." With men like Ramsey and Hayes in the

Administration, he felt sure he and his race would receive justice. From August on he lived with Moses Wester and his family at 29 Wall Street, New York. Wester was the janitor for the Leather Manufacturers' Bank.

Every so often Whittaker's name would surface in an obscure part of a newspaper. On September 4 the *Army and Navy Journal* clipped a New York *Herald* article citing the fact that Hayes had restored four cadets previously promised amnesty on the condition that there would be no hazing at West Point for a year; the time had run out on July 25, 1880, and Hayes had fulfilled the promise. This proved, said the *Herald*, that Hayes did not consider the Whittaker case hazing. The amnesty also proved that cadets had not been responsible for the attack on Whittaker; the *esprit de corps* at West Point would not have allowed placing four cadets in jeopardy for the sake of ill-treating a single black cadet. A week later the same *Army and Navy Journal* reported, insultingly, a sermon on the Whittaker case delivered by a black Canadian minister in a New York black Methodist church and the minister's exhortation to all blacks to come to Canada to escape such acts.[22]

Little direct mention was made of Whittaker in the daily press. Only the organ of the military seemed sufficiently interested to keep Whittaker's name alive. To military men, Whittaker seemed a present specter, not a forgotten ghost of the past. Professor George L. Andrews published his detailed defense of West Point's handling of the court of inquiry; and Schofield, in his printed annual report to the War Department, devoted four pages of the brief pamphlet to the question. He reiterated his oft-repeated position on the affair and on the question of social relations between the races. He just could not bring himself, despite his early call during the Civil War for the use of black troops, to accept the idea of social mingling of the races. He believed in the inferiority of the freedmen which only education and improved morality could remedy. Blacks just did not possess the requisite qualities for success at West

149

Point at the present. It was up to the nation to elevate blacks before they sent them to the Military Academy. Otherwise, unless West Point standards were lowered to accommodate them, blacks would continue to be separated academically. Surely, Schofield said, no American wanted to see the quality of West Point diluted.[23]

Certainly few Americans wished to see West Point change, but that was not the real issue. Unlike Schofield, Americans who thought about this matter focused not on the academic excellence of the Academy but on the guilt or innocence of one black cadet and the validity of West Point's ostracism of all blacks. The Whittaker case was not the *fait accompli* Schofield seemed to consider it. Despite its disappearance from the public eye, it was not forgotten. Whittaker's friends were still working to overturn the inquiry decision and continued to call for a court-martial as the proper vehicle to accomplish this. At the same time, Schofield's fate was also being considered; plans to replace him as Superintendent moved ahead.

In November both issues began to warm up again. Schofield, already aware of the shakiness of his tenure, received yet another shock. On November 3 the Commandery of the State of New York, the Loyal Legion of the United States held an informal reception for General Ulysses S. Grant at Delmonico's restaurant. During the course of the evening Schofield and the former President got into a discussion of the Whittaker case. Grant's words were not exactly tonic to the beleaguered general.

Grant told Schofield that, during the court of inquiry, he had believed the stories he had read in the newspapers—although he now felt he had been deceived. Believing the press accounts, Grant said, he would have acted forcefully to discover the perpetrators of the attack had he still been President. He said he would have suspended all academic activities and kept the cadets at strictly military duties until they had made known the guilty parties.

Schofield, somewhat shaken, assured Grant of the complete cooperation of the cadets and said that, if the cadets had indeed been responsible, he would "have known who they were in twenty-four hours." He also complained of his treatment at the hands of the Republican party despite his long and faithful service to it. Grant listened and said that he knew nothing of plans to relieve Schofield of his West Point command. But he made no offer of help. After this conversation Schofield's enjoyment of the party must certainly have been dampened.[24]

Almost immediately he began to pressure Army authorities for a transfer. Sherman, still faced with the lack of a suitable position for him, urged patience and, in the meantime tried to find a replacement. O. O. Howard, who had received so much support in letters written to the President, wanted the post and asked Sherman for his support; but Sherman curtly told him that his Freedman's Bureau background disqualified him. Howard's views on the subject of Negro rights were "extreme," Sherman said; his appointment at this time would look like a slap at West Point. He said he was prepared "to go as far as the furthest in this question" but felt that "Social Equality must be admitted in civil life, in Congress, Cabinet and Supreme Court before it is enforced at West Point."

In two months approximately thirty letters were exchanged in Sherman's attempt to find a solution to his problem. On December 30, Sherman wrote President-elect Garfield stating his support for Schofield and his opposition to Howard. All was for naught; the decision was made completely opposite to Sherman's desires. Howard was appointed and a new department was created for Schofield out of existing Army departments. Sherman was so upset at this that he wrote to General Phil Sheridan in exasperation: "I was not consulted and wash my hands of the whole thing." He told Schofield that President Hayes had "worked out this scheme himself." He was happy he knew nothing of the plan. "I would not like to burden my conscience with such a bungle."[25]

151

"Bungle" or not, the decision had been made. Schofield was to move out West to become commander of the newly created Department of the Border, and O. O. Howard was to become Superintendent of the Military Academy. At the same time, the person responsible for these changes, Johnson C. Whittaker, was not forgotten. The pressure for a court-martial was increasing.

Ironically the first real mention of a court-martial in the month of November was made in a negative voice. The almost forgotten Martin I. Townsend resurfaced to voice opposition to a new trial. He wrote Secretary of War Ramsey, "I fear that a body of men could not be found in the army free from prejudice sufficient in numbers to constitute such a court." Instead of further court action, Townsend suggested that Whittaker resign his position and go out into the world and make his fortune braced by four years of education and "universal sympathy in his favor."[26]

More forcefully, a group of Whittaker's supporters, including a Congressman-elect, petitioned President Hayes not to order the court-martial that some of Whittaker's other friends had been urging. Whittaker should simply be restored to West Point. By restoring him, Hayes "would only do an act of justice to a friendless youth, subserve the interests of humanity, and give additional evidence of his purpose to recognize no color line in our dealing with American citizens." Hayes, in a November 19 Cabinet meeting, discussed both Whittaker and O. O. Howard but took no action. Less than a month later, Whittaker himself petitioned the President.

The black cadet displayed bitterness over his inquiry and subsequent treatment and asked for either an immediate court-martial or an appointment in some "branch of our country's service."

> I pray your Excellency to give a *just* and an *early* consideration to the case and then accord me what is due—not sympathy for I *scorn* to ask it, not

favors, for justice is *never* a favor—accord me that *justice* which is due every citizen.

Judge me by the testimony of those who know me from infancy and boyhood; judge me by all my acts at school other than the Academy; judge me by my bearing and character during four long years of hatred and worry; judge me by my actions during a long, *unjust* trial, and amid false and malicious accusations. Then turn to the proceedings of the court, see upon what *flimsy, circumstantial* evidence, absurd theories, nonsensical hypotheses, and *mere* opinions the findings are based, and ask has even the *shadow* of justice yet been shown me.[27]

Hayes, receiving this letter, immediately sent it to his soon-to-be-appointed Superintendent, O. O. Howard, and also discussed it with his Cabinet. According to a press account, the Cabinet was split. One group wanted a court-martial; another was opposed to reopening the case and simply wanted Whittaker dropped from West Point because of his failure in philosophy. The latter felt the removal of Schofield and his replacement with Howard were "in themselves a stern rebuke to the abuses and practices" there that had caused the Whittaker affair and showed clearly the Administration's opposition to them. It served no purpose to stir up more problems by exhuming a nearly forgotten incident.

Howard took an opposite tack. After reading Whittaker's letter to the President, Howard recommended that Hayes convene a court-martial mainly composed of non-West Pointers if at all possible. "To remove the fears of a bias on account of the alleged prejudices at West Point," Howard recommended that the court meet in New York City or some other convenient site. Should the court-martial find Whittaker not guilty, the black cadet should be placed in the class below his own. Finally, Howard hoped the entire matter could be "substantially disposed of " before he became Superintendent so his administration might have a calm beginning.[28]

Hayes was apparently impressed with Whittaker's letter and Howard's recommendations, because he decided to give Whittaker his court-martial. Perhaps, too, Schofield's August advice and a petition of fifty to sixty names gathered in Boston near the end of December were also influential. In any case, Hayes ordered the court-martial at a December 20 Cabinet meeting and, following Howard's advice, even had it sit at New York City. Six of the ten board members, including Brigadier General Nelson A. Miles, the president of the court, and Colonel Henry A. Morrow, the second-ranking man, were not West Point graduates. All were Northerners (one was from Maryland) and one of the members, Captain R. T. Frank, graduated from West Point with O. O. Howard. Another court member, Captain J. N. Craig, had had service with a "colored infantry" unit.

The calling of the court-martial and the composition of its panel was favorably received. The New York *Tribune*, on January 3, 1881, editorialized: "The antecedents of none of them raise a suspicion of colorphobia, or suggests [sic] an exaggerated notion of the aristocratic sanctity of West Point." Whittaker's friends, it was reported, were also satisfied with the makeup of the board. Martin I. Townsend called it an "impartial court" and felt confident in leaving "the result with my God and with those engaged in the trial."[29]

Chapter 8

THE COURT-MARTIAL
ORGANIZES

JOHNSON C. Whittaker was to be court-martialed and he was
happy. A person does not usually look forward to being put
on trial, but Whittaker did. He had asked for the court-
martial and his friends had helped pressure the President
into convening it. The strange case was taking yet another
untoward twist. Whittaker's supporters saw a court-martial as the only apparent way to prove his innocence. The
desperateness of his position seems obvious; all other safer
methods must have been exhausted.

The order establishing the court-martial was issued on
December 31, 1880 with the first meeting set for January
20, 1881, in the Army Building at the corner of West Hous-
ton and Greene streets in New York City.[1] In the interven-
ing period both sides were kept busy with preparations.
Whittaker made his choice of lawyers, and the Army began
readying its case. Congress was also heard from. On January 17, 1881, Senator A. H. Garland of Arkansas, on behalf

of the Congressional members of the West Point Board of Visitors, submitted a report to Congress. He and Representative John Philips of Missouri signed the main report, which included a section on the social status of black cadets. They felt there was no reason why blacks and whites should not have "full and equal advantages in the way of education" but denied that social relations could be governed by law. The racial problem should be "left for its cure to time and experience, which may result in its mitigation or the complete separation of the two races in their military education."

New England Senator George F. Edmunds took a different tack. In a series of appended views he argued that blacks had not received their just due at West Point and that this had hurt their academic progress. "While it may be conceded that no law or regulation can rectify the evil ... it is, nevertheless, believed ... that such a course as has existed towards colored cadets is unjust, unreasonable, and inhuman, and that it deserves the severest condemnation." The Academy administration, Edmunds maintained, could help alleviate the problem by their example.

As for the Whittaker case, Edmunds felt that it had been handled incorrectly. White cadets had been taken at their word, while Whittaker, a black cadet, had not been given the same courtesy. The whole inquiry should have been conducted to investigate the event, not to put Whittaker on trial. There was "no insurmountable obstacle to the correction of existing evils by administrative means, and by the wise influence and example of the officers and instructors in charge." If this cannot be accomplished, Edmunds concluded, "it should be a matter of serious consideration whether such a government institution ought not to be absolutely abolished."

Representatives William McKinley of Ohio, a future President, and William H. Felton of Georgia also appended their views. In the matter of social relations they accepted Edmunds' statement but eliminated several sections. They left out the part condemning prejudice and that part criticizing West Point's handling of the Whittaker inquiry. They agreed with everything else, including the threat of abolishment.

In conjunction with this report, Garland introduced a bill (S2039) calling for several basic changes at West Point. He asked that the number of officers detailed to West Point be set by Congress; that no one higher than colonel be assigned there; that the Academic Board have absolute control over dismissals; that the Superintendent, not the Secretary of War, handle the entrance examinations; that the study of German be introduced; and that there be a special Congressional Board of Visitors in addition to the present Board of Visitors appointed by the President. The Congressional Board, Garland felt, should have the authority of an ordinary joint Congressional committee.

This bill was read twice and, on Garland's motion, referred to the Committee on Military Affairs. The report was ordered to be printed but placed on the table. The impact on the Whittaker case was nil, though General Schofield, after reading Senator Edmunds' comments, drafted a letter of protest to Senator Garland. The letter was never sent, Schofield wrote in his official diary, because he was able to make his desired comments during the court-martial.[2]

While the principals prepared and Congress reported, press speculation grew. It was rumored that Whittaker would have excellent defense counsels in the persons of Emory Storrs, a noted Republican campaign orator; Benjamin H. Brewster, later Attorney General; and Daniel H. Chamberlain, the nationally known former Governor of South Carolina. There was no new evidence, it was said, but Whittaker and his supporters, with a better defense, hoped for a more favorable result. The *Nation* even prophesied that the defense plan would be to free Whittaker not by shifting the blame to the cadets but by accusing "some other persons of higher rank." It suggested that, if this was indeed the plan, the defense should make a "clean job of it" and make General Schofield the culprit.

This speculation was quickly laid to rest. It was definitely reported that Daniel H. Chamberlain would be Whittaker's main counsel and would be assisted by Professor Richard T. Greener. Benjamin Brewster would be an adviser.[3] As the trial developed, there was no evidence of Brewster taking any role; after all, he became Garfield's Attorney General in March.

Meanwhile, Asa Bird Gardiner, the judge advocate of the court-martial, was busy, checking with the Secretary of War about the possibility of hiring handwriting experts, including three who had already testified at West Point. He assured the Secretary that he "would—whatever the limit as to compensation—endeavor to secure the evidence at the most reasonable terms." In line with this feeling for economy, Gardiner asked and received permission to hire a reporter to take down the court testimony, a reporter who should "be paid the usual." Concurrently, Gardiner also began to gather his witnesses, asking the Army to order the now graduated Burnett to New York.[4] Little is known concerning the preparations made by Whittaker; apparently he left no record. He was still staying on Wall Street with his friend Moses Wester. Mainly, it seems, he was being coached by his new counsel.

A great deal more is known on the Army side, because Gardiner exchanged many communiqués with the Secretary of War and the Adjutant General. Answering Gardiner's request for handwriting experts, Secretary of War Ramsey left the entire matter in his hands but urged the use of "the utmost discretion in keeping down the expenses of the trial." The tightly budgeted military could not afford an overly expensive court-martial. Despite his concern for economics, Gardiner did use a number of experts in the case and even asked permission to transport the entire court to West Point so that Whittaker's room and surroundings might be inspected first hand. This he said was because "the evidence to be advanced in support of the charges . . . [was] almost entirely circumstantial and depending upon surrounding circumstances."[5]

One lone military voice was raised in support of the black cadet. General Winfield Scott Hancock, loser to Garfield in the 1880 presidential election, in May said he felt Whittaker deserved a court-martial. Hancock believed Whittaker should be acquitted. But General Sherman, who played but an indirect role in the court-martial, mirrored Army and, in many cases, national opinion on the case. He wrote a close friend that Whittaker, "one-fourth black and three-fourths white," was "notoriously deficient in studies" and had "caused one of the most ridiculous scandals ever raised against West Point." Whittaker's blackness was the only reason that there was a court-martial after a court of inquiry had already found him guilty. As Sherman phrased it, "I contend he would have been ignominious [sic] dismissed, but no being one-fourth black—there must be a Court Martial to prove affirmatively these things." Sherman said he did not object to this court-martial but he "did object . . . to believing Whittaker, and discrediting Schofield and the other Officers [sic] of proved patriotism and zeal."

General Schofield, who because of his several reports and public statements had also become an issue in the case, continued to be angry over the entire matter. On January 21, 1881, he relinquished command of the Military Academy and curtly answered the dispatch ordering him to appear at the trial. He could not see how he could possibly be "an important witness in respect to the charges proffered against Cadet Whittaker."[6]

Both pro- and anti-Whittaker newspapers, though not showing as much interest as they had during the court of inquiry, were in basic agreement: The court-martial was a good idea. *Harper's Weekly* felt that the appointment of General Howard to replace General Schofield at West Point and the very establishment of the court-martial indicated that the Hayes Administration "was not satisfied that Whittaker had [had] fair play." The new court was of very high caliber and one from which Whittaker could expect just treatment. If the "conclusion [of the court of inquiry] is confirmed by the present board," *Harper's* said, "there will be no further question." The *Army and Navy Journal*, a consistent supporter of the West Point side of the issue, took a similar position. The two courts, it said, were in reality "two different sets of judges, one representing the Academy, and the other the Army as a whole." Should both come to the same conclusion, "any vestige of unjust prejudice directed against the institution by the former popular excitement over the Whittaker case, ought to be swept away."[7] Significantly, neither periodical speculated about the course to follow if the court-martial board reversed the court of inquiry findings and declared Whittaker innocent. Apparently considerations of guilt were foremost in most minds.

January 20 arrived, and the court-martial convened in Room 14 on the ground floor of the Army Building. The room, which was eventually to prove inadequate for this trial, was undecorated except for an American flag on one wall. The principals in the trial were at one end, sitting behind three tables which formed a semicircle. At the center of the semicircle the court sat at a long table, while Whittaker sat with his counselors at a short table to one side, and Gardiner and the court of inquiry recorder, Captain Clinton B. Sears, sat at another short table on the other side. The rest of the small room was filled to capacity with about twenty people of both races, including the rector of the Episcopal church Whittaker had been attending while in New York.

The center of attraction was, of course, Johnson C. Whittaker, sitting impassively at the side of his counsel in his cadet gray, white belt and white gloves. His appearance had changed but little since the court of inquiry. His hair was black, closely cut but partially curly. He had a "retreating forehead and a prominent chin." His most obvious feature was the lightness of his skin; at a distance it was difficult to distinguish his blackness.[8]

Next to Whittaker sat his counsel, Daniel H. Chamberlain, one of the most interesting men in the history of American politics and race relations. Born in Massachusetts in 1835, he had lived a varied life. As a youth he had worked on his father's farm, gone to the common schools of the area and later attended Phillips Andover Academy. He taught school while preparing himself for college and later graduated from Yale University in 1862 as class valedictorian. The great influence in his life at this time was Wendell Phillips. The abolitionist so overawed Chamberlain that he heard him speak fifty times. Anti-slavery was part of Chamberlain's educational experience.

Immediately after college, Chamberlain entered Harvard Law School and graduated in 1864. Exhibiting his abolitionist leanings, he entered the Union Army as an officer in the all-black Fifth Massachusetts Cavalry Regiment and served in Virginia, Maryland, Louisiana, and Texas.

When the war ended, Chamberlain went to South Carolina to settle the estate of a deceased classmate and decided to stay. He became involved in cotton planting and in 1867 entered the political arena. That year, as a member of the state constitutional convention, he called for the integration of all schools. From 1868 to 1872 he was the state's attorney general and then was a member of the board of trustees that integrated the University of South Carolina. In 1874 he was a successful candidate for the office of governor but lost to Wade Hampton in the 1876 disputed election which was decided when President Hayes withdrew federal troops from the state. Chamberlain soon moved to New York to become part of the law firm of Chamberlain, Carter, and Eaton. He was at this post when the Whittaker court-martial began. On the surface he was only a lawyer, but in reality he was "the prince of carpetbaggers."

Whittaker was represented by a man of wide experience, important connections, and racial concern. Ironically, Chamberlain, the abolitionist, the carpetbag lawyer-politician, was soon to become an anti-black racist, echoing the contemporary white-supremacy theme. He came to defend lynching and put the blame for the black man's degradation squarely on black shoulders, openly repudiating his previous abolitionist beliefs: "Once I did not think as I think now. . . . But do you imagine that I am going to live in 'a fool's paradise' after I have found it out?" During the Whittaker trial, however, there was still Radical Republican blood running through his veins. More importantly, as the case evolved, it became clear that Chamberlain was a competent courtroom lawyer.

The reasons for Chamberlain's acceptance of the case are uncertain, though several guesses can be made. Chamberlain had been a trustee of the University of South Carolina at a time when Whittaker had been a student and Greener a faculty member. Greener had in fact campaigned for him during the 1876 gubernatorial election. Perhaps this connection was the reason for his role. Yet another possibility was his anger at Hayes for deserting him during his 1876 political battle in South Carolina. Chamberlain had been one of the leaders in the carpetbagger attack on Hayes in the spring of 1877. Perhaps he saw the Whittaker case not simply as an opportunity to aid a hapless black youth but also as a chance to embarrass the Administration of the President who, he felt, had done him wrong.[9]

Opposing Chamberlain in the court-martial was Major Asa Bird Gardiner, Corps of Judge Advocates, and a member of General Winfield Scott Hancock's staff. Gardiner had entered the Army during the Civil War as a 1st lieutenant of the Thirty-first New York Infantry Regiment. He served with a number of different units and in 1872 was retroactively awarded the Medal of Honor "for distinguished service during the war while serving as captain in 22nd New York state militia." In 1873 he became a member of the Judge Advocate Corps and established a law department at West Point. By the time of the court-martial he was a highly respected and widely known Army lawyer.[10]

Assisting the main counsels were two familiar faces from the court of inquiry. Captain Clinton B. Sears, though not a permanent assistant counsel, played a significant role at the beginning, helping acquaint Gardiner with the court of inquiry proceedings and decision. Richard T. Greener was permanent assistant counsel and played a leading role in Whittaker's defense. By the time of the court-martial, he was no longer dean of the Howard University Law School, having become Chief Clerk in the office of the Comptroller of the United States. Later he was to become secretary of the Grant Monument Association and United States consul to Vladivostok.[11]

The court-martial board itself was an interesting group, containing individuals of varying backgrounds. The leading figure was Brigadier General Nelson A. Miles. A non-West Pointer who had distinguished himself in the Civil War and even more in the Indian battles of the West, Miles would later during the Spanish-American War hold the office of General of the Army. At the court-martial he sat in the center of the semicircular table, his "ruddy complexion" making him appear the youngest member of the court, even though he was in his forties. Throughout the trial he worked hard to maintain an even temper and on several occasions calmed angry lawyers and court members alike. His status as the most important non-West Pointer in the Army in addition to his role as president of the court-martial board, easily made him the board's most important member.

Sitting on Miles's right was the second senior member of the board, Colonel H. A. Morrow of the 21st Infantry, the commandant of Fort Vancouver, Washington. He was a "broad shouldered, well built" man, on the bald side but with "Burnside whiskers." He was the senior member in point of court-martial experience and was also the most incisive interrogator on the court. He often asked questions which produced answers helpful to Whittaker's case. During the course of the trial he became ill and was unable to take part in the final deliberations.

Sitting next to Morrow was Colonel John M. Brannon of the 1st Artillery of Fort Trumbull, Connecticut. He was short, compactly built, with very alert eyes and a facial scar gained during the Mexican War. He had been a brigadier general of volunteers during the Civil War. To his right were Major E. V. Sumner of the 5th Cavalry of the Department of the Platte and Captain J. N. Craig of the 10th Infantry, Fort Porter, Buffalo, New York. Sumner, it was felt, had a strong resemblance to the fiery Phil Sheridan, while Craig was described simply as a "tall, slender figured officer." Both were non-West Pointers. Craig had been decorated for gallantry at Gettysburg, and Sumner later made brigadier general in 1899.

On Miles's left sat Lieutenant Colonel P. Lugenbeel, Major L. Merrill, and Captain, soon to be Major, R. T. Frank. Lugenbeel was the commandant of David's Island in Long Island Sound and was "probably the oldest man of the court." He was a very short individual, with a clean-shaven face that reminded some of Samuel J. Tilden. He had graduated from West Point in 1840 and had seen action in the Seminole, Mexican, and Civil wars. He had just received word of his promotion to full colonel and would wear the eagle beginning with the next session of the court. He retired less than a year after the trial's completion.

Merrill was stationed at Fort Lincoln in the Dakota Territory and had the appearance of a German officer, a reputation for executive ability, and decorations to match. Frank, of the 1st Artillery, Fort Adams, had spent the period since the Civil War in garrison duty in the South and had taken part in suppressing the railroad strike in 1877. He was to become a brigadier general in 1898. The last

member of the board, Captain M. Barber of the 16th Infantry, a non-West Point Civil War veteran, who in 1901 was
to become a brevet brigadier general of volunteers, was on
his way from Texas and was not present during the first
session of the court-martial. Later in the fall of 1881 when
Henry O. Flipper was court-martialed for allegedly mis-
managing funds, Barber was his counsel.[12]

The court-martial began official proceedings at 11:45
A.M., January 20. The first order of business was to read the
convening order, Special Order #278, and to ask Whittaker if he had any objections to any member of the court.
His counsel, ex-Governor Chamberlain, answered that the
defense had no objection *per se* but wished to question Colonel Lugenbeel to see if there were grounds for an objection.
Lugenbeel was sworn and in answer to Chamberlain's
questions said he had spoken about the case but had not
made up his mind about Whittaker's guilt or innocence. If
there were any objections to him, he would be happy to
retire. Chamberlain was not prepared to challenge Lugenbeel so long as he said he was "unbiased and free from
prejudice" about the case. Lugenbeel appealed to Miles to
disqualify him, but Miles calmly said that as long as there
was no objection from counsels, no member of the court
could retire. Lugenbeel would not get off that easily. Miles
himself, like some of the other members, was serving on the
court-martial board reluctantly.

Gardiner again asked Whittaker if he had any objections
to anyone on the court, and Whittaker answered no. Then
Gardiner administered the oath to the court, and General
Miles followed by swearing Gardiner in. The Court was
declared to be organized.

Chamberlain immediately stood up and asked for more
time to prepare the defense. He had just taken the case, he
said, and since it would be necessary to go through the
massive court of inquiry records, he would need more time.
His purpose was not to delay the trial but simply to have
the opportunity to prepare himself adequately, which

would be only just to Whittaker. Judge Advocate Gardiner joined Chamberlain in asking for a delay. Both lawyers felt that, once they were prepared, the entire court-martial would take no more than two weeks. After some discussion the Court decided to recess until February 3, 1881.

Two charges had been made against Whittaker in the convening order. In the first charge he was accused of conduct unbecoming an officer and a gentleman in violation of paragraph 126 of the Regulations of the United States Military Academy; in the second charge, of conduct prejudicial to good order and discipline. The first charge's specifications accused him of mutilating himself and writing the note of warning "with the design and intention to excite public sympathy, to bring discredit upon the said Military Academy, to obtain notoriety, and further to avoid and escape an approaching public examination." To this end, it was specified, "he deceived his superior officers" and "the public at large" into believing that he had been the victim of a conspiracy. Specifications of the second charge accused Whittaker in effect of lying at the court of inquiry.[13]

The trial actually began on February 3 at 11:00 A.M. The charges of specifications were read and Whittaker replied, "Not guilty." The trial, with testimony totaling over 9,000 pages, lasted not the two weeks predicted but four months, until June 10, 1881. In all that time little new significant information was discovered. In many ways the court-martial was a rehash of the court of inquiry but with greater emphasis on the opinion of experts, both handwriting and medical. Of more significance, Whittaker now had adequate legal representation, and the trial was taking place at a place distant from West Point and at a time removed from the excitement of spring 1880. As a result the entire tone tended to be different. Much counter-evidence was now introduced in opposition to the official case, though only an oblique attempt was made to follow up the possibility that someone else might have written the note of warning and thus might be the real culprit. Whittaker's defense, for the most part, was largely one of reaction. Chamberlain felt that if sufficient doubts could be raised about the government case, Whittaker would have to be found innocent.

The crux of the government case again rested on the findings of handwriting experts, on the claim that Whittaker was guilty because he continually contradicted himself, and on the argument that he was the only person who had a suitable motive to commit the crime. Gardiner pushed these assertions hard.

The defense attacked the government case at all points. It put on the stand its own handwriting experts, who presented evidence that Whittaker was not the author of the note. It denied that Whittaker had any motive for mutilating himself and held that he did not contradict himself so much as contradict the testimony of others about his previous statements. As for the government's contention that Whittaker actually had a favored position at West Point because of his race, the defense countered with examples of prejudice against him. Finally, the defense produced five eminent doctors to show that it was possible for Whittaker to have been unconscious that April morning despite the government's continued assertions, based on Dr. Alexander's testimony, that he was faking.

In sum, the entire court-martial revolved around the issue of the handwriting on the note of warning and the question of Whittaker's unconsciousness. Next in importance were alleged inconsistencies in testimony, alleged prejudice, and the matter of motive.

Chapter 9

THE COURT-MARTIAL:
THE PROSECUTION CASE

THE first witness in the court-martial was Cadet Frederick
G. Hodgson. He lived directly across the hall from Whit-
taker's room, and he had remained with the black cadet that
April morning while Burnett had run for help.

Hodgson testified straightforwardly, reiterating the
points he had made during the inquiry. It was only when
cross-examined by Chamberlain that he introduced some
new ideas. When he began talking about the cut-down cadet belting that had been used to tie Whittaker, he gave the
impression that Whittaker could have broken loose. Chamberlain immediately produced a piece of this belting and
asked Hodgson to break it. Hodgson did so. But when told
to hold the belting in front of him approximately as it had
been in front of Whittaker, Hodgson failed to split it. He
was quick to insist, however, that he still felt Whittaker
could easily have torn loose. But Chamberlain had made his
point.

Later in the cross-examination Hodgson made a statement that Chamberlain did not allow to pass uncontested. Hodgson said that the only conversation he could remember in Whittaker's room the morning of the attack was the waiting cadets' agreement that no cadet had committed the act. Why, Chamberlain asked, was this point brought up at that precise time? Hodgson did not know. Chamberlain asked about his acquaintance with Whittaker. "It was nothing more than I knew him and by sight," Hodgson answered. "I never spoke to him that I recollect, except upon official duty."

Addressing himself to the witness and the court, Chamberlain then asked what it was that had prevented the cadets from going to Whittaker's assistance. Since they supposed that a tragedy had occurred, why hadn't any of them aided Whittaker? Was it because of the belief "common among some ignorant people that it is unlawful to touch a body of a man who had been killed until the Coroner finds them?" The cadets felt they "had no right to touch" Whittaker "in the first place," Hodgson explained; "it would be better at any rate to allow him to be seen by Col. [sic] Piper." He would have acted the same way for a white cadet, he said when Chamberlain asked him. What if Whittaker had been hanging? Then, Hodgson answered, he would have cut him down if any life was evident. At this point Gardiner stepped in to the questioning. His examination emphasized the fact that prejudice was not the reason Hodgson had not gone to the black cadet's aid.

Except for his assertion that it had been "quite difficult" to untie Whittaker's feet because of the tightness of the knots, this was the essence of Hodgson's testimony.[1] Several key points had been made for the defense. Chamberlain had left the impression that more than official duty had prevented Hodgson from going to Whittaker's aid. When the court learned Hodgson was from Georgia, this suspicion was intensified. The picture of cadets callously standing by in Whittaker's room, making no effort to help him and expressing no words of sympathy, was the beginning of the defense contention of prejudice against the black cadet. Hodgson's failure to break the belting and his admission that scissors had to be used to free Whittaker put a crimp in the West Point argument that Whittaker should easily have been able to release himself. Hodgson's testimony, as interpreted by the clever Chamberlain, seemed to offer Whittaker's case some hope.

Several other developments occurred this first day which would later have an impact on the case. It was agreed that no witness would be allowed to remain in the courtroom when he was not on the stand. Only Greener, who had the dual role of counsel and witness, would be an exception. Earlier it had been decided that, if the court wished to question a witness, they would put their queries on notes that would be delivered by the judge advocate. During Hodgson's testimony, however, the court members had so many questions that this formality was dropped. Finally, a letter Gardiner had sent out to the president of the National Bank of North America, asking for handwriting experts, was published. The letter was aimed as much at the public as at the bank president. In it Gardiner expressed his desire to conduct the trial so as to end all doubts concerning the case. Since the evidence was "largely circumstantial and much of it expert evidence as to hand-writing," he wanted the best possible experts and asked for help in finding them. "Whatever . . . the conclusions reached by the experts," Gardiner promised, he would feel duty-bound "to call them and place their evidence on record."[2]

The next two sessions, Friday and Monday, produced heightened interest in the jammed courtroom with the testimony of General John Schofield. The stature of the witness and his controversial testimony caused the first sparks of the trial. The presence of Martin I. Townsend, Schofield's adversary during the court of inquiry and then the appearance of famed churchman Reverend Henry Ward Beecher, added still other notes of the dramatic.

In answering questions put to him by the judge advocate, the defense counsel, and the court, Schofield insisted that he had probably helped the defense more than anyone else in the court of inquiry. For example, he said that he had strengthened the black cadet's defense by first suggesting the possibilities of a swoon and note forgery. To him, Whittaker was a young charge whom he had kept in the Academy over the protest of the Academic Board. "It would be to me," Schofield said, "a matter of no little chagrin if he should prove unworthy of that confidence that I had reposed in him."

Schofield could not see how any of his actions during the court of inquiry, including his General Order exonerating the cadets, could be construed as being prejudicial to Whittaker. His order included Whittaker in its exoneration, though he did admit that, when he wrote it, all the cadets had already sworn their innocence and anti-Whittaker evidence was about to be introduced. There was nothing unjust about the order. All had already testified when he issued it, and he knew that no cadet would change a statement previously given under oath. It was his duty to "relieve . . . [the cadets] from this unjust accusation" that they had conspired to hurt Whittaker.

During the course of Schofield's testimony, Chamberlain attacked numerous aspects of his inquiry activities. He accused Schofield of improperly influencing the court of inquiry board by his constant consultations and suggestions. Schofield's defense was that his actions had been proper since the court members were his "agents for the ascertainment of the truth." Schofield reminded the court that the role of the inquiry was not to investigate the entire corps of cadets; its job was to investigate Whittaker. It was he, after all, who had demanded the inquiry.

Schofield also insisted there was nothing in the history of West Point to indicate that the Corps was capable of an act like the April 6 attack. But, retorted Chamberlain, was not the cadet treatment of Whittaker "peculiarly and especially and continually different from their treatment of any other cadet?" "No," Schofield answered, "by no means." "Had they treated him with the usual personal attention with which they treated other cadets?" Chamberlain asked. "That is a different question," Schofield replied. Well, why did they treat Whittaker so differently? "What was the principal cause for his treatment?" "His color undoubtedly," Schofield said.

Chamberlain pressed the former Superintendent further. Wasn't the very fact the cadets treated Whittaker so differently "a special reason for thinking" they were capable of hurting him? No, Schofield answered, those who knew "the peculiar nature of the Corps of Cadets" would not believe this. But what was so special about the Corps of Cadets that they couldn't be "judged by the ordinary rules of human conduct?" "They are young gentlemen, generally, not roughs, rowdies," Schofield answered. Under pressure, he admitted the cadets were no different than "young gentlemen at any college." But the reputation of the Corps was not central in this case, Schofield argued. The cadets had been exonerated not because of a presumption of evidence but "because of the total failure to find at West Point or anywhere else evidence" against them. The "denial" of the cadets "would have [had] no weight whatever if there had been just ground of accusation against" them.

The real shocker, however, came at the very beginning of Schofield's remarks. This part of the testimony, which took approximately ten pages of transcript to develop, showed dramatically Schofield's thoughts about Whittaker.

At first, Schofield said, he had believed Whittaker was innocent, that he had indeed been the victim of a hostile attack. But then he changed his mind. Chamberlain asked him why.

A: "Well, I began to think after a while that he was too ready in his demand for a court of inquiry. It seemed to me to indicate that he had known what was coming and that he was assured of a strong backing if he got in trouble."

Q: "Do you mean that his promptness in answering charges against him afterward became proof to you that he knew he was to be tried and convicted?"

A: "What I mean is that I afterward thought that perhaps he foresaw at this time the court of inquiry and everything which had happened since then."

Q: "Do you think that a demand for a court of inquiry was a sign of guilt?"

A: "I did not think that a boy would naturally have so much self-confidence as he displayed. If he had been an old officer, I should not have been surprised at it."

Q: "You were able to explain, then, his self-confidence on another ground than that of innocence?"

A: "Yes, I was. I thought perhaps he might rely on the support he would receive outside."

Q: "What do you mean by support from outside?"

A: "I mean the support of those who originated the whole affair. I do not believe that it was originated with Cadet Whittaker."

Outside pressure had influenced the court of inquiry, Schofield continued, causing, for example, the interrogation of cadets after they had already sworn their innocence. Under questioning, Schofield admitted, however, that he had insufficient "legal foundation" for promulgating these suspicions in court.[3]

Since the court of inquiry, press and public interest seemed to have lessened considerably. Press reactions to the court-martial were few and far between. The New York *Tribune* was one of only few papers to respond to Schofield's testimony. But it spoke out strongly. It called Schofield's belief in an outside conspiracy and his presumption of Whittaker's guilt because of Whittaker's promptness in calling for a court of inquiry "more grotesque than anything that has been said yet on the West Point side of the controversy." "What do these mysterious and blood-curdling suggestions mean?" it asked. "Are we to understand that the colored cadet formed a conspiracy with the American people, and then proceeded to whittle his ears?"[4]

Schofield's own reaction to his role in the court-martial again clearly demonstrated his attitude. He told Sherman that he saw "indications of a purpose to *try me* quite as much as the colored cadet." In answer Sherman urged Schofield "not [to] be concerned about that Whittaker case one particle." He "doubt[ed] if it was prearranged and formed part of a great plot aimed at you and the Academy." It was a simple matter: Whittaker maimed himself in order to avoid the examination. If he were Schofield, Sherman said, he would forget about the whole case because "A new series of events . . . [would] soon sweep the case into oblivion or into ridicule."[5]

In the meantime the case proceeded. The judge advocate announced that he planned to call everyone who had been present in Whittaker's room the morning after the attack in order "to ascertain all the probabilities and possibilities surrounding the case." Then, he said, he would attempt to determine the possibility of "outside parties" perpetrating the act. Finally he would introduce the expert testimony.[6]

In accordance with Gardiner's plan, a veritable platoon of West Pointers paraded to the stand in the next several sessions. Generally they expressed belief in Whittaker's guilt and defended as natural the cadets' ostracism of him. Chamberlain took every available opportunity to score points for his client. Perhaps the most significant point made for the Whittaker defense was an opinion offered in passing by Dr. Henry Lippincott, the assistant West Point physician. During his testimony Lippincott made a statement that contradicted the contention of his colleague, Dr. Charles T. Alexander. "It occurred to me during the examination," Dr. Lippincott said, "that he [Whittaker] might possibly have done it to himself; but upon reflection I made up my mind that he had not done it—could not have done as brutal a thing." When asked by a member of the court why he felt this way, Lippincott responded that he "did not think any man would be brutal enough to do so—that was the only reason."[7]

Lippincott's opinion was a tiny crack in West Point's solid front, but it made little impression. The testimony of the next witness, Louis Ostheim, though not as important, caused a much greater stir. Ostheim was one of the cadets present in Whittaker's room the morning after the attack. Instead of taking an oath, he simply affirmed that he would tell the truth and took the witness chair. He answered Gardiner's questions and gave his straightforward account of the incident. When Chamberlain moved into cross-examination, excitement picked up. Very quickly it became evident that Chamberlain was intent on spending most of his time on the question of ostracism. Though he questioned Ostheim on other particulars, most of his inquiries dealt with Whittaker's social position at the Academy. He pressured Ostheim to tell the court why he personally, and the Corps in general, snubbed Whittaker. Ostheim remained noncommittal. He refused to agree with Chamberlain that Whittaker was ostracized for no other reason "except the fact that he was of the African race." He continued to insist that he would have treated a white cadet the same way he had treated Whittaker and felt that social relations among cadets were a private matter. Since Whittaker was a year ahead of him, the black cadet should have made the first move. But, he admitted, even if Whittaker had approached him, he doubted whether he would have responded. The entire Corps ostracized Whittaker, but he himself felt under no pressure to join in. His actions were governed by his own decision.

Ostheim refused to budge, and assistant counsel Greener took over the cross-examination. Why was it, he asked, that Ostheim had affirmed instead of taking an oath? Because he felt that way, Ostheim answered. Were there any religious scruples involved? Greener persisted. "None," Ostheim responded, "except it is the custom of my people to generally affirm."

Q: "To what people do you belong?"

A: "I am a Jew."

Q: "Are you aware that the same prejudice which exists against Whittaker and his race existed against yours in past ages and even exists at the present time?"

A: "I am aware of that fact."

Q: "Do you not think that that fact should lead you to be superior to such prejudice?"

A: "I do not, for any time, desire to have my race brought up in this question. I see no connection whatever with it. I prefer not to answer that question."

Q: "The question of race came up from your own remark."

While this exchange was taking place between the black lawyer and the now uncomfortable Jewish cadet, the court took on a distracted air. Court members either gave one another rapid glances or shuffled the papers in front of them. Chamberlain toyed with his pencil and studied the floor. Whittaker looked steadily at the witness. Finally Gardiner "slowly arose and suggested in the mildest tones" his objection to the line of questioning. Greener accepted the objection but felt his questions had been "pertinent from what the witness said himself."

The effect of this testimony on the court is uncertain, but it is intriguing that the *Army and Navy Journal* ignored the entire exchange. Its report concentrated on the fact that board member Captain Craig had objected to an earlier question dealing with race but had been overruled by the court in a written vote. The Charleston *News and Courier* angrily called Greener "an ignorant, ill mannered, bumptious busybody, whose mission in life is to convince the world that the African is a superior race to the white."[8] However, it made no comment disproving Greener's point.

The next witness was Lieutenant William H. Coffin. Like Lippincott, Coffin produced one statement taking issue with the basic West Point position. He told the court he believed that any cadet who could commit such an act "would very easily lie about it." "Certainly."[9] This was the first time a West Pointer publicly admitted the possibility a cadet would ever violate his oath.

Next a belligerently anti-Whittaker witness testified, Lieutenant Walter Dickenson, at the time of the attack the cadet superintendent, or inspector, of the division where Whittaker roomed. Dickenson made no attempt to camouflage his desire to put Whittaker in the worst possible light. He said the black cadet's hair looked as though it had been cut by Whittaker himself; the blood found on the Indian club looked as though it had been purposely dropped there; and there was hair in the scissors found in Whittaker's room. Furthermore, Whittaker was no gentleman, because he had a tendency to sleep on a pillow without a pillowcase. As for the scraps of burned papers he had found on the floor, Dickenson reported that he had unaccountably lost them. He had been careful to preserve the scraps, indeed he had hung on to most; but several had by mistake been thrown away.

This last bit of suspicious information was quickly skipped over, and attention was centered on Dickenson's firm belief in Whittaker's guilt. "The principal fact was that I didn't believe anybody in the Corps of Cadets would have done it besides Mr. Whittaker and I thought it very improbable that one outside the Corps had done it. Therefore I don't know who could have done it but Whittaker." But why, Chamberlain asked, should Whittaker be suspected more than any other cadet? Whittaker "was in danger of being found deficient in Philosophy," and this was the "only reason" for his suspicions, Dickenson answered. He would have felt the same way had Whittaker been a white cadet.

Dickenson refused to admit that most of his derogatory statements against Whittaker were a result of his belief in the black cadet's guilt. Nevertheless, when asked if the investigation at West Point had been conducted on the "theory that Mr. Whittaker had done it to himself or for the purpose of ascertaining who had done it," Dickenson responded, "On the theory that Mr. Whittaker had done it himself."[10]

After Dickenson's testimony the question of the use of the court of inquiry transcript came up. Gardiner, on February 11, had told the court that he wished to admit the inquiry transcript as evidence in the present trial. Chamberlain objected. This record had been gathered, as he put it, "in an atmosphere of the most chilling and prejudicial character." Besides, Article of War 121 of the Revised Statutes held that in a case involving the dismissal of an officer, oral evidence had to be obtained. Persons should be directly questioned in the court-martial. Their court of inquiry testimony should be used only to refresh memories. Since Whittaker was a cadet, not an officer, Article 121 did not apply, Gardiner pointed out. The thorough court of inquiry testimony would be essential in the work of the court-martial; besides, since Whittaker was accused of lying during the inquiry, the record would have to be introduced to substantiate or deny this charge.

The argument went on for several days at various times during the testimony. Finally the court decided not to allow the introduction of the inquiry record. This should have ended the entire matter, but Gardiner was not so quick to give up. He went over the head of the court-martial board and presented his case to the Secretary of War, Alexander Ramsey. The Secretary, not sure what to do, asked Attorney General Charles Devens. The Secretary of War, Devens replied, had no jurisdictional authority over this court-martial, and thus any opinion or suggestion he might make would be "extra official" and "even embarrassing." He recommended that Ramsey simply refuse to state any opinion on the case. Ramsey accepted the advice and so notified Gardiner.

Gardiner now wrote directly to the Attorney General.

He told Devens that the entire government case was "wholly circumstantial"; the inquiry transcript was needed to learn all the details to determine the truth or falsity of testimony. Devens remained unconvinced, and though Gardiner continued to try to break the legal barrier, the decision stood. The court of inquiry record was not admitted as evidence and was used only to help witnesses check previous testimony or refresh their memories. Judging by Gardiner's vociferous behind-the-scenes activity, the prosecution considered this transcript important to its case and had thus suffered a setback. Whittaker had won one round of legal maneuvering.[11]

While the court and the presidential Cabinet were deciding this matter, a key witness was on the stand, Dr. Charles T. Alexander. He continued to insist that Whittaker had feigned unconsciousness. He had lost only about two ounces of blood, and the blows had been so slight that a sham was the only explanation for his insensible condition. And if Whittaker had been faking unconsciousness, then obviously he had committed the whole crime himself.

From its questioning and its attitude the prosecution put a great deal of reliance on Alexander's testimony. He was after all a doctor, a member of the Army Medical Corps for twenty-four years and a respected member of the West Point faculty. His professional opinion condemning Whittaker carried much weight. He was a formidable witness. In response the defense tried to undercut some of Alexander's eminence. Chamberlain began his cross-examination by showing that although Alexander had long served in the Army medical service, his experience was limited and his opinion thus open to question. The court learned that, during the Civil War, Dr. Alexander had spent no time in the field; he had been mainly an inspector of prisons and purchaser of medical supplies. The unspoken point was that, considering his lack of experience with wounds and unconsciousness, Alexander was not that much of an expert. Furthermore, his examination of Whittaker the morning after the attack had been cursory at best; he was basing his opinions on insufficient data.

Much of Chamberlain's examination dealt with the question of Whittaker's consciousness. Alexander insisted, at Chamberlain's prompting, that Whittaker had passed out at the wrong time. He should have "fainted" during the actual ordeal, not afterward. Alexander said he knew of no case where a swoon like Whittaker's had ever happened. Chamberlain replied that he knew from personal experience that Alexander was wrong. He had once been on a runaway horse and had collapsed only after the "horse had been reined up and the danger was gone." One of the members of the court-martial board, Colonel Morrow, later tried to make a similar point. He asked Alexander if a "timid" person having been awakened in the dead of night, tied, injured, and threatened with death would not have possibly passed out as Whittaker had? After all, said Morrow, Whittaker had been accused of something stronger than timidity. Alexander insisted that, if a person could withstand all Whittaker had without fainting, there was no reason to believe he would faint afterward.

Alexander was on the stand the greater part of two days, February 14 and 16, doggedly defending the correctness of his initial opinion. The defense could not shake his belief in Whittaker's guilt, and he was a strong witness for the prosecution.[12]

The next witness was Lieutenant Colonel Henry M. Lazelle, the Commandant of Cadets and the author of the original damning investigation report used against Whittaker. Lazelle, like Alexander, stuck to his story. However, he did not present his opinions nearly as strongly as he had in his report. During his testimony and cross-examination he admitted having had doubts about Whittaker's guilt, until the evening after the attack. At that time he had noticed the ridges in Whittaker's hair, and these had convinced him Whittaker had cut his own hair and consequently mutilated himself. Dr. Alexander's medical judgment and the absence of any significant injury added further weight in his conviction. Chamberlain and Greener tried to get Lazelle to change or at least modify his story, but they were unsuccessful for the most part. Lazelle continued to insist that Whittaker was guilty. Greener pointed out that it was strange that the room had been cleaned before a thorough investigation was possible. Something of significance might thereby have been lost. He also questioned Lazelle on several points of his pre-report investigation and left the impression that the commandant had done a shoddy job. His failure to check all the cadet rooms, for example, was a substantial oversight. His neglect of the barber's opinion that Whittaker could not have cut his own hair also made little sense. Did this professional opinion not change his own unprofessional supposition about the hair ridges? Greener asked. "It shook it somewhat," Lazelle answered.[13]

On February 17 a whole series of lesser witnesses paraded to the stand, offered their testimony, and departed. Of these, Cadet Lester W. Cornish made the greatest impression. He told of being in Whittaker's room on orders from Major Piper and finding a burned piece of paper containing Whittaker's handwriting in the hall dust box. This was one of the pieces lost by Dickenson. More importantly, he admitted that, like the rest of the cadets, he, a New Englander, had had no social relations with the black cadet. Color was not the sole cause for this, Cornish maintained, however. Whittaker, when spoken to, could not look anyone straight in the eye, and he used a "condiment" in his hair, which, Cornish told a laughter-filled courtroom, could be smelled throughout the hall. Color did play a role in Whittaker's ostracism; but, Cornish intimated, it was a minor consideration compared to eye contact and hair tonic.

Cornish was also asked to give information on the blood found on the Indian club. To facilitate his testimony, he dipped his fingers into red ink and, on a piece of paper

181

rolled to approximate the club, tried to show the court how the blood spots looked. It was during this demonstration that one of the members of the court, Major Merrill, dryly commented that he wanted to get all the evidence he could whenever a witness who had some evidence appeared, "for not many such had been presented as yet."[14]

The court, by this time, had been in session for almost three weeks in cramped quarters with little ventilation, hearing witness after witness expound the same basic story. A decision was made to take a brief recess. After an inconsequential session on Friday, February 18, the court decided not to meet again until Wednesday, February 23. They had received an invitation to attend a battalion drill of the Seventh Regiment of the New York State National Guard on Monday evening and simultaneously inspect the new armory.[15] Nothing else is known of their recess activity nor that of the defense. Whittaker probably spent the time at Moses Wester's home. All sides probably took the time to relax and gird for the long battle still ahead.

The Military Academy, meanwhile, continued functioning. Affairs were progressing smoothly under the new Superintendent, O. O. Howard, whose first month in office seemed to be going well. The Whittaker trial, though some hundred miles distant in New York, was still intimately felt through the participation of the many West Point witnesses. No one connected with the institution was making any public statements on the case, however. The situation changed during the Washington Day ceremonies on February 22. O. O. Howard, making his first formal speech to the Corps of Cadets, told them not to practice ostracism. He was not telling them to associate with thieves, he said; but he felt that "to ostracize a companion for some mere opinion, idiosyncrasy or unpleasant habit not yet corrected . . . [was] wrong."[16]

After Schofield's statements on this same subject, Howard's speech must have come as quite a shock to the cadets and faculty. There is no evidence that Howard took any steps to implement his ideas, however; ostracism continued. With Whittaker on trial, there were no black cadets at the Academy; so one form of ostracism was, of necessity, absent.

On February 23 Whittaker's court-martial resumed its sessions. The participants were probably aware of Howard's speech, but no mention was made of it. Testimony continued as it had before the recess. Gardiner called Mark Finley, a representative of a handkerchief company; Cornelius Ryan, the person who had cleaned Whittaker's room the morning after the attack; Edward McEnearny, the West Point quartermaster clerk; and a number of cadets who had roomed near Whittaker. Finley could not definitely tell whether the handkerchief shown him was made by his company and sold at West Point; Ryan had found and washed off some bloodstains on the inside of the door; McEnearny testified that he had purchased handkerchiefs from Finley's company; and the cadets denied hearing any noise the night of the attack.[17] In short, nothing really new or exciting was discovered. Even Ryan's testimony about the bloodstains caused little stir; the prosecution later surmised that the blood on the door could have been placed there the following morning by one of those who had found Whittaker. The possibility that it might have been placed there by one of the three masked men Whittaker insisted had attacked him was given little consideration.

The following day, February 24, excitement picked up markedly. Lieutenant George R. Burnett, whom a former cadet later described as a person of "no sullenness, nor bitterness, nor perfidiousness, nor enviousness" but "one of the first and most zealous" hazers of plebes, returned from the West to testify. He was, of course, one of the strongest anti-Whittaker witnesses of the court of inquiry and a person who, despite his current post, lieutenant in the 9th Colored Cavalry, was suspected in pro-Whittaker circles of complicity in the attack. The presence of what one newspaper called "the historic bed stead" indicated that Burnett was planning to repeat his controversial inquiry performance.

Gardiner led Burnett through a series of questions which informed the court of Burnett's impressions of the morning of April 6. Again, Burnett displayed his conviction in Whittaker's guilt. As expected, Gardiner asked the former cadet to show the court the manner in which Whittaker had been bound when first found. Burnett approached the mattressless iron bed and quickly tied his legs to the middle of the side rail and his wrists together in front of his body. The court gathered around and closely inspected the knots and the position of the legs and body which, Burnett said, accurately represented the situation on the fated morning. Burnett also demonstrated that in this position he was able to touch his ears and his head and also reach a wide circumference with his body. He also thought he could kick his legs and move the entire bed, but he made no attempt to show this. At Chamberlain's suggestion Colonel Morrow measured the distance between Burnett's bound wrists and found it to be approximately four and one half inches. Burnett was then allowed to stand up to answer other questions.

Chamberlain, beginning his cross-examination, asked Burnett to resume his bound position for the purpose of clarification. Burnett acquiesced and quickly made a slip of the tongue that brought laughter from the assembled crowd. Asked by Chamberlain if his feet were in a position similar to Whittaker's, Burnett responded, "The feet [Whittaker's] were a little closer to the rail when I tied them." The audience laughed at this suggestion of complicity, but Miles gaveled for order, Burnett quickly corrected himself, and the matter was not discussed again. Considering the fact that so much of the court of inquiry and the court-martial cases rested on Whittaker's alleged inconsistencies, one wonders what the reaction would have been had Whittaker made such a slip.

More important than this *faux pas* was a contradiction

Burnett made on another point. He said the knots on the bands were quite tight and later added that the bands were so taut that, while loosening the black cadet, he had had trouble getting the scissors between the bands and the flesh. Other witnesses had mentioned the evidence of imprints on Whittaker's wrists the evening after the attack. There was common agreement that Whittaker had been bound tightly. Burnett, however, said that Whittaker's wrists were four inches apart and that the black cadet could thus have easily broken loose.

This discrepancy was overlooked. More attention was paid to Burnett's rather long statement near the end of his testimony which cited his reasons for suspecting Whittaker. Burnett said he first suspected Whittaker when Dr. Alexander opened the black cadet's eyelid and only white showed. After that, Burnett carefully looked around the room and decided that "the blotch of blood" he noticed on the wall "had [either] been put there intentionally or been the result of a struggle." If a struggle had caused it, then the noise would have been heard in the adjacent rooms. Since no one had heard anything, the conclusion was obvious. The blood on the Indian club also looked to him as if it had been put there intentionally, not having the smeared appearance resulting from "a blow." The location of the hair in a half circle seemed to indicate that Whittaker had bent over a mirror, cut his hair off in bunches, and planted it on the floor. Had someone else done the cutting the hair would have been scattered.

Burnett also found it strange that Whittaker's hands had been tied in front of him instead of behind. Since the black cadet was conscious when the alleged assailants left the room, he could have either called out or banged the floor with the Indian club. Unaccountably he had done neither. Fear of the assailants was not a sufficient reason for silence. Finally, said Burnett, if Whittaker had really been struck by the mirror as he alleged, the glass would have been all over the alcove and not still in the frame.[18]

Burnett's testimony, delivered with an air of assurance and buttressed by a graphic demonstration, was an impressive addition to the prosecution's case. Though he had not tied himself as tightly as it was known Whittaker had been tied—and this later became an important defense contention—Burnett's testimony was very important. The court could now clearly picture Whittaker committing the act. On the other hand, the three masked men, whom the defense accused, remained a cloudy vision.

The next session saw both pro- and anti-Whittaker testimony. Moses P. Wester, the janitor of the Leather Manufacturers' Bank of New York, testified that Whittaker was living with him and his family during the trial. He also acknowledged that a letter held by Gardiner was the one Whittaker had sent him on April 7. Gardiner read the contents of the letter (see page 64), and the court learned of Whittaker's depression the day after the attack and, more importantly, heard his condemnation of West Point.[19]

Next came Thomas Sampson, one of the detectives who had investigated the case at West Point. He offered little real evidence, indicating that most of his investigation had consisted in questioning the black cadet and discovering that Whittaker's story varied slightly each time he told it.[20]

Walter Mitchell, a black West Point domestic, followed Sampson and told the court about his various conversations with Whittaker. He testified that the black cadet had shown him the note of warning the night before the attack but said he had counseled against showing it to the authorities.[21]

Captain Clinton B. Sears, the West Point recorder and Whittaker's professor in his deficient subject, natural and experimental philosophy, testified next. Most of his statement dealt with Whittaker's academic record, and he left the distinct impression that the black cadet was an inferior student. He reminded the court that Whittaker (along with two white cadets) had been put back a year but had still done poorly. Sears said he had to explain material twice as long to Whittaker as to any other student. Sears admitted that the court of inquiry had hurt Whittaker's chances of passing the June examination but left the over-all impression that, even without this interruption, Whittaker would probably have failed.[22]

Chamberlain attempted to refute the idea that Whittaker was in imminent danger of failure and had mutilated himself out of despondency. He closely cross-examined the professor of natural and experimental philosophy, Peter S. Michie. Since Michie was Sears's superior and one of the professorial powers on the academic board at West Point, his testimony was crucial to Chamberlain's contention. Under Chamberlain's prodding, Michie admitted to testifying at the court of inquiry that Whittaker would graduate. He said he believed Whittaker was a "very studious and very attentive" student and one whose "memory" was "excellent." He had placed him in the sixth section, but this did not mean automatic failure. In fact the majority of the sixth section usually passed. Nothing in Whittaker's recitations indicated gloom or despondency. Natural philosophy was a "severe subject" but "generally the last difficult one." Once a student passed it, this usually meant his graduation was practically assured.[23]

Surprisingly, then, Michie turned out to be a favorable witness. His testimony supported the defense's contention that fear of failure could not have inspired Whittaker to mutilate himself.

This encouraging testimony was quickly followed by what seemed on the surface to be a defense setback. The judge advocate, having completed calling his list of witnesses, now wished to advance to the next aspect of his case —the handwriting evaluation. He planned to introduce a number of Whittaker's letters for the sole purpose of analysis. Chamberlain objected strenuously, and the debate that ensued was carried on over several sessions of the court. Chamberlain contended that Whittaker's desk had been "swept" clean of correspondence. If the black cadet had stood on his basic civil right of privacy, the judge advocate would not even have these letters. Even prescinding from this point, it was legally inadmissible to introduce letters only for analysis. If writing was introduced as evidence, then it could also be used for the purposes of handwriting comparison. Correspondence having no bearing on the case could not be introduced solely for analysis. It was also improper to admit evidence gained through a comparison of handwriting when the witness making the comparison had no previous knowledge of the handwriting in question.

Gardiner denied Chamberlain's points, saying that his use of experts and examples of Whittaker's handwriting was perfectly proper and legally acceptable. The court studied the issue in some depth and on Wednesday, March 2, ruled in favor of Gardiner. Whittaker's letters could be admitted for the sake of analysis alone. That same day, Gardiner quickly followed up his advantage by introducing the first of his handwriting experts and a veteran of the court of inquiry, William E. Hagan of Troy, New York. Hagan looked at twenty-four specimens of Whittaker's handwriting and asked for a few days to study.them and make comparisons with the note of warning.[24]

At this point the court-martial took a recess until March 7. One reason was that the soon-to-be-called handwriting experts needed time to make their studies; another was the inauguration of the newly elected President, James A. Garfield. Again Whittaker's case was shunted from the public eye. His court of inquiry decision had been overshadowed by the political conventions of June 1880; now his court-martial lost what little interest it had produced in the press to the inauguration. Excitement over various other events helped push the story of the black cadet even farther from the public eye. In March the Russian czar was murdered; in April Benjamin Disraeli, the great British statesman, died; and in May the commemoration of the Revolutionary War battle of Cowpens took up much news space. As the New York *Tribune* put it, the Whittaker case received "little attention from the public," because the nation "rightly prefers fresh news."[25]

On Monday, March 7, the court-martial ended its second respite. As was quickly evident, the whole tone of the trial had changed. Where previously Gardiner had been attempting to present the circumstantial evidence against the black cadet, now he had moved to a new consideration: the note of warning. The prosecution aim was to prove that Whittaker had written the note and thus had perpetrated the whole incident.

At this very time the March issue of *The Criminal Law* magazine came out with an article discussing the court of inquiry's handwriting analysis. In this anonymous article, almost certainly written by expert Hagan, it was argued that Whittaker alone had written the note of warning. Conventional techniques of analysis were discussed, but the author emphasized the findings of the new science of handwriting analysis, the study of the nonforgeable "nervous characteristic between . . . [the] thumb and fingers." This science allowed experts "to read a man's chirography as a phrenologist [read] his skull, or a physiognomist his face" and showed conclusively that Whittaker had written the note of warning.[26]

From March 7 until the defense began its case on March 31, the court listened to a string of prosecution experts, looked at their charts and slides, and at times fought to stay attacks of boredom. The only break in the monotony came when the prosecution introduced a Portuguese barber, Stephen de Jossa, the last person to cut Whittaker's hair before the attack. De Jossa testified on March 10 through an interpreter that, when Whittaker had come to have his hair cut, he had asked that it be cut short on top and long in the back. The prosecution contended that this was another indication of Whittaker's plot. In asking that his hair be left long in the back he had gone against regulations in order to make it easier for him to gouge his hair the night of the attack. Chamberlain made the barber admit that, at the court of inquiry, he had testified that Whittaker's initial request had been to have his hair cut short on top "and not so very short behind." The wording, Chamberlain pointed out, was important because it indicated a normal request to a barber rather than an indication of a sinister plot.[27]

The novelty of having a witness testify through an interpreter was a minor break in the mass of expert testimony. Most of the court's time from now until the end of the trial was taken up with it. Not only was it minutely detailed and boring; it was also confusing. At times the prosecution experts seemed to be testifying at cross-purposes; and the confusion was compounded when Chamberlain introduced his own set of experts who directly contradicted the prosecution's experts and sometimes themselves.

Gardiner began this section of the trial by introducing three new specimens of handwriting—two of Whittaker's letters to his mother and one requisition for stationery. Chamberlain offered no objection, perhaps feeling that since his objection to the first twenty-four specimens had been overruled he would have no better luck this time.

The first expert to testify was William E. Hagan, who was, like all the prosecution experts, a veteran of the court of inquiry. In his three days of testimony and cross-examination Hagan reaffirmed his belief that Whittaker was the author of the note of warning. Using the microscope, he had found a number of similarities between the way Whittaker wrote his name and the letters in the note of warning. He also felt that there had been attempts to disguise these similarities. Central to his conclusion was his "nerve-tremor" theory. He told the court he had found in both the note and the specimens evidence of "a want of coordination or harmony between the first and second fingers: that is, one finger did not really take up a movement with the pen at the same point where the other left it off." This tremor was distinctive, and no one but Whittaker could have one exactly like it.

In his cross-examination Chamberlain hammered away diligently, but he was not able to get the expert to budge. He asked why Hagan had found resemblances between the note of warning and only four of the ten specimens of Whittaker's writing. Hagan blamed it on tiredness from three days at the microscope. It was true, he said, that he had found dissimilarities. Didn't examples of difference prove as much as examples of resemblance? Chamberlain pressed. "Perhaps so," answered Hagan.

Continuing his cross-examination, Chamberlain zeroed in on the nerve-tremor theory. He asked for specifics, for examples of this tremor, and was joined in this request by Major Merrill of the court-martial board. It seemed to him, Merrill said, that if this habit was a valid device for comparing handwriting, it would have to occur in any two given lines throughout all of Whittaker's writing. Hagan admitted that the same muscular effort was necessary to write any line of writing but could not point out evidences of the tremor in every line.

Chamberlain repeatedly told Hagan either to show graphically what he meant by a nerve tremor or to admit that it was the fabrication of his imagination. Hagan, just as repeatedly, blamed his inability to point out examples not on the fact that there weren't examples but on the fact that the court was unfamiliar with the techniques of handwriting analysis. He admitted that the nerve-tremor theory was newly discovered by him but maintained that, despite its newness, it was accurate. Using it, he was convinced Whittaker had written the note of warning.[28]

When Hagan stepped down, Gardiner viewed his testimony as strengthening the prosecution's case. Chamberlain, on the other hand, saw it as completely worthless. The court was probably confused.

At this point the question of No. 27 was brought up. The judge advocate wished to produce a specimen of No. 27's handwriting in order to investigate the contention of an expert during the court of inquiry that No. 27 could have written the note of warning. Captain Sears, however, refused to produce the specimen, considering it private property. He said he would hand it over only if ordered to do so by the court or by his superior, General Howard. After some discussion the court ordered Sears to produce court of inquiry specimens Nos. 1–30 so that Hagan might inspect them again. Sears obeyed the order without protest.[29]

The next expert to testify was the most controversial veteran of the court of inquiry, Albert G. Southworth. He had matched the edges of the note of warning with the edges of a requisition and of a letter Whittaker had written to his mother, thus indicating that all three had come from the same piece of paper. At the inquiry this disclosure had sealed Whittaker's doom.

Southworth testified he had twenty years' experience in the field of handwriting analysis. He continued to stand by his torn-edge demonstration, and now he added a new element to it. He reported that he had discovered underwriting on the note of warning—partially erased writing which could be seen only with the use of proper instruments. Someone had first written on the note in pencil as a model for the actual message. Later Southworth also found examples of this underwriting on the envelope.

At first Chamberlain concentrated on trying to shake Southworth's contention in regard to the matching edges. He was dealt a severe setback when Southworth successfully matched a number of sheets of paper torn by the defense. Later, however, he gained a significant victory. With the entire board gathered around a stereopticon screen during Hagan's second examination on March 25, Major Merrill noticed that Hagan, though he agreed with Southworth's underwriting theory, did not agree with Southworth's reading of the words that the underwriting formed. Merrill showed, for example, that where Southworth discovered the words "April 4th," Hagan had discovered the word "fixed." The underwriting theory was questionable.

The over-all force of expert testimony ran against Whittaker, however. Through the use of a stereopticon which magnified the writing 400 diameters, Hagan in his second testimony pointed out a new idea. Standing in the strong light with the words "You will be fixed" projected on the back of his bald head, Hagan said that the magnified thumbmark on the envelope had not been caused by a greasy thumb, as earlier suspected. He believed the mark had simply been caused by a person with "a peculiar skin." It took no imagination to determine who Hagan thought had caused the mark. Interestingly, however, Hagan also mentioned similarities between the note of warning and the writing of No. 27.

Another expert, Daniel Ames, also testified that the note of warning had been written by Whittaker. He produced no novel theories; he simply showed the similarities he saw between the warning note and the specimens of Whittaker's hand. He felt that the note of warning had definitely been written by the same person who had written Whittaker's letter to Moses Wester. The disguise in the note was mainly the result of deliberation. Expert James Gayler felt that the note of warning had certainly been written in a disguised hand and that its author was Whittaker. He presented an exhibit of enlarged letters and words to back up his point. Finally, expert J. E. Paine was called. Because of illness, he was unable to attend personally, so his conclusions were presented by Gayler. Paine too believed that Whittaker was the culprit.

As the experts paraded to the stand with their charts, exhibits, and slides, Chamberlain vigorously cross-examined each one. He tried to show weaknesses in their testimony, but he had no success in shaking any of them. They had thought out their conclusions and would not easily be moved. Still, Chamberlain did ferret out some favorable data. He pointed out that since Gayler was a government employee, his objectivity would have to be questioned in acting as a government witness. Ames had admitted making two investigations at the court of inquiry and one at the court-martial and coming up with three different conclusions. The first time he had said No. 23 was the culprit, the second time that either No. 23 or No. 189 but most probably No. 23, and this last time he had said it was Whittaker. What would be the result if he made another examination, Chamberlain asked. Would he come up with a fourth conclusion? Ames answered that he had not made as thorough an examination the first two times as he had the last time, and this last examination "eliminated all the doubt." "How many blunders before you get the right result?" Chamberlain asked. "I don't admit the proposition," Ames answered. "I won't press the point," Chamberlain smilingly replied.

The handwriting testimony, or, more properly, its dullness, had an auxiliary impact. Throughout the trial it had been apparent that the court-martial room was simply not suitable. The board, the counsels, witnesses, and large numbers of spectators combining with the very poor ventilation made conditions oppressive. Perhaps the dullness of the expert testimony made these stultifying conditions even more unbearable. In any case, remedial action came when court sessions had to be cut short due to the poor ventilation. On March 16, as a temporary solution, the number of spectators allowed into the room was limited.

On March 17 Gardiner asked the Secretary of War for permission to move the entire trial to a new location, the United States Court House and Post Office Building in City Hall Park. The present facilities had affected "the health of the counsel and members," he reported. Permission was granted, and on March 21 the trial was moved to the fourth floor of this federal building. The new location, one newspaper felt, gave "to the whole affair a decidedly wholesome and business-like aspect." There were ample facilities for visitors, and the room was again crowded with spectators.

With the move accomplished and the prosecution's expert testimony all but complete, a minor controversy broke out. On March 28 Captain Sears was recalled, and Chamberlain asked him point-blank to identify the author of specimen No. 27. Sears again refused to cooperate without direct order. The judge advocate objected to Chamberlain's question, but the lawyer countered that, since one of the experts had mentioned No. 27, the court should know his identity. This was an important clue and ought to be followed up. The writer of specimen No. 27 had nothing to fear unless he had actually written the note and in that case disclosure was essential. The court should have all the information available in determining the guilty party.

Major Merrill objected to the line of Chamberlain's argument and began to cite his reasons for disagreement. Quickly he was interrupted by Major Sumner, and the court-martial board erupted into open disagreement. Sumner insisted that Merrill's reasons should be put in writing. Merrill refused and continued speaking but was again interrupted, this time by Captain Craig, who denied the right of any member of the court to air his views in public. Sumner, becoming excited, jumped up and renewed his motion, only to be told by General Miles that he was out of order. Calming a bit, he suggested that the entire matter be discussed behind closed doors. Miles agreed, but Colonel Morrow began to express concern for Chamberlain's rights. Sumner demanded to know who was running the court. "I'm running it for the moment," Morrow retorted. "Well, I object to any more speeches being made," Sumner said. Finally Miles ruled that the entire matter would be discussed in private, and the court proceeded with its business. The next day it agreed with Gardiner that No. 27 should not be named. His identity continued to remain a mystery.[30]

After introducing forty washing lists in Whittaker's

handwriting and entering into evidence the scissors and necktie found in Whittaker's room, Gardiner rested his case. After almost two months of sessions and mountains of testimony the prosecution case against the black cadet was complete. It was now the defense's turn.

Chapter 10

•··❦··•

THE COURT-MARTIAL: THE DEFENSE REBUTS

THE court-martial moved into a new phase. Up to this time Chamberlain and his assistant, Richard T. Greener, had been able to react only to prosecution presentations and witnesses. Now they could go on the attack and present their own witnesses. Gardiner had to be the reactor; it was his task to try to weaken their case.

Chamberlain made no opening statement because, he said, it made more sense to avoid repetition and get directly into the examination of witnesses. The first witness he called was the accused, Johnson C. Whittaker.

One can only guess what had been going on in Whittaker's mind throughout this trial. He was mentioned only briefly in the court-martial transcript and the press. When his name did appear in the press, it was only to report his reactions to some statement. A flit of a smile would cross his lips, then he would return to his impassive gaze. He was living with Moses Wester and his family at 29 Wall Street

197

and attended a nearby Episcopal church, but his other activities were never mentioned. He had become an impersonal object during the trial, his humanity lost sight of in the maze of technical information spewed out by the handwriting experts. He was not a person; he was a subject for analysis.

Perhaps Chamberlain decided to put the black cadet on the stand to counteract this impersonality. Whittaker had made a favorable impression during the court of inquiry, Captain Sears's summation notwithstanding. His quiet determination and steadfastness in the face of hard questioning had had an impact. Perhaps, Chamberlain reasoned, he would produce a similar effect now, particularly since the court-martial board seemed more favorable than the inquiry board had been. But there was a risk. If Gardiner could trip the black cadet, could cause him to contradict himself, he would go a long way toward proving his case. The performance of the black cadet in this new encounter in the witness box was crucial to his hopes.

At first Whittaker reiterated his story about the mutilation. The court and the three to four hundred spectators listened carefully and followed his every nuance. More than one opinion must have been made. Whittaker told his story simply and briefly and seemed quite at ease. He "apparently commended himself to the spectators," at least according to one newspaperman.

Chamberlain, using a cross-examination technique, led Whittaker through his testimony. On several occasions Gardiner objected to what he considered were leading questions and attempts to avoid the main points raised during the court of inquiry. Chamberlain was scarcely ruffled, and Whittaker's story was promulgated, differing but little from his previously stated accounts. He had received the note of warning, had been attacked in the night by three masked assailants, had been cut, bled, lost consciousness, and had not come to until the next morning. He now expressed certainty that he had extinguished the gas-

light on going to bed and did not think it had been on
during the assault. Though no cadet had anything to do
with him, he had no reason to suspect any cadets. As for the
possibility of cadet aid on the night of the attack, Whittaker
felt that his treatment precluded any overanxiety on the
part of the Corps to help him. The spectators broke into
applause. Miles, at Gardiner's insistence, threatened to
clear the room.

Apparently satisfied that Whittaker's story had been
adequately presented, Chamberlain took his seat and
turned the black cadet over to the judge advocate for
cross-examination. Gardiner performed his task with a
dogged persistence, but he could not find a substantial
flaw in Whittaker's story. He concentrated on trying to
discover specific details about the attack, the position of
the attackers' hands when they dragged Whittaker from
his bed, exactly how Whittaker had been handled, and
so forth. In more than a few instances Whittaker either
said he did not know or prefaced his answer with "I
think," "perhaps," or "maybe." He also contradicted his
testimony at the court of inquiry in regard to some details; but, when shown this, he responded that he stood
by his earlier testimony because the details had then
been fresher in his mind. The similar behavior of other
witnesses, especially Dr. Alexander, was excused on the
ground that time had erased the memory of all the minute details. In Whittaker's case, however, it was viewed
by the prosecutor as evidence of guilt.

Whittaker seemed determined to guard against any
statement that might injure his position, so at times he
avoided answering the most direct, pointed question. He
was frequently told by the judge advocate to answer un-
equivocally, at times questions were repeated, and on occasion reread by the stenographer. "The session," the
New York *Tribune* noted, "was marked by the persistent
efforts of the Judge Advocate to make the witness [Whit-
taker] answer questions which he could not, and by the

refusal of Cadet Whittaker to answer questions that he easily could answer."

Gardiner's main strategy was obvious. He wanted to get Whittaker to contradict himself. He asked the black cadet, for example, about his treatment by other cadets, and Whittaker wisely gave a noncommittal answer. When pressed, however, he admitted having had problems with several cadets because of his race. The then Cadet Dickenson had often prefixed his morning order to fall out with an oath and had refused to march alongside of him. Other cadets had expressed and displayed similar anti-black feeling. To courtroom applause Whittaker said that the effect of this treatment was to convince him that no cadet would come to his aid the night of the attack. Since they would not even sit with him at chapel, he did not think they would help him in his time of need. Had he cried out, he believed the assailants would have carried out their threat to kill him before cadet help would have arrived.

Pressed further, Whittaker repeated a statement he had previously expressed only briefly late in the court of inquiry. He changed his earlier court-martial testimony and told the board that he suspected three cadets of having committed the attack: Burnett, McDonald, and Blake. These three had seemed the most openly hostile and could have been the assailants.

As the cross-examination proceeded, Whittaker stood his ground and at times even scored a point or two. When Gardiner asked why he made so much of his slight wounds, the black cadet answered, to the apparent satisfaction of the spectators, that he attached little real importance to the wounds themselves. What he considered important was the attack itself and "the accompanying principle." At another point during the questioning Gardiner asked Whittaker how, considering his testimony, he could account for the doctor's statement that he had bled only a few tablespoons full of blood. Giving the lawyer a lesson in legal niceties,

Whittaker answered, "I do not account for anyone's statements except my own."

On Thursday, March 31, Chamberlain interrupted Whittaker's testimony by introducing, over Gardiner's objection, another witness, a lawyer named Henry D. Hyde, who was to testify to the incompetence of one of the prosecution's handwriting experts. Hyde described to the court several cases in which the handwriting expert Southworth had made mistakes. In the "Buffalo whiskey fraud case" in 1867, for example, Southworth had said he was so positive about a handwriting analysis that, if he were on a jury, he would hang a man on it. During the trial it was conclusively shown that someone else had penned the piece of writing. On cross-examination Hyde admitted that he had not meant to impugn Southworth's integrity. He believed him to be a "man of veracity" who "would not knowingly falsify a case." But he had become a "monomaniac"; "he claimed to see things which no one else could see." He would believe Southworth only so far as he himself could verify the findings.

The prosecution's handwriting case had suffered a setback; the credibility of the leading prosecution expert had been effectively called into question. Though Hyde's testimony lost some of its impact by being sandwiched as it was between the two portions of the black cadet's testimony, it raised the question of the reliability of the handwriting analysis. If Southworth had been so positive yet so wrong in the past, how could one be certain he was not wrong again?

At the end of the Friday, April 1, session with Whittaker still on the stand, the court recessed until the following Wednesday as the result of an illness in Colonel Morrow's family. On Wednesday the court reconvened and the black cadet returned to the stand. The Whittaker–Gardiner duel of words continued unabated. The judge advocate asked questions of varying answerability, and the black cadet answered some and evaded others. One encounter revolved around the question of the position of Whittaker's body and his resistance to having his legs tied to the bed rail. Gardiner asked Whittaker if it would have taken two men, exerting all their strength, to tie his legs if he had raised his knees and put up a struggle. Whittaker answered, "If they were very strong men, no, not necessarily. If strong men, or less strong than I, yes." The court, confused by the ambiguity of this answer, left the room for a consultation. On returning, General Miles explained the question to Whittaker, and the black cadet answered that he thought a great deal of strength had been necessary to tie him. He could not speculate whether his assailants had been using their full strength. Gardiner objected that Whittaker was the only person who could give an opinion on this matter; it was part of a series of important questions which would attempt to determine the exact position of all the attackers during the assault. General Miles commented that the whole matter seemed to revolve around the right of the court to compel a witness to give an opinion. He did not resolve the issue, however; the questioning simply passed to other matters.

Another point of controversy centered on the mirror. Gardiner insisted that, if the mirror had been smashed over Whittaker's head as the black cadet had told Dr. Alexander and Lieutenant Colonel Lazelle, its pieces would have fallen out of the frame. Actually, the mirror was found broken but intact. Whittaker's answer to this was that he had never said the mirror had been smashed over his head; he had said that his attackers had broken it on his forehead, after forcing him to view himself. Gardiner displayed the word "smashed" in Whittaker's letter to Moses Wester and the black cadet was forced to retreat. Whittaker was believed to have been guilty of an inconsistency.

There were many other similar exchanges between Whittaker and Gardiner which, Gardiner insisted, demonstrated Whittaker's untruthfulness. In all cases, however, the inconsistency would have to be considered minor; even Gardiner did not contest that. He felt that an accumulation of small inconsistencies pointed to falsehood.

On the other side of the coin, Whittaker continued to hold his own against his experienced interrogator. On one occasion Gardiner asked Whittaker if, as a candidate for an officer's commission, he did not consider courage to be a prerequisite to obtaining a commission. Whittaker responded affirmatively. Then, said Gardiner, considering his candidacy, wasn't it Whittaker's duty "to submit to the threat of death rather than submit to such an outrage?" "No, sir," Whittaker responded to appreciative laughter, "because death would have ended my candidacy."

On another occasion Whittaker said he had not really been deficient in the June examination even though the Academic Board had declared him deficient. Gardiner responded sarcastically by asking why the Academic Board should find him deficient unless he really was. "To get rid of me and the case," Whittaker coldly replied.

The testimony continued all that week; and on Friday, Chamberlain asked a series of questions revolving around the matter of ostracism and the reasons for Whittaker having suspected three specific cadets. Whittaker's answers were full of so much bitterness over his ostracism that he even said his life as a slave had been better than his treatment at West Point. He could never treat anyone the way he had been treated.

Finally in response to Chamberlain's questioning he denied having any defect in the second finger of his writing hand which would produce a peculiarity in his writing. He expressed willingness to make as many copies of his own handwriting style as the court might desire and wrote with both a long and short pencil to display his manner of writing.

Finally Whittaker was excused.[1] The exact impact of his testimony is uncertain. Gardiner seemed happy with the inconsistencies he later claimed Whittaker exhibited in his testimony, and Chamberlain in his own summation concentrated on the examples of ostracism that Whittaker had discussed. Judging by the reaction of the audience, it was on the black cadet's side, but applause and laughter meant little to Whittaker's fate. Only the court would decide that, and their impressions have not been recorded.

As the defense moved to other aspects of its case, its strategy became apparent. Whittaker's testimony was the vehicle for presenting the facts of the assault as seen by the defense; most of the remainder of the argument was based on technical testimony. Chamberlain tried to discredit the prosecution's handwriting experts and then put his own experts on the stand to present evidence favorable to the black cadet. He also presented medical experts to try to undercut Dr. Alexander and to prove that Whittaker could have been unconscious. Finally, Chamberlain introduced witnesses and depositions to establish the high quality of Whittaker's character and morals and to show that he was not the type of person capable of self-mutilation and perjury.

The first witnesses to follow Whittaker on the stand were individuals called to discredit the prosecution's handwriting experts. John Dewee, chief inspector of the Canadian Post Office, testified about a case in which Paine and Southworth had been handwriting experts. Both had settled on a certain individual as the writer of a specimen in question. Paine was so convinced, in fact, that he wrote Dewee that, if he was wrong, "the experience of his own life-time had been in vain." It turned out that both he and Southworth had been wrong. Someone else had written the specimen. An inspector of a Montreal police station and several other persons also testified against the prosecution's experts, particularly Southworth. The impression being made was that Southworth was overly enthusiastic and tended to find what he thought those who had hired him wanted him to find. He was not viewed as dishonest, rather incompetent or, more accurately, as lawyer Hyde had put it, a "monomaniac."[2]

Two West Point barbers appeared on Saturday, April 9, and presented again a piece of evidence that the prosecution was never able to overcome. They both agreed that Whittaker could not have cut his own hair. The first of the two barbers was Max Rappenhagen, the hairdresser for West Point officers. Rappenhagen testified that he had never cut Whittaker's hair, but before and during the court of inquiry Lieutenant Colonel Lazelle and others had asked him to inspect the cuts made in the black cadet's hair. When he had looked at the cuts he had reported to the commandant that, considering their appearance, Whittaker had not done the cutting himself. Having measured them, he had found the cuts to be at least one and one half inches longer than the scissors found in Whittaker's room. He had so testified at the court of inquiry and had not changed his mind since then. He believed that Whittaker had not cut his own hair and that the scissors found in his room were not large enough to make the cuts.

Judge Advocate Gardiner spent most of his cross-examination trying to get Rappenhagen to change or at least modify his story. Did Rappenhagen know, Gardiner asked, that barber de Jossa at Whittaker's request had left the back of the black cadet's hair longer than the front? Wouldn't this have made it easier for Whittaker to cut his own hair? Rappenhagen agreed that longer hair would have made the job of cutting easier. Still, he said, that didn't prove Whittaker had done the job. Couldn't a person have produced a larger cut with smaller scissors, Gardiner asked, by continual cutting with the same stroke? Rappenhagen didn't think so. Despite Gardiner's vigorous attempts to shake him, he stuck to his story. An extremely valuable point had been made for the defense. How could Whittaker have cut his own hair if the only scissors in the room were said by an experienced barber to be insufficient for the job? And if Whittaker didn't cut his own hair, who did?

Chamberlain called another West Point barber, Charles Rappenhagen, who corroborated his brother's statement. He said he had even tried to cut his own hair in imitation of Whittaker's cuts, but he had been unable to do it. He also felt that the scissors found in Whittaker's room were about one inch too small to make the cuts found in his hair. Though he felt that de Jossa's testimony meant it would have been easier for Whittaker to make the cuts, he still felt the black cadet hadn't done it.[3]

The barbers' testimony, rather than indicating Whittaker's innocence, might have meant that Whittaker had been aided in his self-mutilation by another person. During the court of inquiry Louis Simpson had been suspected of this. To try to put this suspicion to rest, Chamberlain called Simpson to the stand. The black former West Point attendant described the few times he had spoken to Whittaker around the time of the attack; during none of those instances had he and Whittaker spoken very long. The only exception was the time they had discussed the note of warning with two other blacks, Simpson's father and Walter Mitchell. Then the conversation had lasted about twenty minutes. Because of previous plans Simpson had departed for Washington three days after the attack. Washington was really his home. In fact, his wife lived there.[4]

Since Gardiner made little effort to question Simpson, Chamberlain had effectively quashed the remains of any suspicions against him. The prosecution's case remained centered on Whittaker as the sole culprit. Consequently, the importance of the barbers' testimony loomed that much larger. Strangely Chamberlain did not emphasize this as much as he might have.

The court-martial now recessed for a week in order to allow both sides badly needed time to prepare further arguments and to relax from the strain. The court was given the chance to synthesize the mountains of detail presented before it. The crux of the defense case still lay ahead, and the all-important summations were yet to be written. The case was far from over despite its already extended term of session. The early prediction by both counselors that the trial would take only two weeks now seemed like a bad joke.

On Monday, April 18, the court resumed its sessions, and Colonel Morrow, who had been absent since April 1, reclaimed his seat. There was some debate over whether Morrow could legally return after so protracted an absence; but, since Chamberlain did not object, Morrow was allowed to resume his place.[5] He had proved to be the most effective questioner of witnesses and procedures as far as the defense was concerned; so there was never any danger of defense challenge. Chamberlain would not want to lose a board member who had shown himself so sympathetic to the defense cause.

With Morrow again in attendance, the defense presentation resumed. Chamberlain called a series of experts to counteract previous prosecution evidence. Dr. T. E. Satterthwaite, a New York physician; John Phin, editor of the *American Journal of Microscopy*; and James McDonough, the vice-president of the American Bank Note Company, all testified as experts in the use of the microscope. They stated that they had studied the note of warning and had found evidence neither of underwriting nor erasures. McDonough said he had found marks on the note of warning, but they were simply the result of "finger creasing." He contended that only "a little stretch of the imagination" was needed to discover any words or letters a person wished to see.[6] The underwriting theory was again under fire.

Leaving the note of warning for a moment, Chamberlain introduced a procession of witnesses for the purpose of establishing Whittaker's reputation and character. The witnesses were a diverse group, enthusiastic in their endorsement of the black defendant. Some, like the Reverend

Edward M. Pinkney, a black Methodist Episcopal minister, had known Whittaker since his boyhood days in Camden. Pinkney had, in fact, helped prepare Whittaker for entrance into the University of South Carolina. Others, like the Reverends Henry J. Fox of Massachusetts, A. W. Cummins of Wellsville, New York, and Professor W. Main of Brooklyn, had been Whittaker's professors at the University of South Carolina. All spoke in glowing terms of their former student. Cummins, for example, said Whittaker ranked third out of a class of forty at the university.

Chamberlain also read a series of depositions, mainly from Southern whites and blacks, attesting to Whittaker's character. Some of the whites' depositions, like that of James Chesnut, were obviously written as a favor to Whittaker's mother in the spirit of *noblesse oblige*. Whether or not they impressed the court is unknown. Taken as a whole, the witnesses and the depositions were an important part of the defense contention that Whittaker's past private and academic life gave no reason to suppose he was capable of self-mutilation and perjury.

The judge advocate did not offer much comment on most of the testimony and heard the reading of the depositions in silence. However, he did try to use one of the defense witnesses, Pinkney, to serve a prosecution purpose. He tried to show that Whittaker's academic preparation had been poor and that it, not ostracism, helped explain why he was a poor student at West Point. He also tried to indicate that Pinkney's statements represented nothing but his own outdated opinion. In his condescending cross-examination of Reverend Pinkney, Gardiner made the black minister admit that he did not know the leading citizens of Camden, South Carolina, on an intimate basis and thus could not accurately say that blacks and whites there thought highly of Whittaker. Moreover, since he had not seen Whittaker for five or six years, he could not know if the black cadet's personality had changed in the meantime.

Mainly Gardiner questioned Pinkney on his knowledge

of the subjects in which he had tutored Whittaker. He left the distinct impression that the minister was an academic incompetent and that Whittaker's preparation had thus been weak. Chamberlain objected to this line of questioning on the ground that Pinkney was not on the stand as an academic expert but simply as a character witness. Gardiner retorted that his questions were important but declined to pursue the matter any further.[7] He did not have to; his point had been made.

Actually, Gardiner's attempt had little real impact. The sum total of depositions and witnesses favorable to Whittaker far outweighed the minor consideration of Pinkney's academic qualifications. Whittaker was seen as an honorable man of adequate though hardly overwhelming intellectual ability.

Chamberlain now introduced his own handwriting experts to present the conclusions of their investigation. As had the prosecution experts, the defense authorities used charts, enlargements, and all sorts of other paraphernalia to document their case. As before too, boredom quickly overcame initial interest.

On Wednesday, April 20, M. Cochran, a teacher of penmanship from Pittsburgh, testified that he had studied the note of warning and the specimens of Whittaker's writing and had come to the conclusion that the note was a forgery. The letter "h," for example, was present 798 times in the specimens of Whittaker's writing but was never as perfect as the "h" found in the note of warning. He did not believe Whittaker could have made such a perfect "h." There were so many other differences between the note and the specimens that he was convinced Whittaker could not have authored the note.

Cochran was on the stand for three days, continually insisting on Whittaker's innocence. His testimony was undermined on Friday when the judge advocate showed him a number of new specimens. Cochran looked at them incredulously, then announced his belief that they had been prepared by the prosecution to trap him. Unfortunately for his credence, it turned out these specimens had been written by Whittaker at the end of his testimony in that very courtroom.[8]

The next defense handwriting expert, George L. Stimpson, was an important witness. He told the court he had had wide experience in analyzing handwriting primarily as a bank receiving teller for fifteen years. He had compared the note of warning with the specimens provided him and had come to the conclusion that the writer of specimen No. 27 was the writer of the note of warning. He had found over six hundred similarities. On the other hand, he felt there were countless dissimilarities between the note and specimens of Whittaker's handwriting. He was convinced No. 27, not Whittaker, had written the note.

In cross-examination Gardiner attacked Stimpson's reputation and competence even more than he attacked his conclusion. He drew a picture of a person who had repeatedly made mistakes in handwriting analysis. Stimpson was well known, Gardiner argued, for flashing his card and offering his services as an authority to anyone in need of handwriting analysis. Stimpson was just too anxious to please, and his opinions could therefore not be trusted.

Chamberlain inconsistently protested. Forgetting his similar attacks on Southworth, he objected that Gardiner's whole approach was irrelevant to the issue of the note of warning. The objection was overruled. Gardiner continued his attack on both the witness's opinion and his competence.

By now the same issues were being belabored to the point of ridiculousness. Every letter in the brief note of warning was undergoing the most minute scrutiny, and the various analyses confused rather than clarified the issue. In the hopes of speeding matters up, the court asked the Secretary of War for permission to begin holding sessions longer than the four hours—11:00 A.M. to 3:00 P.M.—established by the convening order. On April 28, just two days after the application, the President authorized the change. But it had little real impact on the trial's pace.

The trial was in a rut. A Boston detective named Pinkham and a Judge Fox of Massachusetts buttressed lawyer Hyde's statement that Southworth was incompetent. Fox provided no new evidence, but his prestige lent new force to the defense assertion that Southworth's opinion was not to be trusted. Chamberlain introduced several more character witnesses and depositions, but they added nothing new to the defense contention that Whittaker's reputation was spotless.[9]

Chamberlain called another expert witness to try to counteract the judge advocate's contention that Whittaker had written the note of warning: Charles K. Burt, for many years an engraver with the Treasury Department, an expert who had originally been contacted though never used by Judge Advocate Gardiner. Burt emphatically said he saw "no distinguishing underwriting" on the note of warning and punched another hole in the prosecution case.[10]

The key defense expert now mounted the stand. Dr. Richard U. Piper, a graduate of Harvard Medical School and the author of numerous works dealing with the use of the microscope, attacked all aspects of the prosecution's handwriting case. He was the defense's Southworth—an indomitable focus for controversy. His testimony appeared destined to last forever, and the court clearly resented his long-windedness.

Piper presented enlarged microscopic pictures of letters from the warning note and the Whittaker writing specimens. He denied that the several similarities proved Whittaker was the author. Whittaker's writing consisted of many awkward curves, while the note of warning was written by a practiced penman. It was obvious Whittaker was not the writer of the note of warning.

Piper then attacked the prosecution's underwriting theory. Again using photos and microscopic evidence, he argued that any piece of paper would have underwriting.

This "spirit underwriting" was evident on the note. There was, however, no evidence of erased handwriting; none of the note paper's fibers were broken. The very fact that the prosecution experts had found different words on the same spot in the supposed underwriting showed just how invalid the entire point was.

As for the so-called nerve-tremor theory, Piper dismissed it as "poppycock." The matching of the edges of the note of warning with Whittaker's letter to his mother and the requisition was also erroneous. Piper displayed photos of the highly blown-up edges of the papers in question and argued that these photos proved the edges did not match. In fact, the different tints in the photographs showed that the chemical composition of the papers was even different.

Finally, Piper argued that the note of warning had been written not by Whittaker but by the writer of specimen No. 27. He demonstrated on photos of enlarged letters the similarity between letters in the note of warning and in the writing of No. 27. He was positive that No. 27, not Whittaker, was the author.

Gardiner's cross-examination was intense. He insisted Piper was not the microscopic and optics expert he claimed to be and thus his conclusions were suspect. He could not, however, shake the doctor.

The court listened to Piper expound his theories for a week and began to lose its patience with the repetitiousness of the testimony and the disinclination of both lawyers to bring it to an end. The court must have agreed with the New York *Tribune* that this case had "embroil[ed] and confuse[d] and set by the ears the whole fraternity of penmanship experts." On Monday, May 9, Colonel Morrow introduced a resolution to try to speed things up. To cut down on the costs and to end the case as quickly as possible, he resolved that the court limit the examination of witnesses to two hours and cross-examination to a like period. The limitation on the concluding arguments would be six hours, with only one counsel per side to be heard. Morrow explained his reasoning for this resolution as an attempt "to bring the trial to a close within a reasonable life-time." The court and spectators reacted with approving laughter.

Chamberlain responded that he still had some medical experts to present and felt he would need three hours for this purpose. He urged an extension of the limit. The court took the resolution under advisement but took no action. Gardiner continued his cross-examination of Piper.

On Monday, impatience surfaced again. Gardiner was debating Piper's contention that his microscopic drawings were correct to one-millionth of an inch and debate was becoming increasingly technical. An exasperated Colonel Morrow interrupted and asked the purpose of all this technical information. Gardiner responded that he was simply attempting to show that Piper was not the microscopy expert he claimed to be. Well, Morrow asked, would Piper "now have to bring in experts to attest to his expertness? If so, where will this all end?"

The next day, Tuesday, another speed-up resolution was introduced. Major Merrill called for the court to hear no more handwriting experts. He argued that the tribunal felt "competent to deal justly with the question" of the note of warning without taking any more time. Again the court took no action. Naturally enough the next witness testified about the note of warning.[11]

New York photographer David N. Carvalho was described by the anti-Whittaker *Army and Navy Journal* as "one of the shrewdest as well as the most practical of the long list of experts" heard at the trial. He brought in two giant-sized photographs of a very much enlarged note of warning. He pointed out breaks between the letters, for example between the "x" and the "e" in "fixed," arguing that someone had retraced the note with a lead pencil and joined the originally separate letters. The prosecution experts, he said, mistook this coupling of letters for a peculiar characteristic in Whittaker's handwriting. The supposed "nerve-tremor theory" was in reality the result of the joining of letters and was invalid. As for the underwriting theory, Carvalho called it nothing but "an optical delusion." In cross-examining Carvalho, Gardiner was unable to detect any substantial flaws in the photographer's important statements.[12]

The following day another member of the court, Major Sumner, offered yet another resolution for speeding up the court's proceedings. He moved that the court begin sitting at 9:30 A.M. instead of the customary 11:00 A.M. The court cleared the room to discuss the motion in private. When the doors were opened again, the court announced a continuation of the 11:00 A.M. beginning and a determination to consider all future resolutions in secret session. The court's zeal for finishing the trial apparently did not include an earlier starting time. General Miles, however, was becoming so frustrated that, on May 13, he asked General Sherman to relieve him. His request was refused and Miles stayed on.[13]

Richard T. Greener, Whittaker's friend and former teacher and Chamberlain's assistant counsel, now became a witness. He recounted how he had chosen Whittaker for West Point from about two hundred applicants and how confident he had been of Whittaker's success. He had corresponded with Whittaker at the Military Academy and had been present for most of the court of inquiry at the Secretary of War's request. Thus he knew both Whittaker and this case very well. He did not believe the note of warning had been written by Whittaker, and he did not think noise carried very well in Whittaker's hall. The opening around the pipes so often alluded to was not as large as reported. He had had to get down on his hands and knees in order to see the room below. He had also noticed thirteen to fifteen big blotches of blood on Whittaker's floor. They had still been visible in May when he and a New York *Tribune* reporter had visited the room. Some of these bloodstains were the size of his hand, some the size of a half dollar, some the size of a ten-cent piece. They had withstood washing and scraping and were silent witness that much more of Whittaker's blood had been spilled than Alexander and others had alleged.

Greener also reported having been told by Professor Michie while he was at West Point during the court of inquiry that Whittaker was in no particular academic danger. To buttress this point, Greener introduced a detailed, West Point-compiled abstract of Whittaker's grades from September 1879 to June 1, 1880. He argued that there was no evidence of deficiency, not even in philosophy. His overall average for the year was passing; "his only deficiency was purely on the examination mark" in June.

In his cross-examination Gardiner protested Greener's use of the abstract. As a lawyer, Greener knew he should not have added the explanatory pencil notations nor attempted verbally to explain it. Only the person who had drawn the abstract could do this. In any case, the abstract was irrelevant. The Academic Board based its deficiency decision on the term's work *and* the June examination. The fact that Whittaker was not deficient on the eve of the examination meant little.

As for the bloodstain testimony, this was hearsay evidence and the court could not be sure Greener had not seen ink or fruit stains, not blood. Greener agreed and admitted that, in a regular court of law, this type of evidence would not be admissible. But in a court-martial, "which has more latitude," it should be admitted. He was no expert on stains, but he could tell the difference between blood, fruit, and ink.[14]

The trial seemed to have come full circle. Talk of blood rather than writing loops and curves filled the courtroom. The human element was back, and charts, photos, and stereopticons were left behind. The last remaining witnesses again focused on human aspects of the trial, bringing Whittaker back into the spotlight. The question of unconsciousness was discussed by five defense medical experts; all five agreed that, contrary to the testimony of Dr. Alexander,

Whittaker could have lost consciousness the night of the attack. In fact, his symptoms, rather than proving his guilt, showed that he had indeed been unconscious.

The first of the medical experts was Dr. George K. Smith of Brooklyn, who testified that it was possible for a person to be unconscious for two or three hours. Therefore Whittaker could have been unconscious for the long period he claimed he was. The cutting down of his feet and the handling to which his body was subjected for a space of twenty-five or thirty minutes would account for his immediate restoration when ordered to get up. If he had been faking, his heartbeat would have been rapid, not normal as reported.

Smith compared this assault situation with another, made on Secretary of State William H. Seward at the time Lincoln was assassinated. All Seward could remember about the attack made upon him was the impressive figure of the conspirator Payne entering his bedroom. He remembered nothing about the assault, not even one blow. Perhaps Whittaker had undergone a similar blank, Dr. Smith conjectured.

The next witness was Dr. George L. Beard of New York. Dr. Beard felt that, contrary to Dr. Alexander's contention, the condition of Whittaker's eyelids, the natural response of his pupil to light, the normal pulse, the difficulty of rousing him, the quick recovery proved he had indeed been unconscious. He had seen many such instances in his studies of the correlation between the mental and the physical. He knew cases where people in such shock had slept on for days and weeks before being roused.

Beard had wide experience with such cases. Since his graduation from the College of Surgery of New York he had specialized in the treatment of nervous disorders. But, asked Gardiner, did Dr. Alexander's wide experience not give him the ability to diagnose the Whittaker case accurately? No, said Beard. Whittaker's case was a very unusual one; "another like it might not appear for 1,000 years."

"Old and experienced surgeons" like Alexander were being deceived every day.

After a Sunday break, three other doctors testified that Whittaker had not shammed. He had truly been unconscious.[15]

The court-martial was now over—except for some closing fireworks. Whittaker had testified that a scar on the second knuckle of his left hand had been the result of the attack. Gardiner, therefore, recalled Drs. Alexander and Lippincott, who testified that the slight abrasion noticed there after the attack could not have produced such a scar. Whittaker was again lying. Chamberlain retorted that an abrasion could produce a scar and had in this instance. The matter was further complicated by the fact that no one could remember exactly where the abrasion had been. No conclusion was really reached.[16]

One more witness testified. Cadet McDonald, one of the cadets suspected by Whittaker, made a surprise appearance on the stand. When Chamberlain protested his appearance, Gardiner answered that the only reason for McDonald's presence was the "needless suspicion" thrown on him by the defense. The best "rebuttal," he said, was "to put the witness upon the stand, and give the counsel if he desired, the opportunity to examine him." Chamberlain made no response and McDonald retired.[17]

Without warning, Gardiner tried to introduce as evidence several of the specimens of Whittaker's handwriting being used for the purpose of analysis. He said Whittaker's statement in his letter to Moses Wester that he had never dreamed before the attack that anyone at West Point would injure him had real significance when compared to Whittaker's later accusations against West Point. Chamberlain was taken aback by this maneuver. He admitted that he learned something new every day but he never thought he could learn that "a defendant could be compelled to furnish evidence" against himself. The prosecutor might just as well have picked Whittaker's pocket as use for its content a letter which had been supplied by the defense for use in handwriting analysis. Nowhere did the law allow such practice. The court reserved judgment, but the next day announced that it accepted Gardiner's arguments. It admitted the letter. But it refused to accept a last-minute deposition from ex-Attorney General Devens in support of Southworth.[18]

With all the evidence finally in, the defense rested at 1:25 P.M., May 17, 1881. In order for the counselors to prepare their summations, the court recessed until June 1. A collective sigh of relief could be felt in the courtroom, and, according to one newspaper, the only persons sorry to see the case completed were two "loafers" who realized "that the cool court room would little longer afford them a loafing spot."[19]

Chapter 11

THE COURT-MARTIAL: THE FINAL WORDS

On June 1, 1881, with four months of detailed and at times tedious testimony completed, Daniel H. Chamberlain presented his closing statement to try to exonerate Johnson C. Whittaker from the stigma of self-mutilation. In his three days' summation, he carefully covered the main parts of the prosecution's argument attempting to point out inconsistencies and weaknesses.[1]

Chamberlain quickly reviewed the charges and specifications made against Whittaker in the court-martial convening order. Gently but firmly he reminded the court that it was not up to the defense to prove Whittaker's innocence; the prosecution had to prove him guilty. Suspicious circumstances were not enough. Without conclusive proof, Whittaker's innocence had to be assumed and the verdict had to be not guilty.

The motive for Whittaker's act, according to the prosecution, was a desire to avoid the June examination or to gain sympathy. But Whittaker did not even miss one day of duty. Chamberlain knew of no example of anyone scratching his ears or his head to avoid a specific duty. Whittaker was a "youth of a singularly irreproachable character," and up to that time everyone agreed he had lived a blameless life. Yet the prosecution would have the court believe that he had suddenly changed "like the monster that Goethe pictures in one of his short studies, the youth springs into a monster of wickedness in one brief moment." It just made no sense, Chamberlain insisted.

The defense counsel said he did "not propose to try West Point," as some argued should be done, but he felt certain points about it had to be mentioned. It was ludicrous to watch three to four hundred persons completely ostracize a young man of blameless record and then argue that they should be taken at their word, while he be assumed guilty. Who was more worthy of belief—the blameless youth or the cadets doing "daily and hourly outrage against his sacred right?" Moreover, if the argument that no cadet would commit such an act was indeed valid, why did it not apply to Cadet Whittaker?

In essence, Chamberlain said, the prosecution had to prove three basic issues to document Whittaker's guilt conclusively. They had to show that Whittaker had indeed tied and mutilated himself, that he was feigning unconsciousness at the time of his discovery, and that he wrote the note of warning. The defense did not have to prove Whittaker's innocence; the prosecution had to prove his guilt. Showing he *could* have done it was not enough.

The prosecution had argued that, had someone else bound the black cadet, they would have tied his hands behind his back, not in front as he was found. But, retorted Chamberlain somewhat unconvincingly, all the assailants wanted to do was to keep Whittaker's hands out of the way. Tying his hands in the back was no better than tying them in front for this purpose. In any case, this was not a key point. The tightness of the bands around Whittaker's wrists was more important. Witnesses had testified to the extreme tightness of the bands around Whittaker's wrists and the resulting day-long skin indentations. How could Whittaker have tied himself so tautly and why should he have inflicted extra and unnecessary punishment to himself, anyway?

Cadet Burnett's demonstration with a mattressless bedstead was dramatic but of little worth. Whittaker's wrists had been bound very closely to each other; there were four and a half inches of space between Burnett's wrists. Whittaker's legs had also been tied higher on the bed rail. Burnett's demonstration showed only that a person could tie himself the way Burnett had. It did not prove a person could tie himself the way Whittaker was found.

Another government contention, said Chamberlain, was that the semicircle of hair bunches proved Whittaker's guilt. All this really proved was that whoever had cut Whittaker's hair had cut it in bunches. Moreover, two barbers, one of whom had originally been consulted by Commandant Lazelle, had testified that Whittaker could not have cut his own hair. The scissors found in the room were approximately one and a half inches too small to produce the cuts found in his hair. Obviously, someone else using other scissors must have done the job. Whittaker's request to his barber a month before the incident, to cut less hair off the back than the top, proved nothing.

Other weaknesses in the government case were equally important, Chamberlain insisted. The government never really made it clear what instrument Whittaker had allegedly used to cut his ears. Drs. Alexander and Lippincott could not even agree on the exact location, size, and number of Whittaker's wounds and abrasions after the attack. The question of the position of the broken pieces of the mirror, the blood on the Indian club, and the condition of the gaslight were not essential points. To argue that the handkerchief used to stop the bleeding was obviously the black cadet's made no sense since over one hundred and

221

fifty cadets had purchased identical ones. In a similar vein, it was ridiculous to argue that the citizen's necktie found in Whittaker's room after the attack had to be his. No one had seen him with one since his 1878 furlough. Finally, what sense did it make to accuse Whittaker of ripping a part of his Bible and burning it as a taper? The Bible meant too much to him to be so callously torn and burned. As for the matter of the nosebleed, the physician never checked Whittaker's nostril carefully, so the government attempts to deny Whittaker's assertion had no validity.

The summation, thus far, had consumed the entire period from 11:00 A.M. to 3:00 P.M. Consequently the court-martial recessed. At 11:00 A.M. the following day Chamberlain resumed his argument, turning his attention to the question of Whittaker's ability to free himself. Chamberlain pointed out that a constant prosecution contention during the trial had been that Whittaker, had he wanted to, could have freed himself after the assailants had left the room. The original Lazelle report, in fact, had placed much emphasis on Whittaker's supposed ability to free himself with a few kicks of his feet. Considering Burnett's involved demonstration, his failure to do this was significant. More importantly, the difficulty in freeing Whittaker the next day showed how firmly he was lashed to the bed. A few kicks of an exhausted man would have accomplished nothing.

If Whittaker could not free himself, why did he not call for help? But would anyone, being placed in Whittaker's predicament, have trusted the cadets? The fact that no one heard the attack was no proof of Whittaker's guilt. The building was solidly constructed, Chamberlain pointed out, and noise did not travel well. What with inspections and all, the cadets were probably immune to nocturnal disturbances and slept through even louder noises than the relatively minor sounds of the attack.

The entire controversy over the scar on Whittaker's hand and the introduction of the numerous letters Whittaker had written to his mother and friends were equally specious, Chamberlain contended. Whittaker had nothing to gain by lying about the scar, and his anger and discouragement over his treatment at West Point expressed in private letters proved nothing. The prosecution, with the trial ending, was simply grasping at straws.

Chamberlain similarly disposed of the government's contention that Whittaker's inconsistencies and contradictions proved his guilt. He argued that the black cadet had not changed his story during the court of inquiry and the court-martial. The supposed contradictions were not in Whittaker's accounts; they were between details of his story and what some other person remembered him saying. In any case, what difference did these minor points make? What difference, for example, did it make that one time Whittaker could not remember how long it had taken to cut his hair and the next time he had thought it had taken five minutes? The important consideration, Chamberlain insisted, was not minor variation but the absence of "even one essential contradiction."

Chamberlain now turned once again to the matter of the motive and attacked the government assertion that fear of academic failure had inspired Whittaker to mutilate himself. The facts showed that Whittaker was in no academic danger. He had fallen into the sixth, or last, section, but this was not sufficient motive for self-mutilation. As for missing the June examinations, it made little sense to injure himself two months early. Whittaker simply had no motive to commit the acts. And without an adequate motive, the government did not have a case to convict him.

Chamberlain, having completed the first of the three points, now moved to his second area of discussion, the government contention that Whittaker had feigned his unconsciousness. As during the trial, Chamberlain tried to isolate Dr. Alexander against the five defense medical experts in the hope of discrediting his crucial testimony.

Expressing the greatest respect for Dr. Alexander,

Chamberlain nonetheless emphasized his cursory examination of Whittaker and his lack of experience with brain conditions. At the same time he credited Alexander, despite his erroneous conclusion, for at least noticing the symptoms, the normal pulse, temperature, breathing, eye condition, appearance, feel of the skin and the lack of dizziness, nausea, or stomach pain upon revival. Five different physicians, two of whom were specialists in neurology, when told these symptoms unanimously concluded that Whittaker had indeed been unconscious. All five agreed that

> Dr. Alexander's statement shows that Whittaker was in a state of unconsciousness, caused by a powerful mental shock and exhaustion acting on his nervous system and producing profound sleep —a sleep so deep as to hold all faculties in trance; . . . the theory of shamming is utterly incredible and impossible; . . . the pulse alone puts that theory out of the realm of rational consideration.

Since it was 2:35 P.M., the court decided to recess. At 11:00 A.M. the next day, Chamberlain began debating his third necessary point of proof for Whittaker's conviction— that the black cadet had written the note of warning. If Whittaker had written the note, it was almost positive he had been involved in the assault.

Unfortunately, the result of the long hours of questioning on this matter was a mass of "shapeless testimony," considered by some to be worthless. Chamberlain said he believed it had value and should be considered as long as it was understood that the burden of proof belonged to the government. "I propose to show that each and every one of these [government] experts are unworthy of credence or confidence when tested by their work in this case alone."

Chamberlain retraced the role of the government experts back to the court of inquiry to show their lack of consistency. During their first inquiry testimony, Gayler and

Paine could not give a positive opinion because, they said, the note of warning had so little writing on it. Hagan said Whittaker had written the note; Ames said either Whittaker had written the note or it was a "skillfully executed simulation of Whittaker's handwriting"; and Southworth said No. 27 was the writer. In short, the preponderance of the evidence was favorable to Whittaker.

West Point officials were not satisfied and recalled all but Hagan. Presenting the four experts with eighteen pieces of writing, some with Whittaker's name on them and some of the still unnamed No. 27, they asked for another opinion. This time three experts said Whittaker was the writer and Ames still said it could have been either Whittaker or No. 27. The reason Hagan was not recalled, West Pointers said, was because he had made a positive identification. The fact that Southworth had positively said No. 27 was the note's author was ignored. So was the intriguing development that, so long as the experts had not known the writers' identities, the majority had come up with evidence favorable to Whittaker. It was only when they knew what Whittaker had written that they settled on him as the note's author.

Of all the government experts, Chamberlain said, Hagan was the most important because he consistently held Whittaker had written the note. He did not, however, base his conclusion on the usual loops and forms method but on his own theory, what the expert himself called the "discordant motion of the first and second finger." Chamberlain ridiculed this theory by calling it a number of other names and then brushed it off by saying it had "no scientific basis." It was simply "a cobweb of his brain, a figment of his imagination." Hagan wanted the court to "brand Whittaker a perjurer on the sole strength of this absurd, unintelligible, unacceptable and unsupported theory."

Chamberlain now turned to his favorite antagonist, Albert G. Southworth. He ridiculed the expert as a chronic bungler, pointing to his changes of mind in the case combined with a later discovery of matching edges and under-writing. "The mingled boldness and stupidity of . . . [his] statements are among the most remarkable exhibitions of my experience." "He is either the Munchausen or Ananias of this country."

Turning to the defense experts, Chamberlain pointed out that they had shown conclusively that there was no underwriting. Dr. Piper had also demonstrated that the edges did not match and the paper was of different compo-sition. Cochran, Stimpson, and Piper, by conventional tests, had shown that Whittaker was not the writer of the note. The defense had to go no further; they did not have to discover the actual writer of the note to vindicate the black cadet. The burden of proof lay with the prosecution.

In summary, Chamberlain concluded, the prosecution had not proven its case. They had not proven that Whit-taker had tied and mutilated himself, they had not shown a valid motive, they had not proven he was feigning uncon-sciousness the morning he was found, and they had not proven he had written the note of warning. The govern-ment had had superior resources and power in this case when compared to him and the "tireless, unselfish" Greener, but he felt confident, nonetheless, that the truth would win out. "And I reverently believe in a protecting Providence without whose notice not a sparrow falls."

A burst of applause swept through the courtroom as Chamberlain took his seat. He had presented a logical, straightforward summation, emphasizing the idea of rea-sonable doubt and presumption of innocence. Whether he had been able thereby to undermine the government case would be for the court-martial board to decide. But first the prosecution had to be heard. Because of voice trouble and a recent burn to his hand, which had prevented him from taking notes on Chamberlain's summation, Gardiner asked for a postponement over the weekend. The court agreed.

On Monday, June 6 at 11:00 A.M., Major Asa Bird Gar-diner, the judge advocate of the Whittaker court-martial, began his summation. His two-day-long, more than 400-page presentation, though not organized as well as Chamberlain's, was a thorough statement of the government's case. Moreover, like the entire court-martial, Gardiner's summation was not simply a promulgation of legalities. It was a description of the black man's position in late nineteenth-century America.

Gardiner began by congratulating Chamberlain on his summation. It showed clearly, he said, that Whittaker had had excellent legal representation in this case. As for the prosecution, the members of the court knew him well—some from past association—and they knew he would speak up if he did not think there was enough evidence in this case. He had not been happy to receive this assignment in the first place, because he had been busy with another trial and because he did not like the "quasi-political" nature of the case. More to the point, he had been professor of law at West Point during Whittaker's first two years and had helped test him for admission. Be that as it may, there was no doubt in his mind that Whittaker was guilty. He particularly wanted it made clear, too, that he disagreed with Chamberlain's contention about a key legal principle: "It is not that there shall be no possibility of a doubt, but that there shall be no *reasonable doubt.*"

Gardiner carefully traced the entire incident from the discovery of Whittaker that April morning, through the examination by Dr. Alexander to the court of inquiry. He strongly endorsed the court of inquiry's finding that Whittaker was guilty of self-mutilation. The crux of his argument was that Whittaker was the only person with a motive, that he could have committed the act himself, that he wrote the note of warning, and that his inconsistent statements proved his guilt.

Gardiner's argument regarding Whittaker's motive was particularly important. He spent a disproportionate amount of his time on this question, and connected it with the matter of social ostracism, that element of the case which had received the most national attention. Gardiner argued that Whittaker's race had not caused his ostracism. On the contrary, his race had enabled him to receive special treatment not accorded white cadets. For example, Gardiner argued incorrectly, Schofield, by allowing him to repeat a year, had granted a favor not given a cadet for the previous thirty years.

But what about the ostracism?

> He undoubtedly was left alone by many cadets; but whether this occurred because he made himself unpopular by his self-conceit and assumptions or because of certain disagreeable personal peculiarities or because of that want of frankness in his character and appearance which had been manifested here on the witness stand, or whether it was on account of his colored skin merely, or all combined, is something difficult to determine because the sources of want of social assimilation are so varied and complicated.

Whatever the cause, Gardiner argued, echoing again that phrase heard so often, everyone had the right to choose his own friends. Even Whittaker admitted this, so it was clear he could "not pretend to lay claim to any special social recognition by the Cadets." Several of them testified that Whittaker possessed personal habits offensive to them, habits such as sleeping without a pillowcase, using "imguents" on his hair, and not being able to look a person in the eye. Personal habits, like these and Whittaker's own aloofness, not his color, were the main reasons for the ostracism.

Despite the ostracism, the black cadet could mention only two or three "absolutely puerile" instances of real difficulty during his West Point years. In the main, he had been treated fairly. It should be remembered, too, Gardiner repeated again, that at West Point, as at any other college, everyone had the right to choose his own friends. Social relations could not be enforced.

It might be argued, however, that there were persons at West Point who snubbed Whittaker solely because of his skin color. If there were any such people, Gardiner said,

> it was because of a prejudice which is entertained by millions of the inhabitants of this country, a race prejudice, which if ever eradicated, will not be wholly so until the individuals of the inferior race, show themselves in every particular the peers of the race with whom they are not upon terms of social harmony.

Gardiner now made his key point. The important fact about the ostracism, he said, was not that it existed but that it provided Whittaker with the motive for self-mutilation. Even the "lowest order of intellects" could have foreseen that the act would result in Whittaker becoming the "beneficiary of all the sympathy" and West Point being blamed. And this was his motive. "Whittaker calculated upon [the act] as a measure of revenge" for his ostracism. In this light, it made little sense to argue that the cadets had committed the acts. They too could have foreseen the results and would have shrunk from an act destined to make Whittaker a hero. There were too many more efficient ways to remove him, had they so been inclined. Whittaker had the only motive.

A study of the note of warning itself clearly showed the logic of this reasoning. The note had to have been written either by Whittaker, a friend, or an enemy. If written by a friend, why did he imitate Whittaker's handwriting; if written by an enemy, why did he put Whittaker on guard? No, Gardiner said, the black cadet had written the note of warning. His handling of it, his supposed uncertainty as to its disposition, his discussion with the black workers, all were part of the plot.

Leaving the note, Gardiner amplified his motive argument. He said Whittaker had, before his entrance to West Point, been a common laborer with education of the "most elementary and insignificant nature." His tutor, the Reverend Pinkney, knew little himself, Gardiner argued, and "the least said, the better" about the University of South Carolina. Whittaker was ill-prepared for West Point. Even one of the favorable medical experts declared that "his average mental capacity was not, in his opinion, equal to that of whites."

Despite his shortcomings, at the University of South Carolina he had been a leading student.

> He was head boy, foremost among many, and from what you have seen of his instructors you may infer that Whittaker had been petted and purred over as a prodigy, had been coddled and praised until assumption and conceit had formed a vigorous growth in his mind.

At West Point he had neither been coddled nor praised. He found himself in competition with both equals and superiors at an institution which taught manhood, which taught cadets "to stand on their own feet." It was this change which caused the "plant of discontent" to grow.

> And its branches bore morbid fruits of revenge and dislike to those around him. . . . And Cunning that ally of Revenge suggested a plot. It even became impious and caused him to cut from his own Bible certain pages, opposite where he had written religious gush, or holy words, to an unholy use, calling attention to the fact of how good a man he was.

It might still be argued, Gardiner supposed, that racial prejudice caused the cadets to act to get rid of Whittaker. If this was true, why did they wait four years until Whittaker had dropped into the last section and was in danger of deficiency and separation? Cadets had never hazed black cadets before and one had even graduated unmolested. Experienced detectives and the court of inquiry had discovered no evidence to implicate the Corps or any members of it of complicity in hurting Whittaker.

Yet, the black cadet would have the court believe cadets were guilty. Though they were not fools, Whittaker accused the cadets of doing foolish things: sending a note of warning, going to the room without the instruments necessary to commit the act, using no gag but cautioning silence, marking him insignificantly, then stopping even the slight cut with a handkerchief, putting on civilian clothes, thus risking easier disclosure, and, in essence, trying to get rid of him by violence when the demerit route would have been safer and more efficient. The theory of cadet guilt could "not be reasonably sustained." "Too many graduates of West Point have laid down their lives for the country's service," Gardiner summarized, "for us to lightly impute dishonor on those who are being trained in the same identical school, in the same identical way, the identical service."

West Point, argued Gardiner, was an institution of learning designed to serve the government, not the individual. "The survival of the fittest . . . [was] the rule of its conduct." So many young men wanted to attend that only the superior should be there. Despite this Social Darwinian law, Whittaker had received from Schofield "an extraordinary indulgence"; he had in 1879 been allowed to repeat a year. When in the spring of 1880 he found himself failing philosophy and realized his color would not save him again, he devised the plot of self-mutilation. The wounds were indeed trivial, but Whittaker believed they would be sufficient to keep him from separation.

Thus, said Gardiner, there was no reasonable doubt that Whittaker had mutilated himself to obtain public sympathy, to gain notoriety, to bring discredit on the Military Academy, but most of all to avoid the June examination. His mistake was the failure to consider the possibility of discovery.

Gardiner now turned to the matter of unconsciousness and the medical experts. He ridiculed the fact that the defense had had to go all the way to Long Island to get medical witnesses. Did this mean that New York doctors would not go along with the defense suppositions? Were there no Army doctors available? In essence, Gardiner argued, the fact was that a respected physician like Dr. Alexander had made a reasonable diagnosis and the defense doctors really had not shaken it. Dr. Beard, for example, looked less like the expert he kept insisting he was and more like a person selling a liver cure. "His loose, careless, bombastic utterances . . . [were] not those of an experienced scientist." Whittaker's symptoms in no way indicated that he had indeed been unconscious.

Gardiner warned the court that "Negroes are noted for their ability to sham and feign." " 'Playing Possum' is an Africanism that has come to be generally adopted, and the colored person is, according to all anthropologists, endowed with cunning and the power of mimicry, that renders him a lively subject for any form of description." Whittaker's race gave him a special talent to carry out the act.

Gardiner followed up this bit of scientific wisdom by citing a number of learned books which claimed that it was common for men in circumstances like Whittaker's to feign injuries. Whittaker's normal pulse did not necessarily disprove this theory because at least one authority held that a person was capable of controlling his heartbeat. Perhaps Whittaker had willed his pulse normal the morning he was found.

Gardiner continued to attack the statements of the defense medical experts, "visionary enthusiasts," as he called them. He quoted an article from the *Journal of Mental Nervous Diseases*, January 1877, in which expert Dr. Beard had said that the trance was "the hiding place for the world's greatest imposters." Since it was so easy to fake a trance, Dr. Beard had written, a motive was always to be searched for. In this case, Gardiner retorted, there was certainly a motive present.

Before turning to the matter of the note of warning,

Gardiner reiterated his belief that Whittaker had mutilated himself. Both Burnett and Dr. Alexander had shown that Whittaker could have committed the act; it was obvious he had the motive and he certainly had the opportunity because of the free Sunday afternoon and the available hours before reveille. The defense contention that Burnett's hands were not tied as taut as Whittaker's had been made little sense. Burnett was smaller and had smaller fingers than the black cadet, and, besides, because of the presence of ladies, Burnett had been forced to perform in full uniform. Had it been necessary he could have tied himself tighter.

Gardiner then attacked Whittaker's courage. "By his own story the accused has shown himself a coward without one redeeming quality." Even the defense experts with their coma theories "had to predicate them on his innate cowardice—and one of them thought his mental attitude inferior to the average Anglo-Saxon." It was obvious, Gardiner affirmed, that Whittaker was "a person born to obey far more than to command."

Gardiner now turned to the evidence of the handwriting experts and, like Chamberlain, spent a great deal of time discussing it. As Chamberlain had ridiculed his experts, so he ridiculed Chamberlain's. He endorsed Southworth's underwriting theory and Hagan's "nervous tremor" theory. But even without these, he was confident the handwriting analysis alone demonstrated clearly that Whittaker had written the note of warning.

Gardiner defended Southworth's reputation from the defense assaults. He said no person could do such difficult work for thirty years without making some mistakes. Importantly, Southworth denied making errors in some of the cases cited by the defense. Gardiner also endorsed the underwriting theory. He told the court that the erasures on the note of warning were obvious. The fact the defense experts missed them altogether made their entire testimony suspect. In considering this evidence the court should remember that a handwriting expert was like an astronomer. The uneducated eye could look at the sky and see nothing until the skilled astronomer pointed things out. Such was the same case with the handwriting expert. The untrained eye looking at handwriting missed much which the trained expert could see. And all government witnesses "with one acclaim swear that in their opinion Whittaker wrote the note of warning."

The defense experts, Gardiner insisted, could not be trusted because their techniques and conclusions were obviously wrong. Cochran showed himself to be an "incompetent," while "old man Stimpson" was "nothing but a fired bank teller" ignorant even of basic bookkeeping. He wondered if the defense had placed Stimpson on the stand to put expert testimony into disrepute before the court. As for Dr. Piper, who called himself the greatest camera and microscope authority in the world, his testimony was "beneath contempt." He knew nothing about handwriting analysis, answered questions with questions, and did not even know the principles of operation of the camera of which he was supposed to be an expert. In arguing that there were no erasures and thus no underwriting, Piper insisted that, had an eraser been used, it would have rubbed out the blue lines on the paper. But, Gardiner countered, Piper had used an ink pumice eraser, knowing full well that a softer rubber one would not have erased the lines.

There was no question that the writing on the note of warning resembled Whittaker's writing. The government witnesses, going beyond mere resemblance, had proved conclusively he had written the note. Even more, one of the experts, through the use of an ingenious method, had proved this even more completely. Hagan's "nervous tremor" theory had shown that only Whittaker could have written the note. The defense had ridiculed this theory, but courts and jurists recognized its validity. Furthermore, the defense contention that No. 27 had written the note was not tenable. There were some similarities, but that was about it. No. 27's writing did not have the peculiarities Whittaker's handwriting and the note had. Considering all the facts, the only possible conclusion was that Whittaker had written the note of warning.

Gardiner also spent much time pointing out alleged inconsistencies in Whittaker's testimony and story. By viewing these contradictions, Gardiner argued, the court would again recognize Whittaker's guilt. When Whittaker's story was looked at through "the cold strong light of intelligent common sense," no other conclusion was possible.

The note of warning should have been sent Monday, not Sunday, to lessen time of warning. The word "fixed" was not in the cadet vocabulary; it smacked more of the "Ku Klux [Klan] district of South Carolina a few years ago." Whittaker said he thought little of the note, yet he showed it to his two friends and mentioned it in the letter to his mother. If he considered it so unimportant, why had he just not torn it up instead of showing it around?

As for the actual attack, why did Whittaker fall asleep after the first sound? What about the note of warning? How was it that three men could get into his room and get to his bed without his hearing anything, yet he had heard the earlier slight noise? If his nose bled as he said it had, why had the doctors found no evidence the next day? If he had indeed been struck in the head, why were there no marks? How could the assailants have done such a delicate cutting job on his ears since his hands were not tied until after the cutting? Why had the attackers used one of their own handkerchiefs instead of using one of Whittaker's? Why had he not yelled for help or kicked himself loose? Why was it that no one in any of the adjoining rooms heard anything?

On and on Gardiner continued. Every detail that could be used against the black cadet was brought forward. The alleged inconsistencies went on for pages, with Gardiner finally pointing to the matched edges of the note of warning and the papers found on Whittaker's desk. He challenged the defense to refute this key point. Only Dr. Piper disagreed that the edges matched, and his testimony was worth little.

Even more than these inconsistencies, Whittaker's own testimony clearly showed his guilt. He repeatedly contradicted himself and other witnesses. He appeared very calm on the stand, but his reasoning was deficient. He constantly gave himself loopholes and evaded direct answers in order to try to keep the truth back, but contradictions came out nonetheless. He changed details of his story each time he told it, and other witnesses like General Schofield, Dr. Alexander, and the two detectives pointed this out to the court in their testimonies.

The most blatant lie, as far as Gardiner was concerned, was Whittaker's insistence during these sessions that a scar on his hand was the result of the attack, while Drs. Alexander and Lippincott and Lieutenant Knight could not remember the scar being that large or in that exact spot. Some might hold that this contradiction and all the others evident in Whittaker's testimony were of little significance, but he disagreed. If Whittaker could be shown to be lying about one point, this probably meant his whole story was a lie—*"Falsus in uno—falsus in omnibus."* This was hardly good logic, but Gardiner stuck to it for the rest of his summation. Finally he concluded that Whittaker had been contradicted by two civilians, seven commissioned officers, and by the cadets and the officers who slept near him. The only conclusion, he finished, was that Whittaker was guilty. He regretted having to be the prosecutor in this case or the case of anyone in uniform, but he was a soldier and had done his duty to the best of his ability.

When Gardiner sat down, there was a noticeable lack of applause. But the court, not the spectators, would be making the decision, and their reaction was unknown.

Chapter 12

THE COURT-MARTIAL: DECISION AND AFTER

With the witness box now empty and the rhetoric of the rival attorneys but an echo, the court-martial of Johnson C. Whittaker entered its final stage. All that remained was the judgment by the board of Army officers if the evidence presented in the long trial justified a verdict of guilt or innocence. At the least, according to General Sherman, the board's task was "to enforce prompt, exact justice, and not . . . split hairs and extend through centuries." This trial was after all, he told Miles, "a farce from the beginning," aimed at the black vote.[1]

While the court deliberated, a new controversy simmered. Upon finishing his summation, Gardiner had introduced a letter from Colonel Morrow indicating that sickness prevented his presence. The court simply made note of the letter, then adjourned until twelve noon on June 10 to hold its deliberations without Morrow. His absence was a severe blow to Whittaker's chances of acquittal. It kept from the discussions a man who had consistently shown himself to be skeptical of prosecution arguments and might have passed this skepticism to other members of the board.

The defense attorneys realized the significance of Morrow's absence but, for some unknown reason, did not immediately protest. They waited to act until June 10 some two hours before the court was to return. By this time the panel had almost certainly already made its decision. Yet, even though the defense was negligent, the court's handling of the matter was far from satisfactory.

Greener and Chamberlain composed a letter to General Miles asking that the court make no decision until Colonel Morrow was well enough to take part in the deliberations. They argued that Morrow's extensive court-martial experience and "his age and the close attention" he had paid to the evidence made it "extremely desirable that in making up its findings the Court should have the advantage of his presence." Because of the "peculiar circumstances" of the case, the defense argued, a decision should be rendered "by the full Court and not by what is described in the Military textbooks as a 'mutilated' Court."

The letter with its pointed use of the word "mutilated" had no impact. When Greener tried to present it to Miles, the orderly at the door refused him entrance into the deliberation room and even refused to accept the letter. Greener was able to present it only after the findings had been promulgated. At that time Miles simply endorsed it and ordered it sent to the reviewing authority with the rest of the court-martial material. Sometime later Greener sent a copy to D. G. Swaim, the Judge Advocate General of the Army, because he had heard the letter had not been sent as promised.[2]

The outcome of this incident was not a good omen for the black cadet, and the decision presented at noon on June 10, 1881, bore it out. The court-martial found Johnson C. Whittaker guilty of both charges brought against him in the court-martial order.

He was declared guilty, but several significant changes were made to parts of the first charge. In the original court-martial order Whittaker had been accused of mutilating himself and writing the note of warning "with the design and intention to excite public sympathy, to bring discredit upon the said Military Academy, to obtain notoriety, and further to avoid and escape an approaching public examination." The second charge had accused him of lying at the court of inquiry. A crucial part of the prosecution argument had centered on the question of Whittaker's motive and the accusation that he was the author of the note of warning.

In making its decision the court deleted that part of the first charge which accused Whittaker of committing the act for the purpose of gaining public notice, bringing disrepute on West Point, and avoiding the June examination. It also eliminated those parts of the charges which stated that Whittaker had caused the note of warning to be written by someone else.

As a result of these changes the court was saying that Whittaker had mutilated himself and had written the note of warning himself. But he had not committed these acts for the reasons claimed by the government. In short, the court-martial found Whittaker guilty but threw out a fundamental part of the government's argument—the matter of his motive. Considering the importance of the motive to the prosecution's case, this deletion is hard to square with a guilty verdict. It was yet another surprising development in a continually surprising case.

Regardless of the manner of the decision, Whittaker had been found guilty. The court-martial board ruled he was to be dishonorably discharged from the Military Academy, was to pay a $1 fine and be confined at hard labor for one year at a penitentiary chosen by the reviewing authority.[3]

The complicated proceedings now seemed over. But there was more. On a back page of the court-martial transcript, after the report had officially been ended, six members of the court-martial board, including General Miles, recommended that "on account of his youth and inexperience . . . so much of his sentence as related to fine and imprisonment be remitted." Another board member penned a separate addendum urging "clemency" on the part of the reviewing authority.

Whittaker was guilty, but not for all the reasons alleged by the prosecution. He should be punished but not too severely because he was inexperienced—a fitting end to a confused court-martial.[4]

Whittaker's reaction has not been recorded, although it can logically be supposed that he was despondent. His hopes for acquittal had again been dashed, and the avenues for further appeal were limited. The case now went to the reviewing authority, the Judge Advocate General of the Army. Since the court-martial had been convened by the President, it might also be reviewed by him. Even here there was little real hope. Whittaker had twice appealed to military justice and both times had come away with the stigma of guilt fastened even more securely. There was no reason to believe that the new President, James A. Garfield, would wish to get himself involved in the problems of a predecessor. The future did not look promising.

Adding to Whittaker's problems was the fact that, with the court-martial now completed, his status was uncertain. He had received no special orders to appear at the court-martial in the first place, so neither he nor Gardiner knew what to do now that it was over. Gardiner asked his superior for a ruling. The Adjutant General responded that Whittaker had been on furlough since August 1880 and would continue in that status until "final action" was taken in the case. Whittaker thus remained in limbo, still a cadet but not functioning as one. All he could do was wait. He returned to South Carolina sometime during this period, but his activities have not been recorded. No doubt, however, he followed news reports of the court-martial of Lieutenant Flipper. His former black West Point roommate was also on trial[5] for what was called a mismanagement of funds.

The public could only guess at the result of the trial. No public announcement was made; the court transcripts, exhibits, and decision simply were sent to the Judge Advocate General in what one paper called "a large box bigger than a Saratoga trunk."[6]

It was not until December 1, 1881, some six months after the submission of the material and with President Chester A. Arthur in the White House, that something happened. D. G. Swaim, the Judge Advocate General of the Army, rendered his opinion in the form of a report to Secretary of War Robert T. Lincoln, the son of the President who had freed Whittaker. In 101 pages of minute dissection, Swaim decimated the prosecution's case and held the court-martial decision up to ill-disguised contempt. The public was again kept in the dark, however, because this report was for internal government use only.

D. G. Swaim was from an Ohio abolitionist background, a lawyer since 1859 and, during the Civil War, a member of Ohio's Sherman Brigade, so-called because it was recruited by Senator John Sherman, the general's brother. In 1869 he became a member of the Judge Advocate Corps and argued before both circuit courts and the Supreme Court. He was Garfield's personal choice for the post of Judge Advocate General, having served for a time as his private secretary. He was a man of considerable talent and widely respected for his legal abilities.[7]

Swaim saw his job in reviewing the findings of the court-martial first as determining if the court had been "duly constituted" and then as deciding if its proceedings had been "regular," "its ruling and decisions in accordance with the law and evidence."

Attacking the first issue, Swaim concluded that the court had been illegally constituted because the President had no authority to call a court-martial in such a case. According to common law and the Constitution, Schofield alone had the authority. The court-martial proceedings were "therefore void."

Following this eye-opening statement, Swaim examined the charges themselves. Again he concluded that there had been error. The first charge accused Whittaker of violating a regulation of the Military Academy, and the court-martial board agreed. However, Swaim argued, "Crimes and punishments cannot be defined and fixed by a regulation but only by an act of the law making power." Thus the entire charge was void.

The court was correct, Swaim felt, in throwing out that part of the first charge concerned with the motive. From his reading of the transcript he felt Whittaker was in no academic difficulty severe enough to impel him to commit self-mutilation. There was also no evidence that he committed the act to gain public notoriety.

> No adequate motive, therefore, appears from the evidence, impelling the commission of the act and as before stated, the absence of such evidence is reasonably regarded where the fact is doubtful as affording a strong presumption of innocence.

Swaim then moved into the area of ostracism and subjected General Schofield to blistering criticism. He said that the trial testimony showed clearly that Whittaker had been snubbed at the Military Academy. This fact certainly had had an impact on his academic progress. The most disconcerting part, he said, was the attitude of the Academy Superintendent. In his official report for 1880 and in other statements, Schofield had seemed to justify racial ostracism and had criticized the President and Congress for even appointing black cadets to West Point. "To hold that a colored citizen may not be educated there," Swaim argued, "is to say that he is not capable of holding a position under the Government, and is therefore denying him equal rights under the law." Considering the prejudice and ostracism, Whittaker's strength in surviving so long at

West Point certainly was a "strong presumption in his favor."

More than the ostracism, the facts of the case had to be analyzed. Citing exact page numbers of the transcript to document his detailed points, Swaim probed the government case and found it wanting on all counts. In regard to Whittaker's tied hands and feet, for example, Swaim concluded that the evidence was "insufficient to establish beyond a reasonable doubt the fact that Whittaker tied or could have tied himself as alleged." It seemed obvious from the testimony, especially Cadet Hodgson's, that Whittaker had been tied very tightly, certainly more tightly than Burnett had demonstrated a person could tie himself.

As for medical testimony, the prosecution depended entirely on Dr. Alexander, whose examination was superficial, while the defense called five "distinguished surgeons," all of whom felt Whittaker had not been shamming. The evidence of the regular pulse beat was particularly important and could not be overcome by the prosecution theory that Whittaker had perhaps controlled his heartbeat. The ability to control one's heartbeat was "so unusual as to be inconceivable." The evidence, rather than indicating shamming, pointed to an "insensible or unconscious state" produced either by himself or by the acts of others. The fact that Dr. Lippincott noticed a slight wound on Whittaker's head, though he attributed it to a tight hat, was also significant. Alexander never noticed the wound, and Whittaker denied that his hat was tight. This wound could very possibly have been caused by a blow.

Other aspects of the case, Swaim felt, also favored the defendant. Whittaker denied that the knife found in his room was his. The scissors used to cut his hair had to be larger than the ones found. It seemed hard to believe that Whittaker would have cut up his Bible, his constant companion and solace. The assailants probably put the gaslight on and kept it low to avoid attention. When they needed more light to do the job, they used some sort of a taper. The bloody marks on the Indian club were probably caused by the attackers in the process of threatening the black cadet. In all cases, there was no reason to suspect Whittaker.

The actual attack was probably done "for indignity, rather than to do him serious bodily injury." His silence was the result of the circumstances—being awakened from sleep in the dead of night and threatened with death. "A stouter heart" than Whittaker's would have reacted similarly. And consider Whittaker's background:

> A young man born a slave, impressed from childhood with the superior might of the white race; cowed by nearly five years of ignominious treatment on the part of members of that race, separated from his few friends; not naturally robust in constitution, and below the average in the cadet in strength [sic] . . . it is scarcely to be wondered at that a youth thus circumstanced should have failed to display, in such an emergency, the same courage that perhaps other persons might have manifested.

Significantly, the actions of the cadets upon finding Whittaker seemed to bear out his distrust of them. No one made any move to help him; no one even uttered a word of sympathy. Cadets who looked in came not to help but solely out of curiosity. The civilian trousers found in Whittaker's room during the court of inquiry showed that the cadets not only had no sympathy for him but were actually trying to make trouble.

Swaim also concluded that, despite continual and unfriendly questioning, Whittaker's story remained as remarkably consistent "as might reasonably be expected." There were "discrepancies," but these were "plainly to be attributed to the zeal of his numerous interrogators, as well perhaps as to a dazed state to be induced under such circumstances."

Swaim felt Schofield had had no business taking such an

active role in the original court of inquiry. Once he had appointed it, he should have remained aloof and let it do its job. Instead, he conferred with the court on numerous occasions, hired detectives for its use, and even published the order exonerating the cadets before its sessions were over. His anti-black-cadet attitude gave the inquiry an obvious tint, and its proceedings mirrored this. Whittaker was put on the stand first, then brought back several times. He seemed to have been presumed guilty from the beginning.

Finally, Swaim discussed the question of the note of warning. He argued, first of all, that had Whittaker written it he would never have let it get out because of its obvious resemblance to his handwriting. After showing it to his two black friends, he could have destroyed it and not have had the handwriting problem. On the other hand, was it not chivalrous for the conspirators to have given Whittaker a warning?

Swaim mainly concentrated on the admissibility of Whittaker's letter and the expert testimony. He pointed out that the defense had objected to the introduction of examples of Whittaker's handwriting, otherwise irrelevant to the issues, for the purpose of handwriting checks. They had also argued against the "admissibility of testimony, by comparison of handwriting where the witness had no prior knowledge of the handwriting." In both cases the objections had been overruled. Common law and a number of Supreme Court cases showed clearly, Swaim argued, that these objections had been valid. This evidence was totally inadmissible. Even allowing it to stand on its own, however, it did not implicate the black cadet.

> The rebutting evidence offered by the defense on the question of the authorship of the note of warning is material and significant, and inasmuch as it is for the prosecution to prove that the accused wrote it, and not for the accused to

prove he did not write it, there is certainly ample room for doubt.

The whole matter of No. 27 had also never been satisfactorily cleared up, Swaim contended. "I am prepared to hold that the accused has not been shown to be the author of that note beyond a reasonable doubt."

Summarizing, Swaim concluded that the court had been illegally convened by the President, that the proceedings and findings under the first charge were void because a criminal charge could not be sanctioned by a Military Academy regulation, and that the handwriting evidence had been improperly introduced but, in any case, did not prove Whittaker's authorship. "On the whole my conclusion is that the prosecution has fallen short of sustaining the charges and specifications by adequate legal proofs, or such as would be sufficient in law to justify a jury in uniting in a conviction, and that the proceedings, findings and sentence should be, therefore, disapproved."[8]

The matter now rested with the Secretary of War, Robert T. Lincoln, and ultimately with President Chester A. Arthur, the assassinated Garfield's successor. In November one of the defense experts in the court-martial, Dr. R. U. Piper, had asked the President to withhold a final decision on the case because he had some new evidence. He repeated this point in another communiqué in January, promising the material in printed form almost immediately. He told Chester A. Arthur he was planning on having the evidence published in a law review. The first letter was endorsed by anti-West Point Senator John A. Logan and Samuel Fellow, the chaplain of the Illinois chapter of the Grand Army of the Republic.

The promised publication did not materialize until July and August, long after Arthur had made his decision. Mainly it was a repetition of the defense position in the court-martial and again declared emphatically that Whittaker had not written the note of warning. Piper used illustrative plates to show graphically that the pieces of paper Southworth said he had matched were in reality of different chemical composition. Plates were also used to show the fact that, in any case, the edges did not match.[9]

This was, of course, not new evidence as Piper had promised Arthur. It was the same argument that had proved unconvincing to the court-martial board. Even had it been published before Arthur's decision it is doubtful it would have influenced him either.

The existence of the Judge Advocate General's report not surprisingly leaked out to the press in January. The New York *Tribune* expressed its belief that the guilty decision would be set aside because of insufficient evidence, while the New York *Times* talked of the court's allegedly "illegally constituted" nature. The *Nation* magazine received the *Tribune*'s suppositions with astonishment, expressing in questionable legal logic its vigorous disagreement. It pointed out that the court had been carefully selected to ensure officers free of West Point or race bias. Should the Judge Advocate General now set aside its verdict, "it would show that in his opinion he was competent to try the case in the beginning, and that his judgment, formed in Washington, would have satisfied the public, and that the money spent on the court-martial was wasted." This would be "a great mistake," the *Nation* warned, and would have the effect of giving aid to the enemies of West Point. The decision should be left standing.

A month later, on February 16, 1882, with no decision yet promulgated but with Swaim's action generally known, the *Nation* lamented the fact that the Secretary of War, on whose desk the report now lay, was said to be too busy to look at it. The Attorney General, to whom it was rumored Lincoln would refer the entire matter, was also busy. The result was no action and delay of a final determination. The only person happy with this state of events, the *Nation* concluded, was Whittaker! It was "of course delightful" to him because it kept him "from the consequences of his conviction for the moment." The delay also raised the "possibility" that he would never be convicted. "He must often feel puzzled," the Nation wagered, "in trying to account for his good fortune, and for the tenderness which surrounds him."[10]

Whittaker's feelings and, for that matter, his actions are unknown. He waited for a final decision perhaps in New York or Washington but more probably in the South. January and February passed, and there was no movement. Like a becalmed ship, the Whittaker case seemed dead in the water, making no movement in any direction. Finally, in March, Robert T. Lincoln supplied the force to get it moving again. On March 6 the Great Emancipator's son wrote the Attorney General, Benjamin Brewster, for an opinion concerning the admissibility of Whittaker's letters. Considering the speculation in January 1881 that Brewster was going to be Whittaker's lawyer, this was an intriguing development.

The Attorney General, in a four-page answer on March 17, 1882, ruled that handwriting evidence was, according to common law, the Supreme Court, and numerous state courts, inadmissible "where the witness had had no previous knowledge of the handwriting but is called upon to testify merely from a comparison of hands." Only when writing accepted as genuine was already part of the evidence of a case was it admissible. Since in the Whittaker case, Brewster argued, the evidence in handwriting was inadmissible, the case should be set aside. "Justice forbids the enforcement of a sentence which is founded upon a conviction illegally obtained."[11] This was, in part, the same way Swaim had argued.

It was but five days after this opinion that President Arthur made his decision. As part of General Court Martial Orders, No. 18, published on March 22, 1882, and containing the charges, findings, and sentence, Arthur ruled that the findings and sentence were disapproved. Citing the Attorney General's and the Judge Advocate General's concurrence in the belief that the court-martial had improperly admitted Whittaker's letters, Arthur said that this "error in the proceedings of the court in relation to a material issue" therefore voided the decision and the sentence.[12]

Whittaker was, after almost two years, acquitted on a technicality. Unlike the Judge Advocate General, who felt that the case itself did not warrant a finding of guilty, the Administration did not go that far. They simply threw out the case on legal grounds and did not discuss the other issues. Perhaps to avoid political complications, no mention was even made of the court's improper establishment by former President Hayes.

Unfortunately for the black cadet, the decision was not the only thing thrown out by the Administration. On March 21, the day before the promulgation of Arthur's decision, Robert T. Lincoln scrawled out an order to the Adjutant General. "Prepare usual order discharging Cadet Whittaker by reason of failure to pass &c." This was done, and on March 22, the day of Whittaker's acquittal, his short-lived moment of success disappeared when Headquarters of the Army Special Orders No. 66 discharged him from the Military Academy for deficiency in the June 1880 examination.[13] He was not guilty, but was discharged anyway. Ironically, this was the exact advice appended to the court-martial record by a majority of its members. They had found Whittaker guilty but had urged a cancellation of the fine and prison term and the enforcement only of the provision of separation from the Academy. After the court of inquiry an earlier Judge Advocate General had urged separation, as had General Schofield. West Point had lost the battle but won the war.

Not especially surprising, public reaction was practically nonexistent. The public has long since tired of Whittaker's case, and the daily press simply ignored its culmination. Only the *Nation*, the onetime defender of the rights of the freedman but now an accurate barometer of negative national opinions about blacks, made an extended comment. It castigated on questionable grounds the Judge Advocate General's decision but more significantly gave its over-all view of Whittaker and his case. In its words can be heard contemporary nineteenth-century America. When he had been admitted to West Point, the *Nation* said, Whittaker had been done a "moral injury" which was probably "irreparable." His race had also been injured. His failure was not "an individual misfortune simply." Because of his failure he had "left his race worse off by far than if he had not gone to West Point at all. We trust," the *Nation* cautioned, "that when the next trial of a colored cadet is made he will be carefully selected and offer the best guarantees as to his moral and mental stamina."[14]

As if to add the final blow, on March 22, 1882, the day of the decision and the dismissal, D. Wyatt Aiken wrote the Adjutant General. This Congressman from Whittaker's home district, who in 1880 had cut off debate on the black cadet's misfortune by insisting he would protect his constituent, continued to display his lack of concern for Whittaker. He indicated his desire to nominate someone to take the black cadet's place at West Point. The Adjutant General responded quickly, Aiken made a nomination—a white man—and Whittaker's place was taken.[15] Black Americans again had no representative at the United States Military Academy.

That Whittaker must have been bitter over a turn of events which saw him exonerated yet separated from the Academy there can be no question. Still, he told a newspaper reporter that if he were given the chance, despite his belief that he would probably receive "the same as I ever did," he would return to West Point "in a minute." He still wanted his commission and was apparently willing to brave more time at the Academy to get it. And though there was no chance of this happening, a remarkable sense of perseverance, probably nourished by his deep religious faith, continued to cause him to hope he might still be allowed to return.

Sometime during this period he began to make plans to keep his case before the public eye. In May he made an unsuccessful trip to Chicago to secure some sort of a position.[16] In late May arrangements began for him to undertake a national speaking tour. A series of speeches would provide some income but more importantly would give him a chance to tell the nation his story first hand and perhaps fan the embers of his flickering hopes.

The place chosen for his baptism of oratorical fire was Buffalo, New York, in the area of "the burnt over district" once so-called because of its early-nineteenth-century religious and reform fervor. By 1882 the earlier fires had been long out, but Buffalo was undergoing new reform at the hands of Mayor Grover Cleveland. It was an important city of large mixed population and might have been considered an appropriate site for Whittaker to begin a speaking tour. It was also near, yet sufficiently distant from, the West Point and New York trial sites.

Preparations for the inaugural lecture were apparently in the hands of the managing editor of the Buffalo Evening News, William McIntosh. How detailed the advance planning was is unknown, but McIntosh apparently wanted to make Whittaker's first speech a propitious occasion. He wrote Rutherford B. Hayes asking for help.

The editor told the former President of the plans for the ex-cadet to speak in Buffalo on May 31. He said Whittaker would "tell his side of the story to the people of this city," and, if this first venture was a success, he would embark on a national tour. He asked Hayes for "an expression of some kind as to your belief in Whittaker's guilt or the hardship with which he was used." He said that if Hayes could do this it would be much appreciated and would "doubtless greatly aid the young man."

Whether Hayes responded is unknown, but on the McIntosh letter he made a notation that rather strikingly showed his basic disinterest toward the entire matter. Hayes wrote at the bottom of the letter: "Never

251

read the evidence—Can't therefore give an opinion as to the decision."[17]

Despite this lack of a suitable reaction from Hayes, Whittaker still went to Buffalo to deliver his speech on the night of May 31. The site chosen for his address was St. James Hall, at that time an important lecture hall in the city. A rainstorm that evening undoubtedly kept many persons away, but, nevertheless, a racially mixed audience of about 150 appeared to hear the black former cadet deliver his address. The importance of the event in the city was underscored at the very beginning when Whittaker was introduced by the Honorable George W. Patridge, the president of the Buffalo Common Council. The Mayor, soon to be President, Grover Cleveland, was not present, however.

Having received a friendly introduction from the Buffalo politician, Whittaker stepped to the footlights. Behind him was a table piled with books and documents, but Whittaker spoke extemporaneously and made little reference to them. The Buffalo audience was surprised at his appearance as people always were when they saw him for the first time. He did not look like a black man. One reporter said, "He appears to be rather a Caucasian brunette of a pronounced type than a man with negro blood." For this speech Whittaker was smartly attired in a dark suit and "a standing collar and a black tie." His voice was not strong, but it carried to all parts of the hall, and no one had any problems hearing or understanding him.

Whittaker began by putting at ease any of his audience who might have any misapprehensions about a basic contemporary issue. "I am not here," he said, "to discuss social equality of the white and black races. No sensible colored man asks social equality, or wishes to obtrude his society upon any other." Still he insisted, "When a man does right, adheres to duty, he has a claim on your politeness—a claim to be treated as a gentleman." And at West Point a black man, like any other citizen, had a right to "just and gentlemanly treatment."

This statement was well received by the integrated audience, and Whittaker proceeded to the story of his West Point experiences. He told of his ostracism, his ill-treatment at the hands of the cadets and what he emphasized was the blatant unfairness of his court of inquiry and court-martial. He had never spoken in public on these matters before, having resolved not to say anything until military justice had run its course. Now that his case had been completed, however, he felt he had to speak up.

For the next two hours or so he told a captivated audience his tale. Repeatedly he was interrupted by applause. Most of the time he maintained a calm tone and factually presented his side of the case, but often his bitterness came through. He told the audience that he hoped his training would entitle him to a position in the Army. He reminded them, however, how difficult it would be for him to get this wish. "Over the door of the Revere House of Boston, and the doors of a thousand public institutions is the sign 'No niggers enter here,' over the door of the Army it reads 'No niggers enter here as officers, except in time of war and then circumstances alter cases.'"

Yet, he showed himself notably optimistic about the future. Nowhere can this be seen better than in the peroration.

> West Point has tried to take from me honor and good name, but West Point has failed. I have honor and manhood still left me. I have an education which none can take from me. That education has come to me at a fearful cost. The government may not wish me to use it in her service, but I shall use it for the good of my fellow men and for the good of those around me. I stand before you untrammeled by prejudices, unbounded by partisan policies, daring to be independent in thought, independent in politics. Poverty and sneers can never crush manhood.

With God as my guide, duty as my watchword, I
can, I must, I will win a place in life!

The audience exploded into applause and crowded onto
the stage. For a half hour they showered their congratula-
tions on the obviously elated speaker. A reporter was told by
óne of the audience, "I'm a doubter no longer, I believe he's a
square man and has been badly used." Even the *News's* press
rivals were friendly in their reports of the speech. As one
paper put it: "No one, unless it be a West Pointer, a Southerner, or an aristocrat, can listen to him without having his
sympathy excited for the persecuted youth." Whittaker's
initial forensic foray was a success.[18]

Its effect on his life was negligible, however. He told a
reporter the President had referred his application for appointment as second lieutenant to the Secretary of War.
There is no indication, however, that any further action was
ever taken. The Buffalo speech, a similar one in Baltimore in
July, a tour of Georgia churches in September, and perhaps
other public appearances had no real impact. They made
known his feelings, but the audience was either not influential or not inspired enough to take up his side. His case was
viewed more as past history than as a contemporary cause.

Yet he maintained hope. On five separate occasions he
wrote either Robert Lincoln, the Secretary of War, or Judge
Advocate General D. G. Swaim, asking for documents dealing with his court-martial. He did not receive the promised
transcript copy until March 21, 1884. When he wrote in
December asking for the Judge Advocate General's report,
he was told this was a "confidential" document and he had
no right to see it.[19] He never wrote again, probably realizing
at last that his cause was finally and irrevocably lost. There
was no way he could ever resume his Military Academy
career. He would never become an Army officer.

Chapter 13

JOHNSON CHESNUT WHITTAKER: CIVILIAN

JOHNSON Chesnut Whittaker sank from the public eye. Like a shooting star his name had flashed across the skies, but just as quickly it burned out and passed out of sight. He was no longer a celebrity; he became just another black man, trying to earn a living, raise a family and simply survive in late-nineteenth-century, early-twentieth-century America.

It is not known what Whittaker did or where he lived in the immediate period between the completion of his trial in June 1881 and his Buffalo lecture in June 1882. He may have continued living with Moses Wester and obtained some sort of a job in New York City, or he may have visited Professor Greener in Washington. He may also have returned to South Carolina. Since he was not included with his mother and brother as an administrator of his father's will in 1883 he probably did not return to the Camden area.[1]

Sometime in these years, however, Whittaker moved to Charleston, South Carolina, and joined the staff of Avery

255

Normal Institute. This fact was reported in an El Paso, Texas newspaper, in January 1884, indicating that his name was still nationally known.

Avery Institute was a school for blacks founded in 1865 by a Reverend Francis L. Cardozo in a building appropriated for the purpose by South Carolina Freedmen Bureau commissioner General Rufus Saxton. It was at first called Saxton School. In 1866 it was moved to Military Hall on Wentworth Street in Charleston and in 1868 received a new $25,000 building from the American Missionary Association. Ten thousand of the dollars had been donated by Pittsburgh minister Reverend Charles Avery, so the school's name was changed from Saxton School to Avery Institute. Its main task was teacher preparation, but there was also a limited amount of vocational training available to the three hundred or so students.

Unfortunately no records except student rolls remain from this school, so it is impossible to know what Whittaker taught. The 1884 Charleston directory listed him as a teacher at "Charleston Military Academy," but since no such place existed, the listing was a mistake. He was definitely a teacher, however, because in October 1883 he was sent a letter by the State Superintendent of Education enclosing copies of the state school law he had requested. Perhaps the military academy was the Porter Military Academy organized by Reverend A. Toomer Porter, a person Whittaker must certainly have known since he lived at St. Mark's Association, a black literary, educational, and social organization founded by the Reverend Porter. Perhaps Whittaker taught part time at Avery and part time at St. Mark's or the Porter Military Academy or at all three.[2]

His substantial scholastic duties did not keep him completely occupied. Sometime in this period he began to study law. A former justice of the state supreme court, Jonathan Jasper Wright, conducted law classes in Charleston as professor of law of Orangeburg's all-black Claflin College, and, in all probability, Whittaker attended these classes. In his obituary it was later stated that he had studied at Cooper Union in New York, but that school's records do not show it. In any case, he was admitted to the South Carolina bar on May 26, 1885. At first he practiced law in Charleston, but around 1887 he left to begin a thirteen-year residence in central South Carolina.[3]

Sumter, South Carolina, the town Whittaker moved to in 1887, was typical of small Southern towns of the period. The seat of Sumter County, it had in 1890 a population of 3,865, while the county contained 43,605 people. Sumter was predominantly black; 2,042 of its inhabitants were Negroes, and the black population in the county was 31,-792. This proportion of black to white was even higher than the state average of 59.9 percent, which itself was the highest in the nation. Though whites controlled most segments of life, during Whittaker's residency the area was for a time represented in Congress by a black man, Whittaker's former University of South Carolina classmate George Washington Murray, who represented the district from 1893 to 1897. Whether Murray had any influence on Whittaker's decision to settle in Sumter is not known; nor is any relationship between the two men thereafter.[4]

Upon arriving in Sumter, the twenty-nine-year-old Whittaker established a law practice with a man named Edwards. He became an immediate success. It was reported in a local paper that year that the black law firm of Edwards and Whittaker "monopolized nearly all business" during that term of court. Edwards was described as "a very black negro" of "considerable intelligence," while Whittaker was cited as "the famous ex-West Point cadet." Earlier a Columbia newspaper also commented on the success of this firm and the fact that two thirds of the time it appeared for defendants.[5]

In all probability Whittaker, like most black lawyers, was forced by the poverty of his clients to find extra sources of income to meet his expenses. Around 1890 he married Page

E. Harrison, the daughter of a white Sumter city employee and his black wife. Subsequently he fathered two sons, Miller F. in 1892 and Johnson C. in 1896. Two baby daughters were lost at birth.[6] He had new responsibilities and greater needs. Fortunately an opportunity presented itself which allowed him a second front and, more importantly, continued a career which was to become his life's work.

In 1888 the South Carolina legislature granted a charter to the city of Sumter to operate a public school. Consequently the following year two schools were opened—a school for whites in what was known as the old Moses house and a school for blacks "in the Lincoln school house on Council Street, a building long used for educational purposes." Whittaker was a leader in the organization of the black school and, in fact, was elected the school's first principal for the 1890–1891 session. That October there was an enrollment of 305, but an increase was expected "when the cotton picking season was entirely over." For Southern blacks, economic necessity hindered education.

On November 4, 1893, Whittaker received his formal teaching authorization, the highest available, a Grade 1 certificate, and was well established as the teaching principal of Lincoln school.[7] Considering the probable continuation of his law practice, primarily when school was not in session, and the fact that he had a growing family, he was a very busy man.

His own property transactions were enough to keep him occupied. From 1884 to 1902 Whittaker was involved in fourteen real-estate transactions in Camden and in Sumter. In 1884 he and his mother sold a number of Camden lots fronting on King Street for $240, a substantial sum in those days. In 1886 he, his brother Edward, and his mother legally divided the family property on the Wataree River. In 1887, upon coming to Sumter, he purchased a large lot on the corner of Calhoun and Church streets, where he later built a house. Interestingly, he purchased the land from a former Confederate general, Edwin W. Moise, who was later to be defeated for a House seat by Whittaker's black classmate, George Washington Murray. In later years he bought another piece of land in Sumter County. Several sales were made in 1894, probably as a result of the effects of the economic dislocation caused by the Panic of 1893. Whittaker rebought the property when good times returned, but by 1902 had sold everything and owned no property in South Carolina.[8]

On first coming to Sumter Whittaker lived in a house on Calhoun Street that is still standing. Sometime in the 1890's, however, he built a two-story frame home on the corner of Calhoun and Church streets which has since been razed. He lived in what was then and still is a white neighborhood. Nearby, however, was a cluster of black homes in an area called "Yankee Camp," so named because Union troops had bivouacked there during Reconstruction. Most of his friends were light-skinned blacks like himself, but he played a role of leadership in the entire black community. He and his brother-in-law, Dr. C. W. Birnie, a physician and drugstore owner, were widely respected by blacks and whites alike and were key figures in the city.

Whittaker had other responsibilities too. When his father-in-law and mother-in-law died Whittaker took in the remainder of the six Harrison children, accepting the duty his wife felt as eldest child. They all lived together in the substantial house on Calhoun and Church. Each day Whittaker would walk the three blocks from this house and this family to the Council Street school.

Those who knew him in Sumter remember that his military bearing, a remnant of his West Point days, extended into more than his brisk, straight stature and walk. He was a very strict disciplinarian. A still practicing eighty-year-old black dentist remembers Whittaker being a very quiet teacher but one who would "tear you up in a minute" if necessary. He was well liked and respected by the students for his fairness and justice; he was firm but not overbearing.[9]

259

Whittaker's lot as a black school teacher and administrator was a hard one. In 1890, 64.1 percent of the South Carolina population over ten years old were illiterate. Most of these were black. They were also poor and politically powerless. The 1895 state constitution and the 1896 *Plessy* v. *Ferguson* "separate but equal" Supreme Court decision legalized segregation. This, of course, affected education crucially. The ruling whites were not enthusiastic about the prospect of educating blacks, and though schools were provided they were very poor, even by the meager educational standards of the South Carolina of that day. For the 1899–1900 school year, to cite but one typical year, Sumter County had 115 white teachers for 2,771 white students and only eighty-four black teachers for 6,768 black students; the average annual salary for the white teachers was $104.14, for the black teachers $64.26; the total expended on the white schools was $17,645.74, while the black schools received only $8,001.84.[10]

In 1896 one of Whittaker's teachers at Lincoln School had 110 students in her class. By 1899 overcrowding was so bad that each teacher had to care for two classes at the same time. Since funds for a new building were not forthcoming, split sessions were adopted. Each teacher, Whittaker included, continued conducting two classes, but one class met until 11:30 and the other did not come in until the afternoon. The county superintendent of education reported that "the plan was of great benefit to the pupils of the colored schools, and was extremely satisfactory to patrons and teachers alike."[11]

It is doubtful that it was satisfactory to Whittaker, for it was at this time that he moved from Sumter. He was evidently unhappy about something. He left his wife and children and went temporarily to Washington to work for the Census Bureau. While he was gone, Page Whittaker lived many nights in terror as rocks were thrown through the windows of the Whittaker house. When Whittaker returned, the entire family moved to Orangeburg and Whittaker became associated with the four-year-old "Colored Normal, Industrial, Agricultural and Mechanical College." He had been offered a $400-per-year position as professor of natural chemistry and military science on the first faculty in 1896 but at that time had refused.[12] Circumstances had changed enough during the intervening few years to reverse his earlier decision. He now joined the Orangeburg school's faculty.

Though the Colored Normal, Industrial, Agricultural and Mechanical College of South Carolina was a state institution, the state government allotted money reluctantly. Buildings were few and built of wood. The rooms were lighted with either kerosene or acetylene gas, though electricity could have been used if the state had appropriated the necessary funds. In 1903 the newest building received steam heat, but the rest of the buildings continued to depend on wood-burning stoves. The danger of fire was always present. As new buildings appeared slowly on the campus they were constructed mainly by student labor working for fifty to seventy-five cents a day under the direction of members of the faculty. Furniture in student rooms and administrative buildings was of the most spartan nature.

These were hardly the most favorable conditions for learning. In truth, it must be said that the school was a college in name more than reality. In 1908, for example, there was a total enrollment of 683 students, of whom only fifty-nine were in the college department. The rest were scattered among the Normal School, the so-called "Practice School" (elementary), and the Prep School, or Academy. In keeping with what was considered by whites and blacks to be the basic needs of the black population and in keeping with the newly promulgated philosophy of the powerful black leader Booker T. Washington, courses were almost all vocational. The names of the departments show this most clearly: Iron-working and Wheelwrighting Department, Masonry Department, Dairying and Cheesemaking Department, Agriculture Department, Domestic Economy Department, the Harness-Making Department, and so on. There were also over eighty acres of land under cultivation. This, combined with the construction work, left little time for more purely academic pursuits.[13]

When Whittaker moved to Orangeburg and the college, he stepped into a difficult assignment: secretary of the college and principal of the academy. Both positions involved a great deal of responsibility for the now mature man of forty-two. Throughout Whittaker's tenure the academy remained one of the largest elements of the college, and the success of the entire institution depended in large part on Whittaker. The fact that he was a close friend and university classmate of the president of the college, Thomas E. Miller, and indeed had named his first son after him might have made the task somewhat less difficult.[14]

Little is known of Whittaker's day-to-day life during these years. He lived with his family on the campus and, judging by his later life, probably took an active part in the college's life. Whether he practiced any law in addition to his academic work is doubtful, because sometime during these years he gave up his law practice for good.

The decision to give up law had probably been long in coming, but a single event precipitated it. Whittaker was defending a man accused of stealing a pair of trousers off a clothesline. Though he was able to get him acquitted, Whittaker's sense of morality was assaulted: all during the trial the defendant had been wearing the very trousers he was accused of stealing! After that, Whittaker told his family he could not continue to engage in an occupation which was so obviously contrary to his Christian principles. Instead he concentrated on teaching, a profession he considered more noble and one which he was convinced was the way of salvation for his race.[15]

His salary during these years was far from exorbitant, and he could have used supplementary funds from a legal practice. In 1903, for example, he earned only $650 per year. This sum was exceeded only by the $900 salaries of four other professors and the $1,800 annual pay of President Miller. The salary was hardly enough to make him rich, but apparently he and his family were able to subsist. By 1908 he had become one of the four highest paid teachers in the school, at $900 per year.

Compared to other South Carolina college teachers Whittaker was vastly underpaid. Statistics again show graphically the difference between white and black education in South Carolina. In 1908, with an enrollment of 683 students, the total income of the Orangeburg school was $34,550.92, and top professors were paid $900. At the South Carolina College for whites in Columbia, there were 280 students, an income of $69,000, with professors paid $2,000. Instructors received $900. At the white vocational school, Clemson, there were 690 students and the income was $201,477.75.[16]

Whittaker remained in Orangeburg for eight years. In 1908, however, he and his wife made a decision—they left the state college and indeed the state. Unlike most blacks who were to migrate in increasing numbers in the next decade, the Whittakers did not move north, nor did they relocate for economic or racial reasons. They moved west to Oklahoma City, for purely personal considerations. Their son John had a stomach condition and asthma, and it was felt that a higher, drier climate would benefit him.[17]

In 1908 Oklahoma was a newly settled land. It had had a turbulent history as an Indian territory and then as a territory opened to white settlers; it had finally entered the Union in 1907. It was a state where Indians as well as whites had owned black slaves, and it had a substantial black population on statehood day, with more all-black towns than any other state. In 1900 there had been 55,684 blacks in the state, but by 1910 this number had jumped almost two and a half times to 137,612. Still, blacks represented only about 8 percent of the total population.

Like the whites who also flocked into Oklahoma during these years, blacks came for a fresh start in a newly opened area. They had, however, the added incentive of trying to escape the increased segregation and discrimination they were experiencing in the older states of the Union. The newest state might offer hope of a better life.

Unfortunately, anti-black discrimination existed in Oklahoma too. The state had a definite Southern tinge and reflected the Southern attitudes about race. One of the initial acts of the first state legislature, in fact, was to pass a Jim Crow law. Separate train coaches and railroad waiting rooms for blacks and whites were required. Segregation was present in all walks of life, in the law, in jobs, in housing, and in the general attitude of the white population. A 1901 statute had established a separate school system for blacks, and the state constitution accepted this principle. This document, in Section 88 of Article XIII, also reserved the words "colored" or "Negro" for persons of African descent, while the term "white race" was to be applied to everyone else. This meant that Indians, Mexicans, and other racial stocks were legally, at least, considered white.[18] In practice, however, these groups were also discriminated against. The Whittakers were to experience the anti-black prejudice over and over. They had moved to no racial paradise.

After they had lived in Oklahoma City for some time the Whittakers experienced this bias in its most violent form. They purchased a house on South Klein Street in what was then a white neighborhood—a small six-room brown cottage situated on a large wooded lot, part of a still blooming orchard, a house well suited to their needs. A delegation of whites warned them not to move in. The usually mild-mannered Whittaker stood on his rights, quietly but firmly telling the delegation that he and his family had a right to live in the house and that they were determined to do so. He even announced the day and the hour of the move.

On moving day Whittaker, his sons, and several friends

264

were armed with rifles and shotguns as they carried furniture and belongings into the house. No confrontation occurred. It was not until nightfall that trouble began. That
first evening and for some time afterward men on
horseback rode by and fired into the house. The family was
forced to sleep on the floor to avoid the nightly hail of
bullets. True to his character and beliefs, Whittaker demanded legal redress, but city officials did nothing. He and
his family had to face the nightly visitors alone.

Help arrived from an unexpected source. A local newspaper reporter came to interview the family. When he was
shown into the house, he immediately noticed a large
punchbowl on the table filled with ammunition. He returned to his paper, wrote his story, and it was headlined
"Negroes Have Arsenal." From that day on the nocturnal
shootings stopped. Eventually the Whittakers were accepted, made friends, and suffered few racial slights in their
neighborhood.

But slights continued everywhere else. Whittaker was
even insulted on the steps of his own school. He ordered
the two offending white men away, called the police on
them, but never received any satisfaction. Whittaker's son
John was particularly angered over the discrimination he
met after returning from fighting "to make the world safe
for democracy" overseas. He particularly resented not being able to take his wife and daughter to the public park.
Signs warned: "No Dogs Allowed. Whites Only."[19]

But there was opportunity in Oklahoma for blacks, especially for those with the experience Whittaker possessed.
The black and white population had grown at such a rapid
rate in the first decade of the twentieth century that there
was a pressing need for new schools, new teachers, new
administrators. A man of Whittaker's background was a
valuable addition to the community.

On arriving, Whittaker became a teacher at all-black
Douglass High School. He served as assistant principal and
in 1922–1923 became principal. In addition to his adminis-

trative duties he taught chemistry. He was well liked by his colleagues and students, one of whom later became famous —Ralph Ellison, novelist and essayist. Though his students knew of his West Point stint and knew he had had problems because of his race, they knew little else. He never talked about his experiences.

A former student remembers him particularly at recess. Standing rigidly straight as he always did, Whittaker would ring the triangle that was used to call students to attention. Anyone not responding would be quickly brought to task by a stern "Statue, brother!" The culprit would quickly stand still.[20]

As was the case in South Carolina, the black schools in Oklahoma were plagued with financial difficulties. Black teachers were lower paid, buildings were worse, and conditions generally poorer than in the white schools. In 1914–1915, for example, per-capita expenditure for white children in Oklahoma was $14.33 per child, while for black children it was $11.16. Bad as this was, it was at least better than Whittaker's home state. South Carolina at this time spent $10.70 per white child and only $1.09 per black child. Whittaker sent several students from Douglass High School to the black college at Orangeburg, South Carolina, including one who is now an associate professor of music there. And the school did not forget him. At the May 1912 commencement they awarded him a Master of Arts degree for his "meritorious attainments." During the twenty-fifth anniversary celebration of the college he was the main speaker and was awarded a Doctor of Laws degree. That same day the pioneer black educator, Mary Bethune, was awarded a Master of Arts.[21]

Most of the time Whittaker's life followed a regularized pattern. His family was very close, their lives governed most by the deep religion of the father and the meticulous Victorian standards of the mother. Every morning before breakfast Whittaker would gather his family around the kitchen table, where they would all kneel down and he would lead them in extended prayer. He would ask God's blessings on each one individually; the ritual usually lasted at least ten minutes. At night just before bedtime the prayer would be repeated. During the day he would often be seen praying. He belonged to an African Methodist Episcopal (A.M.E.) church and taught Sunday school each week. He was a popular instructor because he always brought nickels and jelly beans for the students. He also taught religion by his daily example. A typical example demonstrates just how religious he was. When Whittaker saw his first grandchild he said nothing but fell to his knees and thanked God for his goodness.

In keeping with his religious faith, Whittaker was a man of apparently infinite patience. His granddaughter remembers him sitting for long periods of time while she combed and recombed his silky long hair. He would take her on walks, and she never remembers him becoming even mildly upset with her childish wanderings. She remembers one particular excursion to Belle Isle Park in Detroit during one of his summer visits. He was a perfect companion but suddenly stopped and wrote something in the little notebook he always kept with him. It was not until after he had died that she saw the notebook and found what he had written there. In tones reminiscent of his jottings in his West Point Bible, he had written of the beauty of the park and the joy of bringing happiness to a young child.

Yet he did have a temper, though it was shown only on rare occasions. One summer while visiting Detroit he heard his son John discipline his granddaughter, Cecil, with a slap. The slightly built silver-haired old man became livid. He announced that he and his wife would not remain in a house where such activity was practiced, got into an argument with his much taller son over child rearing, and proceeded to pack his suitcase. It took him a long time to cool off.

The next year just before the annual visit John took his two children, Cecil and Peter, aside to try to make sure

267

there would be no repetition of the incident. He told them they had best be on good behavior while their grandparents were there. He promised them that if they misbehaved they would be spanked—grandfather or no grandfather. He would pretend he was taking the culprit for ice cream, he said, but would instead head for the nearest alley and administer the punishment there away from grandfather's protecting anger. As a result, throughout the visit, whenever the subject of ice cream came up, the two children were emphatically negative. Whittaker kept wondering out loud how any child could dislike ice cream but never learned the answer.

Whittaker never showed any bitterness toward his West Point treatment and never complained about his life. He discussed politics with his sons only as a training exercise. He would take either side of an issue and force them to stand up to his legally acquired inquisitorial drilling. He voted but took no part in politics. His wife, Page, was much more bitter about her husband's West Point experiences but never discussed them in front of him. She had a scrapbook of clippings of the trials, collected by Whittaker's mother, but, at Whittaker's insistence, burned them. He told her he did not want to keep anything that would embitter his sons and sour their lives.

Twelve years his junior, Page Whittaker always referred to her husband as "Mr. Whittaker" and manifested many of the other trappings of the Victorianism she had learned as a child. As a temperance-union member she was opposed to all drinking, smoking, and card playing. Before her marriage she went to parties but refused to dance because she considered it too intimate. Whittaker himself would dance during their courting days, but he never smoked, drank, or played cards. He would sometimes give her a kiss in front of the family, and she would invariably insist that public kissing was not proper. She often told her granddaughter that her idea of a good time was attending a dance to talk to the ladies and look at the dresses. In Sumter she said she had enjoyed "pink teas." Ladies would gather wearing pink dresses, in a sitting room decorated in pink, to drink pink tea and eat pink cakes. She never got used to the idea that her granddaughter preferred to play tennis rather than sit, embroider, or sew. She considered tennis shorts for girls completely unladylike.

Her entire life was centered on Whittaker. Because of his stomach problems, culminating in an ulcer, she had to be careful of what she cooked. She boiled a chicken before she fried it and fixed plain dishes. He would sometimes make a meal out of buttermilk and thinly sliced corn bread but also enjoyed her favorite, pound cake, and the mashed-potato salad, fruit cake, banana and sweet potato pies she liked to make. She gave him the freedom to take the walks he so enjoyed and the reading he was always doing. She always tied his tie for him (even at home he was never without a jacket and tie). She kept a meticulously clean house, scrubbing pine floors on her hands and knees until they gleamed.

The Whittakers had two sons, Miller and John. Though they knew about the West Point incident, they rarely discussed it with their father. One of the few times it was mentioned was when they returned from World War I both wearing officer's bars. John told his father, "They cheated you out of your commission; now the family has three."[22] Characteristically, Whittaker changed the subject.

Miller received a Bachelor of Science degree in architecture from Kansas State Agricultural College and joined the faculty of the Orangeburg school in 1913. He rose to become the director and later dean of the Mechanical Drawing Department and supervised the construction of many of the college's buildings. For a long time he was the only certified black architect in the state. He served as second lieutenant with the 368th Infantry, 92nd Division in World War I. In 1932 he became president of the state college and held that office until his death. His 1949 funeral at the relatively young age of fifty-seven brought out local city officials, presidents from black colleges all over the South, members of the Board of Trustees, and even the Governor of South Carolina, J. Strom Thurmond.

Whittaker's other son, John, also became a success in life. He studied engineering at the University of Kansas, but left to volunteer for World War I before he received his degree; he served as captain in the 317th Ammunition Transportation Battalion, was commandant of military science at the state college, and later worked with the Detroit and Michigan Highway Departments. He migrated to Michigan in answer to Henry Ford's five-dollar-a-day offer to workers after he had become disconcerted over criticism of his stiff disciplinary practices as college commandant and after he had been slashed by a student guilty of stealing. He worked for Ford and Dodge for about ten years and later was part of the first black surveying crew in state employ. He died in 1946. A son, Peter, served as a flier in World War II, became a lawyer and until his death was dean of the law department at the state college in Orangeburg. A daughter, Cecil, was for a time co-publisher of a black newspaper, the Detroit *Tribune*, and is today a schoolteacher in Detroit. John's four grandchildren include a Harvard Law graduate who is an army officer, a medical student, a runner-up in a recent Miss Michigan contest, and a Fisk University student. John's wife, Marian, is today a retired postal and office worker.[23]

Whittaker and his wife remained in Oklahoma after their sons struck out on their own. Whittaker continued teaching and administering at Douglass High School during this period, helped organize the High School Principals' Association of Oklahoma and was for a long time its treasurer. In 1925, at sixty-seven, at a time when most men are thinking of retirement, he pulled up his stakes, left his teaching position, and returned to South Carolina. He wife had never grown to like Oklahoma, considering it uncivilized compared to the South. Whittaker again took up his position as principal of the academy of the Colored Normal,

Industrial, Agricultural and Mechanical College of South Carolina. Interestingly, he maintained ownership of the South Klein Street house in Oklahoma City.[24]

In many ways the institution J. C. Whittaker returned to in 1925 had remained the same in the eighteen years he had been in Oklahoma. The financial problems were still present, and, though the campus had grown, the budget was still tight. Year after year, despite the college president's yearly plea to the state, the school did not receive enough funds to put screens on all the doors and windows as required by state law. Classrooms were still inadequate, the academy, or high school, continued to be larger than the college division, there continued to be a shortage in housing for the faculty, and necessities like modern refrigeration were missing.

Yet much had changed. The curriculum had been streamlined and the institution began to put more and more emphasis on the college department. The requirements for students and faculty were becoming stricter. A faculty member had gained an advanced degree from Harvard and others had received scholarships to Columbia and Cornell. South Carolina A and M was a better school in 1925 than it had been in 1908.

Upon his return, Whittaker became professor of psychology and education. His main task, however, was the supervision of the academy. As principal he helped streamline its curriculum, raised standards, and generally strengthened it despite inadequate funds and facilities.[25]

Whittaker had changed but little himself. His hair had grown silvery white in Oklahoma, but he still walked as erectly as ever and was as stern and as religious as he had ever been. Though he was principal, Whittaker taught a mathematics class as well. He would open each class by quietly saying, "Rise, please" and then would read a verse from the Bible, say a simple prayer or conduct some similar short meditation. Students found this praying in class rather unusual, but all complied out of respect for him. When a young lady entered the classroom, Whittaker would remind the male students of their manners and have one of them offer her a seat.

He had lost none of his reserve. The only crack in his military bearing was his habit of whistling and humming hymns to himself as he briskly walked on the campus. He also opened his home to students who flocked in to listen to one of the few radios on the campus, constructed by mechanically talented son John. Though he remained a strict disciplinarian, he never raised his voice. If he caught a student in an infraction of the college rules, he would softly say, "I'm sorry but you'll have to do demerits." As a member of the Discipline Committee, he showed the lawyer's training none of the students knew he had. During hearings he would smile courteously and ask questions that would inevitably get at the truth. The "old man" or "old J.C.," as he was known to the students, was not easily fooled.

Students knew Whittaker had had problems at West Point because of his race, but he never talked about them. Once during an assembly a student confronted the gray-haired principal and asked him about that part of his life. As always, Whittaker showed little emotion and quietly evaded the question. He said he did not want to discuss the matter and only hoped the day would come when all Americans could equally share the fruits of the nation.[26]

Beneath the calm exterior, however, there must have been turmoil. Early in his life Whittaker developed a gastric ulcer. He had to be careful of his food intake for much of his adult life, but he never complained about it. He was always thin, never particularly strong but rarely sick. On January 10, 1931, however, the situation changed rapidly. He rose during the night, collapsed, and began to hemorrhage. Four days later, less than a week from the fiftieth anniversary of the beginning of his court-martial, he was dead.

Like his entrance into the world as a slave some seventy-two years previously, Whittaker's death caused little real sensation. The local newspaper did not include his name in its listing of recently deceased persons, although it printed an obituary submitted by the college. It listed a brief history of his life, though it made no mention of his trials and their national prominence. He was buried in a black-only cemetery in a dilapidated section of Orangeburg, where he was later joined by his wife, two sons, and grandson. His gravestone is simple: "Father/J.C. Whittaker/1859–1931." No one looking at it or the cemetery where it today still stands would ever guess that the man buried there had ever been a national celebrity. A man who had lived a truly remarkable life had returned to the obscurity from which he had come.

During his funeral, members of his family saw what they considered was a fitting climax to his life. When the casket was being closed in the college auditorium, a shaft of light suddenly broke through the dark day and shone on it. In the cemetery another streak of light illuminated the casket as his body was being lowered to his final resting place. At the same time a mockingbird broke out into song.[27]

CONCLUSION

JOHNSON Chesnut Whittaker's life was never the same after his arrival at the United States Military Academy in 1876. His experiences there both before and after April 6, 1880, had much to do with determining the direction of his life.

One can imagine the reaction of the young man on first entering the Academy. Born into slavery, educated in a university where whites dropped out rather than attend classes with blacks like him, told all his life that he was inferior, he suddenly found himself in a school that contained only one other member of his race. Not only was he far from home for the first time and afflicted with the usual uncertainties of such an experience, but he was met with cold hostility by all those around him. He was clearly shown he was not wanted.

His very presence was a source of friction. He and other black cadets were disliked not only because of their race but also because they were viewed as the personification of change that an uncertain Military Academy feared. As West Point saw it, Whittaker was a member of a lower order of man. Still, he was the recipient of special favors. His only reason for being there was the political situation in the country.

West Pointers were convinced Whittaker had committed the attack on himself to aid the Academy's enemies and to gain revenge for cadet ostracism. The possibility of anyone else committing the act, especially other cadets, was never seriously considered despite the recent memory of the successful New Year's Eve escapade. West Point's racial prejudice and its concern for itself precluded such a consideration. The Academy acted from bias and fear.

General Schofield showed this attitude most clearly. A talented, successful man of no small intellect, Schofield, when confronted with Whittaker, was notably myopic. He saw only what fit his preconceived notion and acted accordingly. At the same time, he was convinced his actions were just; in fact he saw himself as Whittaker's patron. He sincerely believed that he was not prejudiced and consequently saw criticism of his actions as conspiratorially inspired. Like so many before and after him, prejudice had dulled his sensibilities and obscured the truth.

Johnson C. Whittaker, then, was doomed from the start of his Academy career. His experiences at West Point were full of contradictions. He was told he had all the rights anyone else had, but then was discriminated against because of his background and lack of gentility. He was told that acceptance into polite society required education and gentlemanly refinements and then was prevented from gaining them by constant reminders of his inferiority. When he tried to abide by the rules he was told he was seeking special favor because of his color. When he tried to ignore his ostracism by taking comfort in his Bible and his God, he was called a religious fanatic. Though he was considered inferior on all counts, superhuman acts were expected of him. When he reacted in a human way, this was viewed as proof of his inferiority.

Did Whittaker really commit the nighttime attack himself and then try to shift blame onto West Pointers? There is no conclusive proof of Whittaker's guilt. The facts are circumstantial and his life before and after was blameless —in fact, in many ways exemplary. He might have suffered a momentary aberration, but this seems doubtful. The facts of the case do not justify a guilty verdict, and his entire life makes his guilt improbable.

Perhaps the facts themselves are not as significant as their handling during the trials. There was no real attempt to gather all possible information. The room was cleaned without a prior thorough search. The physical examination by the doctors was cursory, and Colonel Lazelle's official investigation was brief and incomplete. Witness also the reasoning of various people for suspecting Whittaker: Schofield became suspicious because the black cadet had unhesitatingly asked for a court of inquiry. Burnett was convinced of his culpability because of the state of his eyes on being revived. Lazelle was disturbed by the ridges in his hair. Dr. Alexander was known as a stern judge of gold-brickers and suspicious of all cadet illnesses. He immediately thought Whittaker was faking but did not bother to examine him closely enough to make sure. Cadet Dickenson settled on Whittaker because he was sure no one else could have committed the assault.

The nation's handling of the case is also significant. President Rutherford B. Hayes saw the Whittaker imbroglio as complicating his nation-mending tasks, but he was not sufficiently aroused by it to keep fully abreast of its hearings. The failure of a friend's son at West Point was as important to him as the nationally significant Whittaker case. At the same time, however, Whittaker's problem was fraught with enough political danger to cause presidential intervention and to force a change in superintendents. To ameliorate criticism, Schofield was replaced by O. O. Howard, a man with a pro-black reputation. The court-martial was convened for the same reason.

Congress saw the case as both an opportunity and an embarrassment. Whittaker's misfortune gave anti-West Point politicians a temporary issue, but the guilty decision robbed them of it before it could be effectively utilized. In any case, staunch supporters of Negro rights were few and far between in Congress, and, besides, it was hard to wave the bloody shirt over an incident that had happened in the North. The Whittaker case happened at the wrong time and in the wrong place as far as Congress was concerned. One gets the impression that Congressman Aiken's squashing of an investigation was, despite outward protestations, not unhappily received. Certainly little was done to circumvent it.

Public opinion generally viewed the case as little more than a subject for curiosity. Some people became concerned, but most simply watched in fascination. Most Americans, though they might have lamented the lack of fair play at West Point, cared very little for the black cadet. The guilty verdicts were unquestioningly accepted, and by the time President Arthur had reversed the decision the case had long since disappeared from the public eye and no one much cared.

Most newspapers supported the black cadet, but their accounts of the incident contained an undercurrent of paternalism and racism. A few were convinced of his guilt and happy at his predicament. The onetime liberal *Nation* magazine saw in the case a vindication of the South's innocence of charges of anti-black violence. It warned the country not to continue to believe a race which was naturally inclined to lie now that it had seen a black man found out in a lie. The country, long tired of the racial issue, needed no prompting. The next years were to see an increase in anti-black violence and discrimination with little consequent opposition. There were more important problems than black rights, the populace and the press felt. The Whittaker case shows graphically this lack of concern.

The Whittaker trials, then, were important for more reasons than simply to determine the guilt or innocence of a single cadet. They showed in sharp focus the life of the black American. The case of Johnson C. Whittaker is a tale of Gilded Age America's attitude toward and treatment of its newly enfranchised black citizens.

Whittaker's entire life indicates clearly that this plight was not limited to the courtroom nor to one age. He lived during several historical periods when to be black was to have hope and little else. In some ways Whittaker was more fortunate than many of his fellow blacks and, after his trials, did not suffer as acutely as they did the prejudice abroad in the land. At a time long before the saying "black is beautiful" began to have any true meaning, his lightness of skin opened doors to him closed to darker men. He was a man of education and property when such advantages were little known in the black community. He saw his sons become successful when the usual fate for black youth was frustration and failure. He was in many ways not the usual black man.

Yet he was more like his black brothers than different from them. Though so light he could have passed as white, he had an innate sense of pride in his race and its potential and never denied his ancestry. Consequently he suffered discrimination and injustice with all the rest. Perhaps he suffered it more. As a person of talent and ambition, he internally chafed because of the racial restrictions under which he lived. Outwardly he was a model of calmness, but his ulcer shows a battle must have been raging inside. His religion seemed to keep him going, and he suffered in silence.

Disappointed and hurt by his experiences with white society at West Point and during the trials, he withdrew among his own people. He expressed no desire for social equality—i.e., personal contact with whites—yet was firm in his determination to receive what was his just due. A believer in the redemptive powers of education, he was confident in the future solution of the racial issue. His confidence seems most obvious in his insistence that nothing be done to sour his sons and prevent their success.

He was no revolutionary. He dealt with whites both in the law and in education but made no attempts to overthrow, even by word, the oppressive system holding down his people. It was not in his character to do so; he had seen the futility of trying during his trial experiences, and there was little precedent to spur him on. In his time the black leader of most influence was Booker T. Washington, and he too opposed direct action in favor of vocational education and patience. The Jim Crow period of the late nineteenth century produced no flaming black revolutionaries. Blacks had to fight simply to survive. By the time W. E. B. DuBois and the NAACP began to speak of more direct protest, Whittaker was already at a point in his life when a radical change in attitude would have been almost impossible to accomplish.

To his death he personified the typical black leader of the period: conservative, religiously oriented, a believer in vocational education as the hope of the black race, and an exponent of middle-class values. He saw little prospect for immediate change but was sure better days were coming. For what he felt was his right he was willing to stand; for other things which had never been his he did not dispute. It was not for him to lead a revolution.

Johnson Chesnut Whittaker's life clearly shows the failure of American democracy to its black citizens. In Whittaker's life can be seen the stepping stones used by other Americans to improve their status. He was a law-abiding, God-fearing person, a devoted husband and father, educated, reserved, hard-working, and financially secure. He was neither radical nor an exponent of immediate change. All he asked for was what was due him and demanded only what was his absolute right.

J. C. Whittaker was all that white America has always portrayed as a model to blacks. Fulfill these requirements, the black man has consistently been told, and all will be open to you. This was also what Booker T. Washington, whom Whittaker must certainly have read, emphasized. Johnson C. Whittaker did this; he was a model citizen. He was discriminated against anyway. Education, economics, and middle-class values were not tickets to full equality for him. His race determined his place in society. Until this fact is realized, until the true motivations for discrimination are faced, black people like Whittaker will continue to be disappointed and the nation will continue to be the loser thereby. The life of this one black man shows in clear relief the true face of prejudice and puts to lie the theory that education and economics are guarantees of equality.

NOTES

CHAPTER 1

1. The Proceedings of the General Court Martial of Johnson C. Whittaker, United States Military Academy, Records of the Judge Advocate General (Army), National Archives Record Group 153, QQ 2774, Part XV, pp. 1229–32; John Bratt Diary, April 6, 1880, United States Military Academy, Special Collections.

2. C. Vann Woodward, *The Strange Career of Jim Crow* (New York, 1955).

3. Rayford Logan, *The Betrayal of the Negro from Rutherford B. Hayes to Woodrow Wilson* (New York, 1965).

4. Richard Hofstadter, *Social Darwinism in American Thought* (Philadelphia, 1944).

5. Stanley Hirshon, *Farewell to the Bloody Shirt: Northern Republicans and the Southern Negro* (Bloomington, 1962), pp. 25, 251–55;

Vincent P. DeSantis, *Republicans Face the Southern Question* (New York, 1969), pp. 34, 220–21. Both these excellent works document the black man's plight graphically.

6. William T. Sherman Papers, Library of Congress; Sherman Family Papers, University of Notre Dame Archives; William T. Sherman Papers, Ohio Historical Society. There are countless examples in the above.

7. Russell Weigley, *History of the United States Army* (New York, 1967), pp. 270–71.

8. W. Scott Dillard, "The United States Military Academy, 1865–1900: The Uncertain Years," manuscript of Ph. D. dissertation soon to be presented to the University of Washington. (Major Dillard was gracious enough to permit this author to read a draft of this excellent dissertation.) Chapter III, particularly pp. 36, 38, 45. Chapter VI discusses the reform attempts.

9. John A. Logan, *The Volunteer Soldier of America* (Chicago, 1887), pp. 327–460.

10. Dillard, *op. cit.*, Chapter VI, pp. 55n, 64–65, 1.

11. Henry O. Flipper, *The Colored Cadet at West Point* (New York, 1969), p. 73. Hereafter cited as Flipper, *Colored Cadet.*

12. Cadet Physical Examinations, Record Group 94, National Archives; Flipper, *Colored Cadet*, p. 24.

13. *Ibid.*, p. 23.

14. Thomas J. Fleming, *The Men and Times of the United States Military Academy* (New York, 1969), p. 234. Hereafter cited as Fleming, *Military Academy; Regulations for the U.S. Military Academy at West Point, New York* (Washington, 1877), pp. 20–21, 24–28.

15. See, for example, *Official Army Register for January 1880* (Washington, 1880), pp. 259–61.

16. John L. Chamberlain, "Cadet Reminiscences," three-page typewritten manuscript, United States Military Academy, Special Collections. Hereafter cited as Chamberlain, "Cadet Reminiscences." Flipper, *Colored Cadet*, pp. 32–34; see also Chapter 3 of the present work.

17. Stephen Ambrose, *Duty, Honor, Country, A History of West Point* (Baltimore, 1966), p. 222. Hereafter cited as Ambrose, *West Point.* Bernard T. McManus, "Cadet Life at West Point," *Godey's Magazine* (January 1895), pp. 26–35. The latter is a favorable account of life at West Point which, nonetheless, shows its severity.

18. Chamberlain, "Cadet Reminiscences"; see also Chapter 5 of the present work.

19. Ambrose, *West Point*, p. 222; John M. Schofield, *Forty Six Years in the Army* (New York, 1897) pp. 7–8.

20. J. B. and Farnham Bishop, *Goethals: Genius of the Panama Canal* (New York, 1930), pp. 38–51; Chamberlain, "Cadet Reminiscences"; John Bratt Diary, January 1, 2, 1880, United States Military Academy, Special Collections; General Order # 1, January 2, 1880, West Point Order Book, United States Military Academy Archives.

21. Ambrose, *West Point*, pp. 222, 224–26; Fleming, *Military Academy*, p. 246.

22. Flipper, *Colored Cadet*, pp. 61, 104; Ambrose, *Military Academy*, pp. 229–30; *Annual Report of the Visitors of the United States Military Academy Made to the Secretary of War, 1881* (Washington, 1881), p. 5, Record Group 94, National Archives.

23. O. O. Howard, *Autobiography* (New York, 1907), Vol. I, pp. 48–54; Stephen Ambrose, *Upton and the Army* (Baton Rouge, 1964), p. 12.

24. Fleming, *Military Academy*, pp. 238–39.

25. *Ibid.*, pp. 213–14; Thomas Phillips, "The Black Regulars: Negro Soldiers in the United States Army, 1866–1891," Ph. D. dissertation, University of Wisconsin, 1970, pp. 1124–25.

26. Sidney Forman, *West Point: A History of the United States Military Academy* (New York, 1950), pp. 141–42.

27. Peter S. Michie, "Caste at West Point," *North American Review*, CXXX (June 1880), pp. 604–13.

28. George L. Andrews, "West Point and the Colored Cadets," *International Review*, IX (November 1880), pp. 477–89.

29. *Ibid.*, p. 479; Ambrose, *West Point*, p. 232; Fleming, *Military Academy*, pp. 214–20; Ezra J. Warner, "A Black Man in the Long Gray Line," *American History Illustrated*, IV (January 1970), p. 33; William L. Katz (ed.), *Eyewitness, The Negro in American History* (New York, 1967), pp. 351–52; Phillips, *op. cit.*, p. 1123. Chapter XIII of this dissertation discusses Smith in some detail; William P. Vaughn, "West Point and the First Negro Cadet," *Military Affairs* (October 1971), pp. 100–102.

30. Ambrose, *West Point*, pp. 232–33; Fleming, *Military Academy*, pp. 220–25.

31. Flipper, *Colored Cadet*, pp. 106–07, 250, 221–22, 214–15, 207–08, 232–33, 121, 138–39, 175, 256.

CHAPTER 2

1. Mulberry was the main residence of the Chesnuts. Other of their plantations around Camden were Sandy Hill, Sarsfield, Cool Spring, Knight's Hill, and the Hermitage. Since Mulberry was the plantation where they spent most of their time, all references in this chapter will be to it.

2. Johnson C. Whittaker Bible, Exhibit Box, The Proceedings of the General Court Martial of Johnson C. Whittaker, United States Military Academy, Records of the Judge Advocate General (Army), Record Group 153, QQ 2774, National Archives. Hereafter cited as CM Records. In her diary, Mary B. Chesnut calls the twins John and Jeems and seems to imply they were born in 1861. She had spent only about a month in Camden between 1858 and 1861 and this may explain the confusion. Mary B. Chesnut, *Diary from Dixie*, edited by Ben Ames Williams (Boston, 1905), April 20, 1861, p. 44. Hereafter cited as Chesnut, *Diary*. The Manuscript Division of the South Caroliana Library, University of South Carolina, has a copy of a term paper and an annotated copy of the published Chesnut manuscript diary. The author compared the original diary with the published one and found some significant differences. The material used in this chapter was seen to be accurate as published. Louis Pettus "Mrs. Chesnut's Diary—A Reappraisal," unpublished History 287 term paper, University of South Carolina.

3. T. J. Kirkland and R. M. Kennedy, *Historic Camden, Part Two: Nineteenth Century* (Columbia, South Carolina, 1926), chronicles life in Camden though it concentrates on the early nineteenth century and is sketchy.

4. Chesnut, *Diary*, pp. 24, 43–44, 162; Johnson C. Whittaker later said his father left his mother three days after he was born. Buffalo *Courier*, June 1, 1882; Judge of Probate Court Records, Kershaw County, South Carolina, contain the records concerning James Whitaker's 1883 will, which show Maria and her son Edward as administrators of a $233.13 estate. The 1880 census

listed a fifty-six-year-old mulatto named James Whitaker as single and living in nearby Wataree Township, Kershaw County. *1880 Census*, Kershaw County, South Carolina, p. 18, microfilm, National Archives.

5. Chesnut, *Diary*, pp. 433, 465.

6. *Ibid.*, p. 181.

7. Esther S. (Reynolds) Davis, *Memories of Mulberry* (Brooklyn, 1913), pp. 2–15.

8. Chesnut, *Diary*, pp. 21–22, 38, 64, 139, 140, 158, 433.

9. *Ibid.*, pp. 158, 203–04, 368.

10. *Ibid.*, pp. 159, 410.

11. Mary Chesnut said that James Whitaker was "as good as white but not quite." *Ibid.*, p. 64. The two best studies of slave life are Kenneth Stampp, *The Peculiar Institution* . . . (New York, 1956), and Stanley Elkins, *Slavery* . . . (New York, 1959); Maria Whitaker always simply placed her mark on documents she had to sign. See, for example, records concerning James Whitaker's will cited in Note 4.

12. Chesnut, *Diary*, pp. 148–49, 170–71.

13. *Ibid.*, pp. 528–29.

14. *Ibid.*; Joel Williamson, *After Slavery: The Negro in South Carolina During Reconstruction 1861–1877* (Chapel Hill, 1965), p. 24. Hereafter cited as Williamson, *After Slavery*. For accounts of slaves in the Confederacy, see Bell I. Wiley, *Southern Negroes 1861–1865* (New York, 1938), and Charles E. Cauthen, *South Carolina Goes to War* (Chapel Hill, 1950). Chapter XIII of the latter book discusses the legal status of slaves during the war.

15. George B. Tindall, *South Carolina Negroes, 1877–1900* (Columbia, 1952); C. Vann Woodward, *The Strange Career of Jim Crow* (New York, 1955); Williamson, *After Slavery;* William J. Cooper, Jr., *The Conservative Regime, South Carolina 1877–1900* (Baltimore, 1968); Cooper, p. 111, Note 87, is a brief discussion of the differences in the above interpretations.

16. Williamson, *After Slavery*, pp. 245, 298, 300–01, 314–16.

17. Deposition of Joseph Jenkins, Exhibit Box, CM Records; Deposition of Robert M. Kennedy, The Proceedings of the Court of Inquiry in the case of Johnson C. Whittaker, United States Military Academy, Records of the Judge Advocate General (Army), Record Group 153, QQ 1858, National Archives, Part XI, p. 2975; hereafter cited as C of I Records. Title Book DD, pp.

404–05, Clerk's Office, Kershaw County, South Carolina; DeKalb Street is a main thoroughfare in Camden today; see, for example, Title Book, CC, p. 131, Clerk's Office, Kershaw County, South Carolina.

18. Johnson C. Whittaker Bible, Exhibit Box, CM Records; Interview with Whittaker's daughter-in-law, Marian Horton and his granddaughter Cecil Whittaker McFadden, Detroit, Michigan, 7 August 1971. According to the remembrances of the two Whittaker relatives, James Whitaker was a tailor who purchased his own freedom by doing extra work long into the night. Doing such close work by candlelight brought on blindness in later life.

19. Deposition of Angelina Ball, C of I Records, Part XI, pp. 2879–80.

20. Deposition of Monroe Boykin, *ibid.*, Part XI, pp. 2971–72. There is a public monument to Reverend Boykin in Camden today. Deposition of Edward M. Pinkney, *ibid.*, Part XI, pp. 2987–88, testimony, CM Records, Part XLV, pp. 4505–25.

21. Daniel W. Hollis, *University of South Carolina*, 2 Vols., Vol. II, *College to University* (Columbia, South Carolina, 1956), Chapter IV, pp. 61–79. Hereafter cited as Hollis, *U of SC;* Williamson, *After Slavery*, p. 232–33; A very hostile account is contained in Edwin L. Green, *A History of the University of South Carolina* (Columbia, 1916), pp. 410–15; Faculty Minutes Book, October 5, 1874, folio 49–50, Manuscript Division, South Caroliana Library, University of South Carolina; Williamson, *After Slavery*, p. 233.

22. Depositions of Fisk Brewer, Henry J. Fox, A. W. Cummings, B. B. Babbitt, Exhibit Box, CM Records; Cummings supplied the grades.

23. Tindall, *South Carolina Negroes*, pp. 57–67, 150, 204, 218; Hollis, *U of SC*, 76; Reverend G. A. Townsend completed his course at the university in 1876. According to Professor E. Horace Fitchett's article, "The Influence of Claflin College on Negro Family Life," *Journal of Negro History* XXIX (October 1944), p. 431n, the following occurred. "In 1936 when a gold headed cane was promised by the Alumni Association to the oldest living alumnus of the University, Rev. Townsend turned out to be the person deserving the honor. However, when his racial identity was revealed the honor was withheld."

24. Richard T. Greener testimony, CM Records, Vol. LXII, p. 6050.

25. S. L. Hoge to Secretary of War, May 26, 1876, J. C. Whittaker to Secretary of War, June 2, 1876, Johnson C. Whittaker Acceptance Papers, 395–1876, Record Group 94, National Archives; Henry O. Flipper, *The Colored Cadet at West Point* (New York, 1969), p. 165. Hereafter cited as Flipper, *Colored Cadet;* J. C. Whittaker physical examination report, Record Group 94, National Archives; Special Order No. 153, August 31, 1876, Post Orders, United States Military Academy, No. 9, July 1, 1875–July 3, 1880, pp. 170–71, United States Military Academy Archives. Hereafter cited as Post Orders, USMAA.

26. Flipper, *Colored Cadet,* p. 165.

27. Register of Delinquencies 1875–1880, United States Military Academy, pp. 349, 432, 588, USMAA; S.O. 228, December 22, 1876, Post Orders, p. 233, USMAA.

28. For example, S.O. 178, October 7, 1876, pp. 196–97, S.O. 54, March 24, 1877, pp. 264–65, Post Orders, USMAA.

29. W. Scott Dillard, "The United States Military Academy, 1865–1900: The Uncertain Years," Ph.D. dissertation soon to be presented to the University of Washington, p. 8–24; Thomas Phillips, "The Black Regulars: Negro Soldiers in the United States Army, 1866–1891," Ph.D. dissertation, University of Wisconsin, 1970, pp. 1175–76; Flipper, *Colored Cadet,* pp. 281–82.

30. John M. Schofield to the Adjutant General, January 15, 1879, copy, appendix, C of I Records; *Annual Report of the Board of Visitors of the United States Military Academy for the Year 1879* (Washington, 1880), p. 16.

31. Consolidated Marks from Weekly Class Reports from September 1st to December 31st, 1879, January 1st, 1880, to June 1880, Exhibit Box, CM Records; *Ibid.,* Part XVIII, pp. 1529–48; *Ibid.,* Part LXII, p. 6078.

32. This information is cited in a number of testimonies in both the C of I and the CM and is discussed in contemporary newspapers.

33. *West Point Tic Tacs* (New York, 1878), pp. 62–63, Special Collections, USMAA.

34. C of I Records, Part X, pp. 2645–58.

35. CM Records, Part LIV, p. 5435; *Ibid.,* Part LXII, p. 6052; J. C. Whittaker to Moses Wester, August 28, 1879, Exhibit Box, *ibid.*

36. Johnson C. Whittaker Bible, Exhibit Box, CM Records.

37. S. O. 186, December 20, 1879, S.O. 5, January 5, 1880, West Point Order Book, Record Group 94, National Archives.

CHAPTER 3

1. This chapter is based on a correlation of the testimony of witnesses at the Court of Inquiry and Court-Martial, various reports and the prosecution and defense summations. Citation of this chapter would require almost as much space as the text; therefore, citations are made only when more than an isolated fact is involved.

2. Court of Inquiry Extract, April 24, 1880, in The Proceedings of the General Court Martial of Johnson C. Whittaker, United States Military Academy, Records of the Judge Advocate General (Army), Record Group 153, QQ 2774, National Archives. Hereafter cited as CM Records.

3. Williston Fish, *Memories of West Point 1877–1881*, 3 vols. (Batavia, New York, 1957), manuscript edited and reproduced by Gertrude Fish Rumsey and Josephine Fish Peabody, United States Military Academy Archives, Special Collections, I, 174–75.

4. Whittaker repeated this story innumerable times. See, for example, The Proceedings of the Court of Inquiry in the Case of Johnson C. Whittaker, United States Military Academy, Records of the Judge Advocate (Army), Record Group 153, QQ 1858, National Archives, Part I, pp. 5–132. Hereafter cited as C of I Records.

5. *Register of Delinquencies 1875–1880, United States Military Academy*, p. 588, United States Military Academy Archives.

6. Dr. Charles T. Alexander to Adjutant, April 7, 1880, in C of I Records, Appendix, Part XI, pp. 2820–24; Lieutenant Colonel Henry M. Lazelle to Adjutant, April 7, 1880, in *ibid.*, Appendix, Part XI, pp. 2825–29.

7. *Ibid.*, John Bratt Diary, April 7, 1880, manuscript, United States Military Academy, Special Collections.

8. CM Records, Part I, pp. 47–131.

1. Francis B. Heitman, *Historical Register and Dictionary of the United States Army* (Washington, 1903), Vol. I; Williston Fish, *Memories of West Point 1877–1881*, 3 vols., edited and reproduced by Gertrude Fish Rumsey and Josephine Fish Peabody (Batavia, New York, 1957), III, 837, 859, 825. Special Collections, United States Military Academy Archives.

2. A cadet explained the affair in a letter to the family of Major Mordecai, whose father was a West Point graduate himself, in fact one of the oldest still living. E. St. John Greble to Mrs. Rose, Alfred Mordecai Papers, Library of Congress. John M. Schofield to the Adjutant General, April 6, 7, 1881, John M. Schofield Papers, Library of Congress. Hereafter cited as Schofield Papers, LC. Schofield also answered reporters' inquiries about the incident. See Letter Book, Vol. I, pp. 427–28, United States Military Academy Archives.

3. Schofield to William T. Sherman, April 11, 1880, William T. Sherman Papers, Library of Congress. Hereafter cited as WTS Papers, LC.

4. New York *Times*, New York *Tribune*, April 8, 1880; Columbia (South Carolina) *Register*, April 10, 1880.

5. Johnson C. Whittaker to his mother (Maria J. Whitaker), April 7, 1880, The Proceedings of the General Court Martial of Johnson C. Whittaker, United States Military Academy, Records of the Judge Advocate General (Army), Record Group 153, QQ 2774, National Archives. Hereafter cited as CM Records. Whittaker to "Dear Friend" (Richard T. Greener), April 7, 1880. *Ibid.*

6. Charleston *Courier and News*, April 9, 1880; New York *Times*, April 10, 1880; New York *Tribune*, April 8, 1880. Thomas Phillips, "The Black Regulars: Negro Soldiers in the United States Army, 1866–1891," Ph.D. dissertation, University of Wisconsin, 1970, p. 1199. This black paper also reported that a rumor was circulating at West Point that Whittaker's lightness of skin had fooled several cadets for a time into thinking he was white. Their anger when they found out he was "a white nigger" and had fooled them was known by all, the paper said. Charleston *New Era*, April 24, 1880, William R. Perkins Library, Duke University.

7. New York *Times*, April 11, 1880; New York *Tribune*, April 10, 14, 1880.

8. The Proceedings of the Court of Inquiry in the Case of Johnson C. Whittaker, United States Military Academy, Records of the Judge Advocate General (Army), Record Group 153, QQ 1858, National Archives, Part I, pp. 1–132. Hereafter cited as C of I Records. New York *Times*, April 7, 11, 1880.

9. C of I Records, Part I, pp. 132–39, 169–70; *Army and Navy Journal*, April 17, 1880.

10. C of I Records, Parts I, II, pp. 140–69, 170–218; *Army and Navy Journal*, April 17, 1880; New York *Tribune*, April 11, 1880; Erie (Pa.) *Despatch*, April 12, 1880.

11. C of I Records, Part II, pp. 139–40, 219–22; New York *Times*, April 13, 1880; William Wherry to Commandant, April 10, 1880, Letter Book, Vol. I, p. 429, United States Military Academy Archives.

12. Adjutant General E. D. Townsend to Commanding General, West Point, April 8, 1880, Alexander Ramsey to Thomas F. Barr, April 8, 1880, Letters and Endorsements, United States Military Academy, Record Group 94, National Archives; Alexander Ramsey to Schofield, April 8, 1880, Alexander Ramsey Papers, microfilm, Minnesota Historical Society; Confidential Record of John M. Schofield, USA, April 9, 1880, Schofield Papers, LC.

13. *Congressional Record*, 46th Cong. 2nd Sess. (April 9, 1880), pp. 2205, 2248–49; New York *Times*, April 8, 9, 10; Schofield to D. Wyatt Aiken, April 19, 1880 (acknowledging April 16, 1880, letter), Schofield Papers, LC; Erie *Despatch*, April 15, 1880.

14. New York *Times*, April 11, 1880.

15. This theory or parts of it are mentioned with minor varying details throughout the court of inquiry, court-martial, and in the press. The above is taken from the recorder's summation in the court of inquiry. C of I Records, Part X, pp. 2763–69.

CHAPTER 5

1. The Proceedings of the Court of Inquiry in the Case of Johnson C. Whittaker, United States Military Academy, Records of the Judge Advocate General (Army), Record Group 153, QQ

1858, National Archives, Part II, pp. 198–99. Hereafter cited as C of I Records.

2. C of I Records, Parts I, II, pp. 140–218.

3. *Ibid.*, Part II, pp. 223–46, 249–78.

4. *Ibid.*, Part II, pp. 247–49, 325–29.

5. *Ibid.*, Part II, pp. 330–72, 375–438. The testimony cited above was also discussed in the *Army and Navy Journal*, April 17, 1880, and numerous other newspapers.

6. S. L. Woodford to Attorney General Charles Devens, April 12, 1880, Department of Justice Source Chronological Files, Record Group 60, National Archives; Confidential Record of J. M. Schofield, USA, April 13, 1880, John M. Schofield Papers, Library of Congress. Hereafter cited as Schofield Papers, LC. *Army and Navy Journal*, April 17, 1880.

7. Justin D. Fulton to Alexander Ramsey, April 10, 1880, Alexander Ramsey Papers, microfilm, Minnesota Historical Society. Hereafter cited as Ramsey Papers, Minn. Hist. Soc. Ramsey sent a brief return letter telling Fulton all possible was being done for Whittaker. Ramsey to Fulton, April 12, 1880, *ibid.*; Alexander Ramsey to John M. Schofield, April 13, 1880, C of I Records, Appendix, p. 2989; Charles Devens to Martin I. Townsend, April 16, 1880, Letters Sent by the Department of Justice; Instructions to U. S. Attorneys and Marshals, National Archives, Microcopy No. 701; New York *Times*, New York *Tribune*, Washington *National Republican*, April 14, *Army and Navy Journal*, April 17, 1880.

8. Townsend to West Point Adjutant, April 13, 1880, Letters Received, Vol. I, 1877–1880, p. 435, United States Military Academy Archives.

9. Ramsey to Schofield, April 13, 1880, Ramsey Papers, Minn. Hist. Soc.; C of I Records, Part II, pp. 372–74, 404; New York *Tribune*, April 15, 1880. J. M. Schofield to Secretary of War, April 15, 1880, Letters Sent, Schofield Papers, L.C.; Townsend to Ramsey, April 15, 1880, Ramsey Papers, Minn. Hist. Soc.

10. Martin I. Townsend to Alexander Ramsey, May 5, 1880, C of I Records; Confidential Record of J. M. Schofield, USA, April 16, 1880, Schofield Papers, LC; William M. Wherry to Clinton B. Sears, April 16, 1880, C of I Records, Appendix, p. 2990.

11. C of I Records, Part III, pp. 481–535; Townsend to Ramsey, April 15, 1880, Alexander Ramsey Papers, Minn. Hist. Soc.; Townsend to Charles Devens, April 16, 1880, Department of

Justice, Source Chronological Files, Record Group 60, National Archives.

12. New York *Times*, April 15, 1880; C of I Records, Part III, pp. 536–37.

13. New York *Times*, April 15, 1880.

14. *Ibid.*, April 18, 1880.

15. *Ibid.*, April 16, 1880.

16. C of I Records, Part III, pp. 617–21, 638–39; New York *Times*, April 18, 19, 1880; J. M. Schofield to William T. Sherman, April 17, 1880, William T. Sherman Papers, Library of Congress.

17. C of I Records, Part III, pp. 540–615, 621–37, 646–51, 651–59, 659–80, 640–46; New York *Tribune*, New York *Times*, April 16, 1880.

18. Confidential Record of J. M. Schofield, USA, April 16, 1880, Schofield Papers, LC; Washington *National Republican*, New York *Tribune*, New York *Times*, April 17, 1880. Henry Ward Beecher preached a very critical sermon on West Point's handling of the Whittaker case and black cadets in general on April 18, 1880. Charles H. Barth Diary, April 19, 1880, manuscript, Special Collections, United States Military Academy Archives.

19. C of I Records, Part IV, pp. 681–86, 722–28.

20. *Ibid.*, Part IV, pp. 784–814, Part V, pp. 976–85, 997–1003, 1249–52, to cite but a few; *Army and Navy Journal*, April 24, 1880; New York *Times*, April 20, 22, 1880; Erie *Despatch*, April 21, 22, 1880; New York *Tribune*, April 21, 1880.

21. New York *Times*, New York *Tribune*, April 14, 1880; *Puck*, April 21, 1880.

22. John Bratt Diary, April 21, 1880, manuscript, Special Collections, United States Military Academy Archives; Thomas Phillips, "The Black Regulars: Negro Soldiers in the United States Army, 1866–1891," Ph.D. dissertation, University of Wisconsin, 1970, pp. 1198–99. Confidential Record of J. M. Schofield, April 21, May 1, 1880, Schofield Papers, LC.

23. See, for example, New York *Tribune*, April 22, 1880, New York *Times*, April 23, 1880; Schofield to Mrs. John C. Bullitt, May 9, 1880, Schofield Papers, LC.

24. C of I Records, Part VI, pp. 1324–47, 1563–65, 1729–30; *Army and Navy Journal*, April 24, 1880; Confidential Record of J.

M. Schofield, USA, April 22, 1880, Schofield Papers, LC; Erie *Despatch*, April 23, 1880.

25. C of I Records, Part VI, pp. 1432–1508, Part VI, pp. 1568–88; *Army and Navy Journal*, April 24, 1880.

26. C of I Records, Part VII, pp. 1591–1630, 1662–72, Part VIII, pp. 2116–34; *Army and Navy Journal*, May 1, 1880; New York *Times*, Erie *Despatch*, April 24, 1880; Washington *National Republican*, April 26, 1880.

27. C of I Records, Part VII, pp. 1699–1713, 1739–62; New York *Tribune*, April 25, 1880; New York *Times*, April 27, 28, May 5, 1880; Erie *Despatch*, April 28, 1880; *Army and Navy Journal*, May 1, 1880; S. L. Woodford to Charles Devens, April 21, 26, 1880, Department of Justice Source Chronological Files, Record Group 60, National Archives.

CHAPTER 6

1. The Proceedings of the Court of Inquiry in the Case of Johnson C. Whittaker, United States Military Academy, Records of the Judge Advocate General (Army), Record Group 153, QQ 1858, National Archives, Part VIII, pp. 2064–67, 2084–88, 1929–38. Hereafter cited as C of I Records. *Army and Navy Journal*, May 1, 1880; Columbia *Register*, April 30, 1880.

2. C of I Records, Part VII, pp. 1765–68, Part VIII, pp. 2125–30, 2871–76; *Army and Navy Journal*, May 8, 1880.

3. C of I Records, Part IX, pp. 2139–43, 2150–80.

4. C of I Records, Part IX, pp. 2180–84.

5. *Ibid.*, Parts IX, X, XI; *Army and Navy Journal*, May 15, 22, 1880; New York *Tribune*, Erie *Despatch*, May 13, 1880.

6. C of I Records, Part IX, pp. 2232–33; Townsend to Ramsey, May 5, 1880, CM Records and Register, Letters Received, Secretary of War, 1880, copy, Alexander Ramsey Papers, Minnesota Historical Society; *Army and Navy Journal*, May 15, 1880; Richard T. Greener to Secretary of War, May 12, 1880, Register, Letters Received, Secretary of War, 1880, copy, Alexander Ramsey Papers, Minnesota Historical Society; Townsend to Ramsey, April 15, 1880, Ramsey to Townsend, April 17, 18, May 8, 1880, microfilm, *ibid.* Around this time, too, Schofield saw a letter Lieu-

tenant Flipper had written about his suspicions on the case. Schofield told the letter's forwarder to do nothing with the letter because the court of inquiry was handling matters. At the latter's request, Schofield returned this letter. He kept no copy of it. Thomas W. Price to Schofield, May 10, 1880, Schofield to Price, May 14, 1880, Schofield Papers, LC.

7. New York *Tribune*, April 26, 1880; Erie *Despatch*, April 27, 1880; see, for example, E. S. Fowler to Secretary of War, May 12, 1880, Jasper K. Herbert to Alexander Ramsey, May 6, 1880, The Proceedings of the General Court Martial of Johnson C. Whittaker, United States Military Academy, Records of the Judge Advocate General (Army), Record Group 153, QQ 2774, National Archives, hereafter cited as CM Records. *Nation*, May 13, 1880; Confidential Record of J. M. Schofield, USA, May 8, 14, 1880, John M. Schofield Papers, Library of Congress. Hereafter cited as Schofield Papers, LC; G. Reid to Secretary of War, April 28, 1880, Alexander Ramsey Papers, Minnesota Historical Society, contains an attack on Schofield and some pro-Whittaker press clippings from San Francisco.

8. C of I Records, Part IX, pp. 2197–2214, 2220–24, Part X, pp. 2547–48; *Army and Navy Journal*, May 15, 1880; Erie *Despatch*, May 8, 1880.

9. C of I Records, Part IX, pp. 2282–2454; *Army and Navy Journal*, May 22, 1880; New York *Tribune*, New York *Times*, May 16, 1880; Erie *Despatch*, May 17, 1880.

10. New York *Times*, May 17, 1880; New York *Tribune*, May 18, 1880; Charleston *News and Courier*, May 19, 1880; *Nation*, May 20, 1880.

11. Confidential Record of J. M. Schofield, USA, May 15, 1880, Schofield Papers, LC.

12. Johnson C. Whittaker to Mrs. Ferndon, May 20, 1880, Rutherford B. Hayes Library, Fremont, Ohio; the New York *Tribune* on May 17, 1880, reported that Whittaker went to church on Sunday and did not see a newspaper until the afternoon.

13. C of I Records, Part X, pp. 2498–2529, 2530–46, 2480–88; *Army and Navy Journal*, May 22, 1880; Lieutenant Colonel H. M. Lazelle to Acting Assistant Adjutant General, West Point, May 25, 1880, Whittaker to Acting Assistant Adjutant General, West Point, May 30, 1880, Record Group 94, Section 214, National Archives.

14. New York *Times,* May 29, 1880.

15. C of I Records, Part X, pp. 2677–784.

16. *Ibid.,* Part X, pp. 2785–803.

17. *Ibid.,* Part X, 2806–17.

18. New York *Tribune,* New York *Times,* Charleston *News and Courier,* May 31, 1880; *Scribner's Monthly,* XX (June 1880), p. 463; Orangeburg (South Carolina) *Times,* June 4, 1880; *Harper's Weekly,* June 5, 1880.

19. Confidential Record of J. M. Schofield, USA, May 29, 1880, Schofield Papers, LC; William T. Sherman to Henry S. Turner, May 16, 1880, William T. Sherman Papers, Ohio Historical Society; New York *Tribune,* New York *Times,* May 31, 1880.

20. Record of Delinquencies, 1875–1880, p. 588, United States Military Academy Archives; Whittaker to Richard T. Greener, May 27, 30, 1880, CM Records.

CHAPTER 7

1. *Harper's Weekly,* May 1, 1880; New York *Tribune,* May 6; Washington *National Republican,* May 18, 1880; Peter S. Michie, "Caste at West Point," *North American Review,* CXXX (June 1880), pp. 604–13; Michie's article was based on a memorandum from Schofield in which the general asked that his name not be used. Thomas Phillips, "The Black Regulars: Negro Soldiers in the United States Army, 1866–1891," Ph. D. dissertation, University of Wisconsin, 1970, pp. 1207–09, 1267n; New York *Herald,* May 23, 1880; The Michie–*Herald* exchange is discussed in W. Scott Dillard, "The United States Military Academy, 1865–1900: The Uncertain Years," manuscript of Ph. D. dissertation soon to be presented to the University of Washington, p. 8–29.

2. Columbia *Register,* June 3, 1880; Confidential Record of J. M. Schofield, USA, June 2, 1880, John M. Schofield Papers, Library of Congress. Hereafter cited as Schofield Papers, LC.

3. New York *Tribune,* June 5, 6, 1880. Thompson was allowed to delay his entrance examination because of the attack. John M. Schofield to Adjutant General, June 14, 1880, Letter Book, Department of West Point, U.S. Military Academy, Vol. I, p. 466, United States Military Academy Archives.

4. Confidential Record of John M. Schofield, USA, June 3, 1880, Schofield Papers, LC.

5. New York *Tribune*, June 10, 1880.

6. Confidential Record of John M. Schofield, USA, June 4, 1880, Schofield Papers, LC; S.O. #85, June 4, 1880, United States Military Academy Orders, Record Group 94, National Archives; S.O. #57, June 7, 1880, *ibid.*, extended the limits of Whittaker's confinement; John M. Schofield to Adjutant General, June 4, 1880, Letter Book, Department of West Point, U.S. Military Academy, Vol. I, pp. 459–60, United States Military Academy Archives.

7. New York *Tribune*, June 8, 9, 12; Washington *National Republican*, June 12, 1880.

8. *Army and Navy Journal*, Erie *Despatch*, Washington *National Republican*, June 12, 1880; Schofield to D.E.L. Floyd Jones, June 15, 1880, Schofield Papers, LC.

9. New York *Times*, June 25, 1880; *Army and Navy Journal*, June 5, 1880.

10. Register of Letters Received by the Office of the Adjutant General, June 17, 1880, Microcopy No. 711, National Archives; June 25, 1880, Cabinet meeting mentioned in Chicago *Tribune*, June 26, 1880, The Rutherford B. Hayes Library, Fremont, Ohio. Hereafter cited as Hayes Library; R. C. Drum to Schofield, June 25, 1880, United States Military Academy, Letters Received, Record Group 94, National Archives; J. D. Fulton to William M. Dunn, June 11, 1880, Alexander Ramsey Papers, microfilm, Minnesota Historical Society. Hereafter cited as Ramsey Papers, Minn. Hist. Soc. This letter included a June 5, 1880, petition in favor of Whittaker signed by the famous black leader Henry Highland Garnet and a number of other black ministers.

11. Judge Advocate General to Secretary of War, June 30, 1880, The Proceedings in the Court of Inquiry in the Case of Johnson C. Whittaker, United States Military Academy, Records of the Judge Advocate General (Army), Record Group 153, QQ 1858, National Archives, draft and final copy. Hereafter cited as C of I Records.

12. *Army and Navy Journal*, August 14, 1880.

13. Whittaker to Richard T. Greener, June 25, 1880, The Proceedings of the General Court Martial of Johnson C. Whittaker, United States Military Academy, Records of the Judge Advocate

General (Army), Record Group 153, QQ 2774, National Archives. Hereafter cited as CM Records. Phillips, *op. cit.*, p. 1213; Confidential Record of John M. Schofield, USA, June 26, 1880, Schofield Papers, LC.

14. Henry Barnard, *Rutherford B. Hayes and His America* (Indianapolis, 1954), p. 494; Kenneth E. Davison, "Travels of President Rutherford B. Hayes," *Ohio History*, LXXX (Winter 1971), pp. 63–72.

15. George F. Hoar to R. B. Hayes, June 25, 1880, E. B. Buck to Hayes, November 20, 1880, J. P. Grinnell to Hayes, December 7, 1880, Noett McAllister to Hayes, June 5, 1880, James M. Hoyt to Hayes, July 10, 1880, and many others, Hayes Library; E. B. Washburne to Ramsey, April 23, 1880, Ramsey Papers, Minn. Hist. Soc.; Colored Citizens of Mound City, Illinois, to Hayes, August 14, 1880. Johnson C. Whittaker Application Papers, 395–1876, Record Group 94, National Archives; Sallie McLean to Mr. and Mrs. Hayes, J. P. Kilbreth to Hayes with enclosure; King, Thompson and Maxwell to J. K. Kilbreth, July 28, 1880, Hayes Library.

16. Cabinet Meeting Agendas, June 15, July 6, 13, 18, August 3, 1880, Hayes to Schofield, July 9, 1880, Schofield to Hayes, July 8, 1880, H. T. Crosby to Hayes, August 5, 1880, Cabinet Meeting Agenda, August 3, 1880, Hayes Library. Kilbreth never graduated, resigning in January 1882. O. O. Howard to Professor Andrews, January 2, 1882, Adjutant's Letter Book, United States Military Academy No. 5, inserted between pp. 320–21, United States Military Academy Archives.

17. R. B. Hayes, *Hayes: The Diary of a President, 1875–1881*, edited by T. Harry Williams (New York, 1964), July 12, 1880, p. 283; Hayes to M. F. Force, July 18, 1880, in R. B. Hayes, *Diary and Letters of Rutherford B. Hayes*, edited by C. R. Williams (Columbus, Ohio, 1926), III, 613–14; Force to Hayes, July 21, Hayes to Force, July 28, 1880, in *ibid.*, III, 616; Ramsey to A. H. Terry, July 26, 1880, Ramsey Papers, Minn. Hist. Soc.

18. Schofield to Sherman, July 31, August 1, 1880, original in William T. Sherman Papers, Library of Congress, copy in Schofield Papers, LC; Memorandum in Sherman's handwriting on the back of the August 1 letter, WTS Papers, LC; Sherman to Schofield, August 9, 1880, *ibid.*; Schofield to William M. Evarts, August 11, September 12, 1880, Schofield Papers, LC; Schofield to

Sherman, August 11, 1880, *ibid.;* A. H. Terry to Ramsey, telegram, August 2, 1880; T. F. Barr to Terry, telegram, August 8, 1880, Terry to Barr, telegram, August 9, 1880; Ramsey Papers, Minn. Hist. Soc.; Confidential Record of John M. Schofield, USA, August 14, 1880, Schofield Papers, LC; Schofield to Sherman, August 14, 1880, *ibid.;* Sherman to Schofield, August 15, 1880, WTS Papers, LC; Schofield to Sherman, August 16, 1880, Schofield Papers, LC.

19. Confidential Record of J. M. Schofield, USA, August 17, 1880, Schofield Papers, LC.

20. Hayes to Secretary of War, August 17, 1880, S.O. #177, August 19, 1880, Johnson C. Whittaker Acceptance Papers, 395–1876, Record Group 94, National Archives; R. T. Greener to Alexander Ramsey, August 14, 1880, CM Records; *Army and Navy Journal,* August 21, 1880.

21. Confidential Record of J. M. Schofield, USA, August 17, 1880, Schofield Papers, LC. Whittaker, who had always received few demerits, was on August 14, 1880, cited among those cadets with an excess of marks for the last two months. Adjutant to Commandant, August 14, 1880, Adjutant's Letter Book, United States Military Academy, No. 5, pp. 149–50, United States Military Academy Archives.

22. CM Records, Part LIV, p. 5435; *Army and Navy Journal,* September 4, November 13, 1880; Erie *Despatch,* September 4, 1880; J. D. Fulton to Ramsey, with newspaper clipping enclosed, December 28, 1880, Ramsey Papers, Minn. Hist. Soc. In August 1880 an article appeared citing the dangers of convictions based on circumstantial evidence and listed a number of cases to document this point. Benson J. Lossing, "Circumstantial Evidence," *Stoddart's Review* (August 1880), pp. 123–25.

23. George L. Andrews, "West Point and the Colored Cadets," *International Review,* IX (November 1880), pp. 477–98; Henry Cabot Lodge invited Schofield to write this article but the general gave the assignment to Andrews. William M. Wherry to Lodge, May 26, 1880, Letters Sent, p. 120, Schofield Papers, LC; "Annual Report, Department of West Point, United States Military Academy for the Year 1880," Report of the Secretary of War, House Executive Documents, 46th Congress, 3rd Session, Part 2, pp. 223–30. A copy of this report is also included in Confidential

Record of J. M. Schofield, USA, October 18, 1880, Schofield Papers, LC.

24. *Ibid.*, November 3, 1880.

25. Schofield to Sherman, November 5, 1880, Sherman to Schofield, November 12, 1880, O. O. Howard to Sherman, December 7, 1880, Sherman to Howard, December 7, 1880, Sherman to Sheridan, Sherman to Schofield, December 13, 20, 1880, Sherman to James A. Garfield, December 30, 1880, Sherman Papers, LC.

26. Martin I. Townsend to Alexander Ramsey, November 4, 1880, CM Records.

27. J. Hyatt Smith *et. al.*, to Hayes, November 17, 1880, Johnson C. Whittaker Acceptance Papers, 395–1876, Record Group 94, National Archives; Cabinet Meeting Agenda, November 17, 1880, Hayes Library; Whittaker to Hayes, December 13, 1880, C of I Records.

28. New York *Tribune*, December 29, 1880; Howard to Hayes, December 15, 1880, C of I Records; O. O. Howard, *Autobiography of General O. O. Howard*, 2 vols. (New York, 1908), II, p. 486.

29. Citizens of Boston to Hayes, December 28, 1880, Johnson C. Whittaker Acceptance Papers, 395–1876, Record Group 94, National Archives; Alexander Ramsey Diary, December 28, 1880, Ramsey Papers, Minn. Hist. Soc.; New York *Tribune*, December 31, 29, 1880, January 3, 1881. M. I. Townsend to Ramsey, February 19, 1881, Ramsey Papers, Minn. Hist. Soc.

CHAPTER 8

1. S. O. #278, December 31, 1880, Johnson C. Whittaker Acceptance Papers, 395–1876, Record Group 94, National Archives; *Army and Navy Journal*, January 8, 1881.

2. "Report of the Congressional Board of Visitors to the West Point Academy for 1880 dated December 20, 1880," *Miscellaneous Documents of the Senate of the United States*, 46th Cong., 3rd Sess. 1880–1881, and Special Session of the 47th Congress; *Congressional Record*, 46th Congress, 3rd Session (January 17, 1881), p. 667; New York *Times*, January 18, 1881; J. M. Schofield to A. H. Garland, January 25, 1881, Confidential Record, October 1, 1880, to Sep-

tember 11, 1891, John M. Schofield Papers, Library of Congress.

3. *Nation*, January 6, 1881; *Army and Navy Journal*, January 8, 1881.

4. Asa Bird Gardiner to Secretary of War, *c.* January 1, January 17, 20, 1881, Letters Received (Main Series), Adjutant General, Microcopy 666, National Archives. Hereafter cited as M-666, National Archives.

5. Alexander Ramsey to Gardiner, January 21, 1881, Gardiner to the Adjutant General, January 28, 1881, *ibid.*

6. W. S. Hancock to Sherman, May 27, 1881, William T. Sherman Papers, Library of Congress. Hereafter cited as WTS Papers, LC. William T. Sherman to H. S. Turner, January 16, 1881, William T. Sherman Papers, Ohio Historical Society; Sherman to B. H. Grierson, January 4, 1881, WTS Papers, LC; G.O. #1, January 21, 1881, John M. Schofield Papers, Library of Congress. Hereafter cited as Schofield Papers, LC; Schofield to the Adjutant General, January 21, 1881, M-666, National Archives.

7. *Harper's Weekly*, January 22, 1881; *Army and Navy Journal*, January 8, 1881.

8. New York *Times*, New York *Tribune*, January 21, 1881; New York *Tribune*, February 4, 1881; New York *Times*, April 7, 1881.

9. W. B. Fowler, "A Carpetbagger's Conversion to White Supremacy," *North Carolina Historical Review*, XLIII (Summer 1966), pp. 286–304; Springfield (Mass.) *Republican*, April 14, 1907, from Harvard University Archives; Harold M. Hyman (ed.), *The Radical Republicans and Reconstruction . . .* (Indianapolis, 1967), p. 416; Henry G. Thompson, *Ousting the Carpetbagger* (Columbia, 1926), p. 176; Daniel H. Chamberlain, *. . . Open Letter to the Right Honorable James Bryce, M.P., of England* (n.p., 1909), p. 7; Daniel H. Chamberlain, "Reconstruction in South Carolina," *Atlantic Monthly*, LXXXVII (April 1901), pp. 473–84; Richard T. Greener to Isaiah Wears, Jacob C. White Papers, Moorland-Spingarn Collection, Howard University Library; Vincent P. De Santis, *Republicans Face the Southern Question* (New York, 1969), p. 104. The few scattered Chamberlain letters in various depositories contain nothing on Chamberlain's role in this trial.

10. Francis B. Heitman, *Historical Register and Dictionary of the United States Army* (Washington, 1903), vol. I; Ernest R. Dupuy, *Where They Have Trod . . .* (Washington, 1940), p. 320.

11. "Twenty Fifth Anniversary Report Harvard Class of

1870," Harvard University Archives; *Dictionary of American Biography*, p. 578.

12. New York *Times*, January 21, 1881; *Army and Navy Journal*, January 29, 1881; Heitman, *op. cit.*, vol. I; H. O. Flipper file in Carter G. Woodson Papers, Library of Congress.

13. S. O. #278, December 31, 1880, Johnson C. Whittaker Acceptance Papers, 395–1876, Record Group 94, National Archives; *Army and Navy Journal*, January 22, 1881; New York *Times*, January 22, 1881.

CHAPTER 9

1. The Proceedings of the General Court Martial of Johnson C. Whittaker, United States Military Academy, Records of the Judge Advocate General (Army), Record Group 153, QQ2774, National Archives, Part II, pp. 25–111, hereafter cited as CM Records; *Army and Navy Journal*, February 5, 1881.

2. CM Records, Part II, pp. 112–19; A. B. Gardiner to William Dowd, January 31, 1881, in *Army and Navy Journal*, February 5, 1881, and Erie *Despatch*, February 4, 1881.

3. CM Records, Part III, pp. 120–215, Part IV, pp. 217–48, Part V, pp. 305–15; the long quote is a capsulized version of Schofield's testimony which appeared in New York *Tribune*, February 5, 1881. Interestingly, A. B. Gardiner wrote a letter to new Superintendent Howard in late December attacking the Schofield superintendency and expressing happiness at Howard's appointment. A. B. Gardiner to O. O. Howard, December 31, 1880, O. O. Howard Papers, Bowdoin College. The reason for the attack was probably Schofield's involvement in the controversy over Gardiner's role in the Fitz John Porter court-martial. See Box 82 (1877–1881), John M. Schofield Papers, Library of Congress.

4. New York *Tribune*, February 5, 1881.

5. John Schofield to William T. Sherman, February 8, 1881, WTS to Schofield, February 10, 1881, William T. Sherman Papers, Library of Congress. Hereafter cited as WTS Papers, LC.

6. CM Records, Part V, p. 339.

7. *Ibid.*, Part V, pp. 340–83.

8. *Ibid.*, Part V, pp. 383–90, Part VI, pp. 396–431; New York

Times, February 10, 1881; *Army and Navy Journal,* February 12, 1881; Charleston *News and Courier,* February 14, 1881.

9. CM Records, Part VI, pp. 431–82.

10. *Ibid.,* Part VII, pp. 507–87.

11. *Ibid.,* Part VIII, pp. 610–16, Part IX, pp. 723–27, 742–44; New York *Tribune,* February 12, 1881; Erie *Despatch,* February 12, 1881; New York *Times,* February 11, 12, 15, 1881; A. B. Gardiner to Secretary of War, February 16, 1881, Office of the Adjutant General, Letters Received (Main Series), Microcopy 666, National Archives; hereafter cited as M-666, National Archives; Alexander Ramsey to Attorney General, February 18, 1881, Department of Justice Source Chronological Files, Record Group 60, National Archives; hereafter cited as R.G. 60, National Archives; Attorney General to Secretary of War, *c.* February 16, 1881, M-666, National Archives; Gardiner to Attorney General, February 21, 1881, R.G. 60, National Archives; Attorney General to Secretary of War, February 25, 1881, M-666, National Archives; Gardiner to Attorney General, February 27, 1881, R.G. 60, National Archives; *Army and Navy Journal,* February 19, 1881.

12. CM Records, Part VIII, pp. 650–79, Part IX, pp. 682–756, Part X, pp. 758–852; New York *Times,* February 15, 16, 1881.

13. CM Records, Part X, pp. 852–69, Part XI, pp. 877–978.

14. *Ibid.,* Part XII, pp. 988–1071; New York *Times,* February 18, 1881; *Army and Navy Journal,* February 19, 1881.

15. CM Records, Part XIII, p. 1105; *Army and Navy Journal,* February 18, 1881.

16. O. O. Howard to John A. Logan, January 31, 1881, John A. Logan Papers, Library of Congress; New York *Tribune,* February 23, 1881; Howard was also preparing a loyalty oath to the federal government for the cadets to emphasize "the folly of the idea of 'State supremacy' "; O. O. Howard to John A. Logan, February 15, 1881, John A. Logan Papers, Library of Congress.

17. CM Records, Parts XIII, XIV, pp. 1132–61; New York *Times,* February 24, 1881.

18. Williston Fish, *Memories of West Point 1877–1881,* 3 vols. (Batavia, N. Y., 1957), edited and reproduced by Gertrude Fish Rumsey and Josephine Fish Peabody, manuscript, Special Collections, United States Military Academy Archives, I, 363. CM Records, Part XV, pp. 1229–1339; New York *Times,* February 25, 1881; Washington *National Republican,* February 25, 1881.

19. CM Records, Part XVI, pp. 1339–43.

20. *Ibid.*, Part XVI, pp. 1343–63.

21. *Ibid.*, Part XVI, pp. 1363–67.

22. *Ibid.*, Parts XVI, XVII, pp. 1369–1503; New York *Tribune*, New York *Times*, February 26, 1881.

23. CM Records, Part XVIII, pp. 1529–48; *Army and Navy Journal*, March 5, 1881.

24. CM Records, Part XIX, pp. 1554–58; New York *Tribune*, March 2, 1881; Erie *Despatch, Army and Navy Journal*, March 3, 1881; New York *Times*, March 8, 1881.

25. R. T. Greener was a member of Garfield's Inaugural Executive Committee. Inauguration program, Rutherford B. Hayes Library, Fremont, Ohio; New York *Tribune*, March 2, 1881.

26. "Anonymous," "Calligraphy and the Whittaker Case," *The Criminal Law Magazine*, II (March 1881), pp. 139–73.

27. CM Records, Part XXIII, pp. 1958–60; New York *Times*, March 11, 1881.

28. CM Records, Parts XX, XXI, XXII, pp. 1674–1931; New York *Tribune*, New York *Times*, March 8, 1881; Erie *Despatch*, March 10, 1881; *Army and Navy Journal*, March 12, 1881.

29. CM Records, Part XXIII, pp. 1958–61; New York *Times*, New York *Tribune*, March 11, 1881; *Army and Navy Journal*, March 12, 1881.

30. CM Records, Parts XXIII–XXXV; New York *Tribune*, March 17, 18, 19, 22, 24, 26, 1881; *Army and Navy Journal*, March 12, 19, 26, April 2, 1881; New York *Times*, March 11, 22, 26, 29, 1881; Erie *Despatch*, March 15, 1881; Gardiner to Secretary of War, March 17, 1881, M-666, National Archives; R. C. Dunn to Gardiner, March 17, 1881, Office of the Adjutant General, Letters Sent (Main Series), Microcopy 565, National Archives.

CHAPTER 10

1. The Proceedings of the General Court Martial of Johnson C. Whittaker, United States Military Academy, Records of the Judge Advocate General (Army), Record Group 153, QQ 2774, National Archives, Parts XXXVII–XLII, pp. 3487–4199. Here-

after cited as CM Records. *Army and Navy Journal,* April 2, 9;
New York *Tribune,* March 31, April 1, 2, 7, 8, 9, 1881; New York
Times, March 31, April 1, 2, 8, 9, 1881.

2. CM Records, Parts XLII, XLIII, pp. 4200–334; *Army and
Navy Journal,* April 16, 23, 1881; New York *Times,* April 9, 1881.

3. CM Records, Part XLIII, pp. 4290–320.

4. *Ibid.,* Part XLIV, pp. 4334–58.

5. *Ibid.,* Part XLIV, pp. 4359–71.

6. *Ibid.,* Part XLIV, pp. 4371–441; *Army and Navy Journal,*
April 23, 1881; New York *Tribune,* April 19, 1881.

7. CM Records, Part XLV, pp. 4504–52 and exhibit collection;
New York *Tribune,* April 26, 1881; *Army and Navy Journal,* April
23, 1881.

8. CM Records, Parts XLVI–XLVIII, pp. 4568–883; *Army and
Navy Journal,* April 23, 30, 1881.

9. Stimpson had offered his services to West Point during the
court of inquiry. George Stimpson to Adjutant General, West
Point, May 18, 1880, Letters Received, Vol. I, 1877–1880, Depart-
ment of West Point, U. S. Military Academy, p. 453, United
States Military Academy Archives. CM Records, Parts XLVII–
LIV; *Army and Navy Journal,* April 30, May 7, 1881; New York
Tribune, April 21, 1881; New York *Times,* April 30, 1881; S. O.
#97, April 28, 1881, CM Records; *ibid.,* Parts LIV, LV, pp. 5423–
46; New York *Times,* New York *Tribune,* May 1, 1881.

10. CM Records, Part LV, pp. 5446–98; New York *Tribune,*
May 3, 1881.

11. CM Records, Parts XLVIII–LIV; New York *Times,* May 6,
10, New York *Tribune,* May 5, 1881; *Army and Navy Journal,* May
7, 14, 1881.

12. CM Records, Part LXI, pp. 5948–6042; New York *Times,*
May 11, 1881; *Army and Navy Journal,* May 14, 1881; Carvalho had
offered West Point authorities his services during the court of
inquiry but Schofield had politely refused it. John M. Schofield
to D. N. Carvalho, May 3, 1880, Letters Sent, John M. Schofield
Papers, Library of Congress.

13. CM Records, Parts LXI, LXII, pp. 6042–46; William T.
Sherman to Nelson Miles, May 16, 1881, William T. Sherman
Papers, Library of Congress.

14. CM Records, Part LXII, pp. 6046–101; *Army and Navy Journal,* May 14, 1881; New York *Times,* May 12, 1881.

15. CM Records, Parts LXII–LXVI; New York *Tribune*, May 12, 1881; *Army and Navy Journal*, May 21, 1881; New York *Times*, May 12, 13, 15, 1881.

16. CM Records, Part LXV, pp. 6450–62; Part LXVII, pp. 6856–59.

17. CM Records, Part LXVII, pp. 6765–67.

18. *Ibid.*, Part LXVII, pp. 6767 ff; New York *Times*, May 18, 1881; *Army and Navy Journal*, May 21, 1881.

19. New York *Times*, May 18, 1881.

CHAPTER 11

1. The summations of Daniel H. Chamberlain, Defense Counsel and Asa Bird Gardiner, Judge Advocate, discussed in this chapter may be found in Parts LXVIII to LXXII of The Proceedings of the General Court Martial of Johnson C. Whittaker, United States Military Academy, Records of the Judge Advocate General (Army), Record Group 153, QQ 2774, National Archives.

CHAPTER 12

1. William T. Sherman to Nelson A. Miles, May 16, 1881, William T. Sherman Papers, Library of Congress. Hereafter cited as WTS Papers, LC.

2. Richard T. Greener and Daniel H. Chamberlain to Nelson A. Miles, June 10, 1881, Exhibit Box, The Proceedings of the General Court Martial of Johnson C. Whittaker, United States Military Academy, Records of the Judge Advocate General (Army), Record Group 153, QQ 2774, National Archives. Hereafter cited as CM Records. Greener to D. G. Swaim, n.d., attached to above letter in *ibid.*

3. *Ibid.*, Part LXXII, pp. 7621 to unnumbered; General Court Martial Order # 18, Headquarters of the Army, March 22, 1882, Johnson C. Whittaker Appointment and Acceptance Papers, 395–1876, Record Group 94, National Archives. Hereafter cited as Whittaker Appointment Papers, National Archives.

4. CM Records, Part LXXII, unnumbered back pages.

5. Gardiner to Adjutant General, June 28, 1881, Adjutant General to Gardiner, July 1, 1881, Whittaker Appointment Papers, National Archives; *Nation,* September 29, October 6, November 17, 1881. Flipper was found guilty, and as late as 1922 attempts were made to clear him. He had the misfortune of being aided that year by Secretary of the Interior Albert Fall, himself soon to be implicated in the Harding scandals. Henry O. Flipper File, Carter G. Woodson Papers, Library of Congress.

6. New York *Tribune,* Erie *Despatch,* June 14, 1881; *Army and Navy Journal,* June 18, July 2, 1881.

7. James A. Garfield to Rutherford B. Hayes, with attached memorandum, December 1, 1880, original in Indiana Historical Society, copy in Rutherford B. Hayes Library, Fremont, Ohio.

8. D. G. Swaim to Robert T. Lincoln, December 1, 1881, CM Records.

9. R. U. Piper to the President, November 8, 1881, January 27, 1882, CM Records; R. U. Piper, "Expert Testimony . . . Whittaker Case," *The American Law Register,* XXX (n.s. XXI) (July, August 1882), pp. 425–42, 489–507.

10. New York *Tribune,* n.d., discussed in *Nation,* January 12, February 16, 1882; New York *Times,* January 4, 1882. The February 16, 1882, New York *Times* published a story that Richard Greener was representing Louis Simpson in the latter's demand for redress because of alleged "improper and illegal" treatment during the court of inquiry. This point was never mentioned again.

11. Robert T. Lincoln to Benjamin Brewster, March 6, 1882, CM Records, also in Department of Justice Source Chronological Files, Record Group 60, National Archives; Brewster to Lincoln, March 17, 1882, CM Records, also in *Official Opinions of the Attorney Generals* . . . (Washington, 1890), vol. XVII, pp. 310–13.

12. General Court Martial Order No. 18, Headquarters of the Army, March 22, 1882, Whittaker Appointment Papers, National Archives; CM Records, Part LXII, last page.

13. Robert T. Lincoln to the Adjutant General, March 21, 1882, Whittaker Appointment Papers; S.O. No. 66, Headquarters of the Army, March 22, 1881, *ibid.*

14. *Nation,* March 30, 1882.

15. D. Wyatt Aiken to the Adjutant General, March 22, 1882, Adjutant General to Aiken, April 20, 24, 1882, Office of the Adju-

tant General, Letters Received, Record Group 94, National Archives; D. Wyatt Aiken to Secretary of War, December 9, 1880, Adjutant General to Aiken, December 15, 1880, United States Military Academy Endorsement Book, *ibid.* The latter two citations indicate how early in the case Aiken tried to nominate a replacement for Whittaker's slot at West Point.

16. *Army and Navy Journal,* March 25, 1882; Thomas Phillips, "The Black Regulars: Negro Soldiers in the United States Army, 1866–1891," Ph.D. dissertation, University of Wisconsin, 1970.

17. William McIntosh to Rutherford B. Hayes, May 22, 1882, Rutherford B. Hayes Library, Fremont, Ohio.

18. Buffalo Evening *News,* Buffalo *Courier,* Buffalo *Express,* June 1, 1882; Buffalo *Commercial Advertiser,* June 1, 1882, clipped and printed in New York *Times,* June 4, 1882.

19. Buffalo *Courier,* June 1, 1882; Phillips, *op. cit.,* pp. 1257–58; Whittaker to Robert T. Lincoln, September 7, 1882, Whittaker to D. G. Swaim, August 5, 1883, undated but received September 23, 1883, March 4, 1884, Whittaker to Lincoln, December 24, 1884, Lincoln to Whittaker, January 5, 1885, Exhibit Box, CM Records.

CHAPTER 13

1. Records of the Judge of Probate Court, Kershaw County, South Carolina.

2. El Paso *Lone Star,* January 26, 1884, information provided in letter to author, May 16, 1971, by Elinor Wilson, biographer of James Beckwourth; George B. Tindall, *South Carolina Negroes, 1877–1900* (Columbia, 1952), p. 224. Hereafter cited as Tindall, *South Carolina Negroes.* Burchill R. Moore, "A History of the Negro Public Schools of Charleston, South Carolina, 1876–1942," Master's thesis, University of South Carolina, 1942, pp. 46–47; *Charleston City Directory 1884* and research which indicated the absence of records on Avery conducted by Mrs. Granville T. Prior, Director, South Carolina Historical Society, letter to author, May 26, 1971; A. Coward to Whittaker, October 18, 1883, Letter Book, State Superintendent of Education, No. 26, from January 16, 1884, South Carolina Department of Archives and History, Columbia. Hereafter cited as S.C. Archives. Mrs. Gran-

ville T. Prior to author, August 1971; 1883 Charleston *Yearbook*, pp. 205–8. An anecdotal account of the Porter Military Academy can be found in A. Toomer Porter, *Led On! Step by Step* . . . (New York, 1898), pp. 340–99. There is no mention of Whittaker.

3. Tindall, *South Carolina Negroes*, pp. 144–45; Orangeburg (S.C.) *Times and Democrat*, January 17, 1931; Herbert Lieberkindt, Cooper Union Director of Admissions and Registrar, to author, July 9, 1971; Frances H. Smith, Clerk, the Supreme Court of South Carolina, to author, April 21, 1971; *Charleston City Directory 1887*; In the North, at this same time, one last fleeting memory of the court-martial surfaced. Daniel H. Chamberlain wrote to Martin I. Townsend asking for handwriting expert Hagan's address in order to utilize his services. Whether the former protagonists joined forces is unknown. Chamberlain to Townsend, January 6, 1887, Manuscript Division, South Caroliana Library, University of South Carolina.

4. Bureau of the Census, *Bulletin 8. Negroes in the United States* (Washington, 1904), pp. 219, 277, 16; Anne King Gregoire, *History of Sumter County* (Sumter, S.C., 1954), is a detailed study of this county, with practically nothing on blacks. Pages 396–400 discuss legal action against Murray over a land transaction.

5. (Sumter) *Watchman and Southran* (sic), March 3, 1887, note card found in Anne King Gregoire's manuscript card file in Charleston Historical Society, Mrs. Granville T. Prior to author, June 29, 1970; Columbia *Daily Register*, February 24, 1887, cited in Tindall, *South Carolina Negroes*, p. 147, 147n.

6. *Ibid.*, p. 147; Gravestones, Orangeburg Cemetery; Interview with Whittaker's daughter-in-law, Marian Horton, and his granddaughter, Cecil Whittaker McFadden, Detroit, Michigan, August 7, 1971. Mrs. Horton, since remarried, was the widow of John Whittaker. Mrs. McFadden is the daughter of John and Marian Whittaker. Hereafter cited as Horton-McFadden interview.

7. John Kershaw, chairman, Sumter County Board of Commissioners, to James H. Rice, State Superintendent of Education, June 13, 1889, asking for help in securing funds for Sumter schools, Papers of Superintendent of Education, 1886–1890, S.C. Archives; Hugh Stoddard, "A History of the Public Schools, Sumter, South Carolina, 1888–1925," Master's thesis, University of South Carolina, 1937, p. 94; "Register Book 1891–1892, 1892–

1893, Jon T. Greene, School Commissioner," inside front leaf, Sumter County, Office of Superintendent of Education; "Records of Certification of Teachers 1871–1920," p. 89, *ibid.*

8. Title Books, Clerk's Office, Kershaw County, South Carolina, DDD, p. 358, OO, pp. 95, 96, QQ, p. 213, SS, p. 582; Title Books, Clerk's Office, Sumter County, South Carolina, Z, p. 577, DDD, p. 442, EEE, pp. 309, 491, FFF, p. 309, NNN, p. 205, OOO, p. 288, PPP, p. 716. Edward Whittaker remained a farmer in the Camden area until he died. He and his brother were so different they had little to do with each other. Horton-McFadden interview.

9. Separate interviews in Sumter with Attorney George D. Shore, Jr., E. C. Jones, DDS and W. F. Bultman, Sr., June 14, 1971; Mr. Bultman interviewed Mrs. Anna Louise McDonald, a niece of Mrs. J. C. Whittaker, and forwarded the results. Bultman to author, June 27, 1971; C. W. Birnie will, Judge of Probate Court, Sumter County, South Carolina.

10. Thirty First Annual Report of the State Superintendent of Education in *Reports and Resolutions to the General Assembly* (Columbia, 1900), Part 2, information forwarded to author by a member of the S.C. Archives staff, T. M. Bolivar, July 2, 1971. Hereafter cited as *Reports and Resolutions.*

11. Stoddard, *op. cit.,* pp. 95–96.

12. Horton-McFadden interview; William R. Lowman to Whittaker, August 29, September 9, 1896, in possession of Mrs. Cecil Whittaker McFadden; Nelson C. Nix, *South Carolina State College, Orangeburg, South Carolina, A History* (Orangeburg, 1937), p. 22. Hereafter cited as Nix, *SC State.* Mr. Nix was longtime dean at the college and a contemporary and friend of J. C. Whittaker.

13. Reports of the President and the Board of Trustees of the Colored Normal, Industrial, Agricultural and Mechanical College of South Carolina for the years 1900 to 1908, included as part of the Annual Report of the State Superintendent of Education in *Reports and Resolutions,* 1901–1909. Hereafter cited as SC State Report.

14. Nix, *SC State,* p. 22; Horton-McFadden interview.

15. *Ibid.*

16. SC State Reports, 1903, 1908, in *Reports and Resolutions,* 1904, 1909; no breakdown on teacher salaries at Clemson was

discovered, but it is safe to assume that they were substantially higher than at the black school.

17. Horton-McFadden interview.

18. Edward E. Dale and Morris L. Wardell, *History of Oklahoma* (New York, 1948), p. 471; Edwin C. McReynolds, *Oklahoma: A History of the Sooner State* (Norman, 1954); Joseph B. Thoburn and Muriel B. Wright, *Oklahoma, A History of the State and Its People*, 2 vols. (New York, 1929), vol. II; Nathaniel J. Washington, *Historical Development of the Negro in Oklahoma* (Tulsa, 1948), pp. 35–40, 42–45; Carter G. Woodson, *A Century of Negro Migration* (New York, 1969), pp. 144–46. Woodson also discusses the 1879 migration into Kansas and the debate over it between Frederick Douglass and Whittaker's lawyer and friend, Richard T. Greener, *ibid.*, pp. 134–44.

19. Horton-McFadden interview.

20. D.A. Wisener, a colleague of Whittaker's on the Douglass faculty, to author, June 28, 1971; a letter was sent to Mr. Ellison, but no reply was received; interview with Professor Reginald Thomasson, South Carolina State College, Orangeburg, June 9, 1971. Hereafter cited as Thomasson interview.

21. Henry A. Bullock, *A History of Negro Education in the South From 1619 to the Present* (New York, 1967), p. 180; Thomasson interview; Nix, *SC State*, pp. 34, 49; South Carolina Agricultural and Mechanical College *Bulletin* 1922–23, p. 72.

22. Miller received a second lieutenant's commission. John first received a first lieutenant's commission, later received one to captain. Technically this was a promotion, but he considered it a new commission because he possessed two separate commission documents. Cecil Whittaker McFadden to author, October 10, 1971.

23. Horton-McFadden interview; *The Collegian* (South Carolina A and M student newspaper), December 1949; Orangeburg *Times and Democrat*, November 15, 17, 1949; Miller F. Whittaker's death certificate, Orangeburg County Health Department; gravestones, Orangeburg Cemetery; interviews with Mrs. Charliese P. Sheffield, assistant college librarian, and Mr. T. J. Crawford, registrar, South Carolina State College, both of whom knew the Whittaker family, June 9, 1971.

24. Nix, *SC State*, p. 52; Horton-McFadden interview; Page E.

Whittaker will and accompanying papers, Records of the Judge of Probate Court, Orangeburg County, South Carolina.

25. SC State Reports, 1925–1931, in *Reports and Resolutions,* 1926–1932.

26. There is a book in the college library, formerly Whittaker's property, called *The Golden Gems of Life,* which provided material for some of these class meditations. Its short homilies remind one of some of the cards and clippings Whittaker kept in his Bible while at West Point fifty years previously. Interview with T. J. Crawford, South Carolina State college registrar and former Whittaker student, June 9, 1971; Horton-McFadden interview.

27. J.C. Whittaker death certificate, Orangeburg County Health Department; no will was registered in Orangeburg County, so Whittaker evidently did not leave one; Orangeburg *Times and Democrat,* January 17, 1931; gravestone, Orangeburg Cemetery; Horton-McFadden interview; Whittaker's death certificate and gravestone both list 1859 as the year of his birth. His West Point Bible, however, lists August 23, 1858, as his birthday. Other documents (e.g., West Point applications) corroborate the Bible date.

INDEX

INDEX

INDEX